The Welland Canal Company

A Study in Canadian Enterprise

by
Hugh G.J. Aitken

St. Catharines, Ontario, Canada
Canadian Canal Society
1997

Originally published in 1954
by Harvard University Press

Reprinted with the permission of
Harvard University Press by:

Canadian Canal Society
P.O. Box 23016
Midtown Postal Outlet
124 Welland Avenue
St. Catharines, Ontario
Canada L2R 7P6

First reprinting, April 1997

CANADIAN CATALOGUING IN PUBLICATION DATA

Aitken, Hugh G. J.
   The Welland Canal Company : A Study in Canadian Enterprise

Includes bibliographical references and index.
ISBN 0-9681987-0-8

1. Welland Canal Company - History.   I. Canadian Canal Society.
II. Title

HE401.25.W4A37 1997   386'.47'06571338   C97-930696-5

Cover Illustrations: Stock Certificate, printed in: Thomas C. Keefer, *The
Old Welland Canal and The Man Who Made It.* (St. Catharines: The Print
Shop, 1920), p. 14.
   Advertisement, printed in: *The Farmers' Journal, and Welland Canal
Intelligencer.* (St. Catharines), December 2, 1829.

Printed and bound in Canada by:
Lincoln Graphics Inc., St. Catharines, Ontario.

INTRODUCTION

Professor Hugh G.J. Aitken's opening words in the first chapter of *The Welland Canal Company: A Study in Canadian Enterprise* suggest briefly and modestly that his book is "about the building of a canal in the British colony of Upper Canada in the first half of the nineteenth century" with the "principal emphasis ... placed on the element of entrepreneurship." From our current perspective, we think Professor Aitken was too modest.

Numerous books, pamphlets and articles, as well as several theses, have been written about the four Welland canals. While some of these accounts have dealt at length with the colourful and exciting history of the canals, the vast majority unfortunately are all too brief in their treatment. A handful are scholarly undertakings, with an emphasis on research, but aside from them, the rest are the work of non-academic historians. Moreover, the lion's share of published material on the canals, regardless of length or scholarly value, was written in the period following the opening of the St. Lawrence Seaway in 1959. Quite a few titles are of even more recent vintage, having appeared in the wake of the sesquicentennial of the opening of the first Welland Canal, in 1979. For the most part, they deal with the canal's influence on the development of local communities and industries; their contribution to the local and wider Canadian (even world) economy; and William Hamilton Merritt, the canal's leading visionary and promoter. Interest in the Welland Canal shows no sign of abating.

Professor Aitken's book, however, stands above and outside any other treatment of the Welland Canal. It is the only substantial study of the Welland Canal Company, that remarkable group of men who pooled their talents and resources to build a canal to join Lake Erie to Lake Ontario. Professor Aitken examines in wonderful detail their motives and decisions as well as the means by which they achieved their lofty and daring goal within the circumstances and limitations of the geographical, social, political and economic conditions of their time.

The Welland Canal Company remains a fine example in the canon of works on the history of entrepreneurship in Canada. Factual, superbly written and thoroughly engaging, it was in a relatively new field of historical research when it was published in 1954. This book is an indispensable introduction to the Welland Canal saga, and has stood well the test of time and criticism. It rightly deserves to be brought back into print.

The Canadian Canal Society is proud to have undertaken this task. The text has been reproduced in its entirety with the permission of the author and publisher. A Note on Sources, and an Errata list, have been compiled by Society member Roberta M. Styran.

John Burtniak
Michael Power
Roberta M. Styran
Canadian Canal Society
April 1997

ACKNOWLEDGEMENTS

The Canadian Canal Society extends very special thanks to Hugh G.J. Aitken for his interest and cooperation in the reprinting of his classic work, *The Welland Canal Company, A Study in Canadian Enterprise*. The Society is pleased also to recognize Harvard University Press for granting permission to reprint this volume.

Louis J. Cahill, Honorary Life Member of the Society, was the first to suggest that Professor Aitken's study deserved a renewed life. The Society sincerely appreciates Mr. Cahill's abiding interest and involvement in this project.

NOTE ON SOURCES

For the convenience of today's researchers, it should be noted that some of the documentary material cited by Aitken is now on microfilm - for example, the Merritt Papers, a large collection of which is held by the National Archives of Canada in Ottawa (formerly the Public Archives of Canada), as well as the smaller collection in the Archives of Ontario in Toronto. Microfilm copies of these collections are available in the Special Collections Department of the St. Catharines Centennial Library. The National Archives' Series C and Series G are also on film, and there are finding aids to assist in locating individual volumes.

Material <u>not</u> available to Aitken, but now held by the National Archives, includes the three *Minute Books* of the Welland Canal Company, as well as several *Letterbooks*. The second of the *Minute Books*, covering the period 7 December 1825 to 3 April 1837, is also available on microfilm at the St. Catharines Centennial Library. It forms part of a collection of Welland Canal records microfilmed by the Archives of Ontario from material loaned for the purpose by the St. Lawrence Seaway Authority. Most of this material is now in the National Archives, although some items are held by Special Collections, James A. Gibson Library, at Brock University in St. Catharines. This microfilm is also held at the St. Catharines Centennial Library, the St. Catharines Museum, the Brock University Library and, of course, at the Archives of Ontario in Toronto.

There are two main series of records in the National Archives which deal with the Welland Canals - those of the Department of Public Works (RG 11), and the Department of Railways and Canals (RG 43). The Department of Finance records (RG 12) contain one volume (2536) of documents relating to the transfer of Welland Canal Company shares from the private stockholders to the Government of the United Canadas, which was completed in 1842.

ERRATA

Most of the information given below has been taken from the second *Minute Book* (RG 43, Vol. 2099). Aitken was quite right to be suspicious of information in J.P. Merritt's biography of his father (see Aitken, p. 152, n. 58), but in the absence of this *Minute Book*, was not aware that the *Third Report* (see Aitken p. 156, n. 71) was not always complete or correct, especially in the matter of dating.

p. 46	Scottish-born Francis Hall was trained by Thomas Telford, not John Rennie. Hall used this connection several times as an entrée into the British North American colonies.
p. 46	There are at least two occasions recorded in the *Third Report* in which James Clowes is referred to as the son of Samuel [p. 253, evidence of Merritt; p. 277, Samuel Clowes' evidence - there may have been another James, a brother, but this cannot be substantiated].
p. 52	The ground-breaking ceremony was on 30 November 1824, not the 20th. There is a terse note in Merritt's journal, "Tuesday attended the ceremony."
p. 66	Contracts for the Lake Erie extension were let "late in June." However, there is at least one contract dated 3 June, to Lewis, Little and Garrison for sections 15, 16 and 19 [RG 43, Vol. 2087, File "Welland Canal Correspondence"].
p. 71	Welland Canal Company petition to the Provincial Government submitted 1 November 1836 - the Board did not meet on that date. On 2 November they resolved to submit petitions "to the three branches of the Legislature" [RG 43, Vol. 2099, p. 444], and the text of one, addressed to the Legislature, is given under 4 November, p. 448-9. An earlier petition had been addressed to the Lieutenant Governor, text given under 4 August 1836 [RG 43, Vol. 2099, p. 431].
p. 73	This map is incorrect in one detail: the cut from Port Maitland, with the Broad Creek lock connection to the Feeder, was not accomplished until the 1840s.
p. 76	The Act of 5 July 1841 marked the end of the Welland Canal Company "for all practical purposes." - This is

true, but the third *Minute Book*'s last entry is dated 3 February 1842. On 29 January 1842, the Company's Secretary, George Prescott, wrote to H.H. Killaly, Chairman of the Board of Works, that the necessary two-thirds of the private stock had been transferred to the Government and that "the Canal has now become Government property according to the terms of the Act" [RG 43, Vol. 2102 (*Letterbook*)]. *De facto*, as opposed to *de jure*, control had, as Aitken states, been assumed by the Government at least by early October 1841. On 2 October Killaly wrote to S.B. Harrison, Secretary West, recommending that the Canal Company's Board of Directors be authorized to procure a loan - to be contingent "on the effective control by the Board of Works" [RG 11, Vol. 116 (*Letterbook*), #319].

p. 111   The Board meeting of 7 September 1825, at which the appointment of Merritt as Agent was recommended, actually took place on 7 December 1825. Aitken's reference on p. 167, n. 1 is to the *Third Report*, p. 268. The correct page is 269.

p. 123-4   The Board read Merritt's letter on 23 December 1831. Aitken's reference on p. 168, n. 18 gives 10 March 1831 as the date of this letter. The letter, as quoted in the *Third Report*, p. 138, is dated 10 November.

p. 124   Merritt offered to relinquish his property in 1835. Aitken's reference, p. 168, n. 19 is to the *Third Report*, p. 192, which gives the date as 1825. However, the letter itself is given in the *Third Report* on p. 57, and is dated 2 September 1835.

p. 162n. 53   14 February 1827 should read 1828.

p. 165n. 100   The Board met on 19 February 1833. According to the *Minute Book* the Board met on 13 and 27 February. Incidentally, the Board meeting date 18 February on p. 531 of the *Third Report* should be dated 28 February, just one of several examples of incorrect dating.

THE WELLAND CANAL
COMPANY

STUDIES IN ENTREPRENEURIAL HISTORY
PUBLISHED IN COÖPERATION WITH THE
RESEARCH CENTER IN ENTREPRENEURIAL HISTORY
HARVARD UNIVERSITY

THE WELLAND CANAL
COMPANY

A Study in Canadian Enterprise

By HUGH G. J. AITKEN

HARVARD UNIVERSITY PRESS
Cambridge, Massachusetts
1954

Distributed in Great Britain by Geoffrey Cumberlege
Oxford University Press · London

Library of Congress Catalog Card Number 54-5993
Printed in the United States of America

It is true, that what is settled by custom, though it be not good, yet at least it is fit; and those things which have long gone together, are as it were confederate within themselves; whereas new things piece not so well; but though they help by their utility, yet they trouble by their inconformity. Besides, they are like strangers; more admired and less favoured.

Bacon, *Of Innovations*

PREFACE

THIS BOOK IS THE WORK OF A JOURNEYMAN HISTORIAN, BARELY out of his apprenticeship and not yet within sight of the status of a master craftsman. To say this is to explain, if not to excuse, its limitations. No very profound level of analysis has been attempted; the method of presentation is, in general, straightforward narrative. It may be that more refined techniques might reveal other things which are true of the Welland Canal Company and its history. In this book my aim has been more modest: it has been to set down nothing which further inquiry or more penetrating analysis might prove false. It has been my hope that in this way my work might contribute in some degree to knowledge of the history of Canada and of the history of business enterprise.

The research has been carried out in the conviction that an adequate understanding of the rate, style, and direction of economic change in a society requires that attention be paid to the forms of business enterprise and the patterns of business behavior which have developed in that society; and, further, that these forms and patterns are cultural phenomena which are not to be explained solely in terms of the great achievements of great men. It is possible that this conviction is no more than a personal bias. But it seems reasonable to suppose that overemphasis on the creative role of particular individuals may deflect attention from certain underlying factors of a social and cultural nature which are, to be sure, less conspicuous in the historical record but which nevertheless exercise a pervasive influence upon actions and aspirations.

To guard against misunderstandings, I feel bound to make it clear at once that this book is not and does not purport to be a biography of William Hamilton Merritt, the promoter of the Welland Canal Company. Anyone who reads these pages in the expectation of finding therein a word-picture of Merritt's personality, his virtues and his defects, will be disappointed. The book is no more a biography of Merritt than it is a biography of J. B. Yates, the Albany lottery manager, or John H. Dunn, Upper Canada's receiver general, or any of the other persons who played a part in the activities of the Company. The focus of interest is not on these men as individuals, but on the jobs which they performed and the roles which they played in the Company.

So far as Merritt in particular is concerned, I have preferred to leave the reader to form his own opinion; for those who find this difficult, literary characterizations are conveniently available in standard works on the development of the Canadian canal system. Certainly these pages contain little that is not consistent with, for example, the character sketch provided by M. J. Patton in the tenth volume of the series, *Canada and its Provinces*. The evidence which I examined in preparing this book was not so richly informative as to encourage any more subtle analysis of his personality.

I may perhaps be pardoned, nevertheless, for inserting a personal impression that Merritt, like so many other nineteenth-century entrepreneurs in North America, was far from a romantic or exciting figure. It was only in matters connected with transportation that his imagination seemed to catch fire and his vision to outrange by far the mental horizons of his contemporaries. Hard-working to a fault, conscientious and desperately in earnest in everything he did, he seems to have been entirely lacking in humor and incapable of lightheartedness. These qualities, which make it difficult for later generations to feel toward him any emotion save a certain awed respect, were of course the very characteristics which made him effective as promoter and manager of the Welland Canal Company.

It may also be prudent to add a warning that the particular case of business enterprise which this study undertakes to examine does not fit easily into the conventional stereotype of "private" enterprise. It lies rather — as do so many other large enterprises in the Canadian story — somewhere in the middle range of the spectrum between state entrepreneurship on the one hand and complete private responsibility on the other. There appear to be good grounds for believing that this renders it more rather than less representative of enterprises performing similar tasks in North America during the first half of the nineteenth century.

For any errors of fact or interpretation which this book may contain I am, of course, solely responsible. But it is both necessary and pleasant to record my indebtedness to the many friends and colleagues who have assisted and encouraged me in my work. A special debt is due to the senior members of the Research Center in Entrepreneurial History at Harvard University, who have aided me in more ways than probably they are aware: Professors Arthur H. Cole, Alexander Gerschenkron, Oscar Handlin, Leland H. Jenks, and John E. Sawyer. The research and writing for this book have been carried out during my tenure of an appointment at the Research Center in Entrepreneurial History and would not have been possible without the assistance, both financial and intellectual, which that institution provided. To the late Professor Harold A. Innis and to Professor W. T. Easterbrook of the University of Toronto I am sincerely grateful for first turning my attention to research in Canadian economic history and for assistance given in many ways, not only while I was a graduate student at the University of Toronto, but also in later years. To Professor J. L. McDougall I owe a unique debt for permission to consult and use his pioneering dissertation on the Welland Canal Company, submitted to the

University of Toronto in 1923. The staffs of the Public Archives of Canada and the Department of Archives of the Province of Ontario have proved extremely helpful and coöperative and merit my most sincere thanks.

Certain sections of this work have appeared in the form of articles in the *Canadian Journal of Economics and Political Science* and in the *Bulletin* of the Business Historical Society. My thanks are due to the editors of these journals and to the University of Toronto Press for permission to reproduce this material.

H.G.J.A.

CONTENTS

TABLES

MAPS

CHARTS

CHAPTER ONE

UPPER CANADA:
THE INLAND PROVINCE

THIS IS A BOOK ABOUT THE BUILDING OF A CANAL IN THE British colony of Upper Canada in the first half of the nineteenth century. Such a topic can be discussed from several different points of view and different aspects of the story can be selected for emphasis. In this study the principal emphasis will be placed on the element of entrepreneurship. For present purposes this means that we are chiefly interested in the men responsible for the construction of the canal, their motives, their decisions, and the organization which they developed to carry out their task. But it is not possible to discuss these matters sensibly unless we also take into account the environment — geographical, social, political, and economic — in which these men lived and worked. What they did and what they failed to do can be understood only in terms of the possibilities and limitations which they saw in the world around them. It is necessary, therefore, before we take up the story of the canal, to examine the circumstances in which the project was conceived.

If we look at a map of North America which emphasizes the political boundaries, our attention is likely to be caught first of all by the long, smooth sweep of the Canadian–American boundary across the prairies along the forty-ninth parallel. When we look at the eastward half of the continent, we see something very different: a kinked, seemingly haphazard boundary, winding its way along rivers and through lakes, dipping deep into the United States as far as the forty-second parallel before turning northeast up the St. Lawrence River and across the height of land to the Atlantic.

If we turn to a map which shows the contours and geological structure of the land, we get a somewhat similar impression: to the west, the flat lands of the prairies; to the east, the ancient rock mass of the Pre-Cambrian Shield, pushing southward from Hudson Bay, crowding down on the north shore of Lakes Superior and Huron, touching the very margin of the St. Lawrence at Prescott before retreating to envelop the lowlands of Quebec. Along the southern edge of the shield lie the Great Lakes and the

St. Lawrence River, through which runs, roughly speaking, the international boundary.

The correspondence in the eastern half of the continent between the fringe of the shield and the Canadian–American boundary is sufficiently marked to strike even the unsophisticated eye. But it is by no means exact. If it were, Canada as we know it today could never have come into existence, for the territory which nature so grudgingly spared between the shield, the lakes, and the river has been the nursery of the Dominion, the base for expansion, the supply center which made the westward movement possible. Besides the arable lands of Quebec and the Ottawa valley, there is the peninsula of southern Ontario, the hundred thousand or so square miles of fertile land between Lakes Ontario, Erie, and Huron, which is now one of the major industrial centers of Canada.

This peninsula, pointing like a spear at the heart of the American union, is the scene of the story which we are about to tell. Between 1791 and 1841 it was known as Upper Canada, the first inland colony in the British Empire. Before 1776 it had been a wilderness, with only a few lonely fur-trading posts and military forts to mark the presence of civilization. Its settlement began with the American Revolution, when, beginning as a small trickle in 1775 and swelling to a steady stream in later years, United Empire Loyalists from the Atlantic colonies sought refuge in British territory. One detachment of these Loyalists, about seven thousand in number, settled in what was then the western part of the province of Quebec — principally along the north shore of Lake Ontario and in the Niagara peninsula — and formed there a series of small agricultural communities. If we neglect the Indians, these Loyalists were the first sedentary population of Upper Canada.

In 1791 the old province of Quebec was divided into two new provinces, named Upper and Lower Canada. This division was in essence a recognition and formalization of the cultural differences between the recently-arrived Loyalists and the French. The French in the lower parts of the St. Lawrence valley had been guaranteed the preservation of their rights and privileges by the Proclamation of 1763 and the Quebec Act of 1774. Wise policy therefore clearly indicated (or so it was believed in London) that separate provision should be made for the English-speaking inhabitants of the country beyond the Ottawa and the immigrants of similar stock who would follow them. What decided the matter was the intention of the British government to grant a measure of representative government to the new provincial legislatures. Secretary of State Grenville, for example, argued that

> every consideration of policy seemed to render it desirable that the great preponderance possessed in the upper district by the King's ancient subjects, and in the lower by the French Canadians, should have their effect and operation in separate legislatures, rather than that these two bodies

of people should be blended together in the first formation of the new
constitution, and before sufficient time has been allowed for the removal
of ancient prejudices by the habit of obedience to the same government
and by the sense of a common interest.[1]

Granted the difference in levels of political education and aspiration
between the British and French inhabitants, together with the so-called
establishment of the Roman Catholic Church by the Quebec Act, the survival of feudal land law, and the persistence of the French language even
for official purposes, the problem of government seemed insoluble except
by division. The demands of the English-speaking inhabitants were for
institutions and laws which they believed to be their right. To the French,
on the other hand, representative Assemblies, habeas corpus, and freehold
tenures were strange innovations in which they saw at best little value, at
worst a threat to their cultural integrity. Conflicting interests such as these
could not be overlooked, but in no way other than by separation did it
appear that they could be reconciled.

The establishment of the province of Upper Canada was an attempt to
reconcile two hard facts: the fact of the American Revolution, with its
consequence, the proscription and expulsion of a large number of British
subjects; and the fact that in Canada there already existed a French-
speaking civilization, old-established and closely-knit, which, it was believed, could not absorb these alien immigrants and would not readily be
absorbed by them. So far as Canada was concerned, the most urgent immediate problem left by the Revolution was the appearance of a Protestant
English-speaking population side by side with a Roman Catholic French-
speaking community. These communities, alien to each other in language,
religion, and culture generally, were now separated by a political act
which gave to each its own jurisdiction. Yet their futures were inextricably
linked together. Not only were they both members of the British colonial
system; they also had a common stake in the St. Lawrence River, that artery
of communication which seemed to promise such easy access to the interior
of the continent and which linked them to the British metropolitan economy.

What manner of people were these Loyalists who had come to live in
the wilderness around Lakes Erie and Ontario? One important characteristic they had in common: all had opposed, or were held to have opposed,
armed rebellion against the British Crown; all had supported, or had
been unable to refute the accusation of supporting, the maintenance of the
British connection. It is not necessary to attribute to them any perfervid
universal loyalty to the British Crown; this characteristic was acquired
later, when Loyalist descent had become matter for pride, a means of dis-
tinguishing oneself from later arrivals, an important status symbol. As
indicated by such things as education and property, the Loyalists (thirty-
two thousand or so in number) who went to New Brunswick and Nova

Scotia were of somewhat higher social position than the six to seven thousand who found their way to the interior.[2] Certainly they were more articulate. The Loyalists who came overland to Canada were mostly of humble station — Highland crofters, or German farmers, or American frontiersmen.[3] Few of them had more than a rudimentary education.

Whatever their previous social station may have been, these Loyalists constituted the original population of the new province of Upper Canada. The role which necessity thus forced on them was one which in general they were well fitted by experience to play. Many of them were experienced frontier farmers.[4] The terrain, soil, and climate of Upper Canada were not radically different from the conditions they had known in Pennsylvania, New York, or New Jersey. The novelty which was inherent in the establishment and development of the new province lay not so much on their shoulders as on those of the British government, whose responsibility it was to provide the framework of order, law, protection, and good government generally within which development and settlement might proceed.

The first lieutenant governor of Upper Canada, John Graves Simcoe, who arrived to take up his appointment in November 1791, had very positive ideas regarding the mistaken policies which had led to the loss of the thirteen American colonies. To the deep belief in the necessity for order and authority in human affairs with which his military experience endowed him, he added the prejudices and preconceptions of the English squirearchy into which he had been born, and a profound detestation of democracy and all its works. As commanding officer of the Queen's Rangers, a partisan corps raised in Connecticut and the environs of New York and composed mainly of Loyalists with a sprinkling of British regulars, he had witnessed the Revolutionary War from start to finish. His command of Loyalist troops had convinced him that the Atlantic colonies had been lost through folly and bad generalship rather than through any clash of social philosophies or economic interests. Americans were to him, by and large, Englishmen who had been led astray by a handful of ambitious demagogues. He believed that the great majority of Americans would have no serious objections to living under British monarchical institutions, so long as these institutions guaranteed protection and freedom from want. And he entertained the lively hope that some, perhaps all, of the American states and territories might be induced to rejoin the British colonial family.[5]

Before ever he left England, Simcoe had a very clear idea of what he intended to do in Upper Canada. From merchants and maps he learned what there was to be known about the resources and geography of the colony, and provisionally settled upon the site of a new provincial capital which, with a sublime disregard for existing trade routes and settlements but with a careful eye on the probable direction of American invasion, was to be situated at the forks of the River La Tranche, renamed the Thames, almost thirty miles inland from Lake Erie. The principal aim of his lieutenancy, he announced, would be to preserve Upper Canada for the British Crown; to that end, he would institute in the colony a form of government and an administration so pure and perfect that none who experienced it could conceivably desire change, and which by its example would tempt the American states back to loyalty.[6] In the phrase which he was to wear thin by repetition, Upper Canada had been granted the very image and transcript of the British constitution. The present population was loyal, else they would not have been in Upper Canada, and later immigrants would remember their forgotten loyalty when they experienced the palpable excellence of British rule.

The first need of Simcoe's colony was for settlers. The Loyalists would, he confidently expected, provide the core around which the new society would grow, but development demanded immigrants. To obtain them, Simcoe looked to the United States, not to Britain. Only in the United States could be found the experienced frontier farmers whom Upper Canada needed. One of Simcoe's first acts on reaching Canada was therefore to prepare a proclamation advertising the terms on which land was available. Extensively circulated in the United States through British and West Indian newspapers and through the activities of special agents, this proclamation achieved substantial results. American settlers received two hundred acres of land free of all but nominal charges. Larger grants were made to settlers who had large families, or substantial capital, or who for any reason appeared likely to be able to keep a larger area under cultivation. This "open-door" policy of encouraging American immigration was maintained right up to the outbreak of war with the United States in 1812.

It may seem strange that the lieutenant governor of Upper Canada, a country settled by people who had recently suffered at the hands of Americans, should have exerted every effort to encourage an influx of these same Americans, and that the development of the colony should have been based so firmly on the advent of men who had lately been enemies. Yet such was the case; and it is certain that had Simcoe been a man of different convictions — had he, for example, set his face against American immigration and rested his hopes on immigration from Great Britain — the political history of Upper Canada would have been profoundly altered and its economic development considerably retarded. Simcoe's immigration policy cannot be understood apart from his complete lack of faith in the practicability of the American political system. He found it impossible to believe that any thinking person could prefer to live under the "wild and phrenetic democracy" of the American republic when the opportunity was open to enjoy the benefits of monarchical institutions. The American Revolution, in his opinion, called for no radical change in the principles or practice of colonial government. Its chief cause, he believed, had been "the want of an aristocratic power which might afford a legal provision for the fair claims and just ascendancy of honorable ambition and not suffer it to waste its energy in dissatisfaction and discontent." That defect was now to be remedied.

These beliefs colored his whole immigration policy. The well-known incident described by La Rochefoucault is illuminating:

> We met . . . an American family who, with some oxen, cows, and sheep, were emigrating to Canada. "We come," said they, "to your Governor," whom they did not know, "to see whether he will give us land." "Aye, aye," the Governor replied, "you are tired of the Federal Government; you like not any longer to have so many kings; you wish again for your old father" (it is thus the Governor calls the British monarch when he speaks with Americans) ; "you are perfectly right; come along, we love such good Royalists as you are; we will give you land." [7]

It made no difference to Simcoe from where the immigrant came, so long as he was a "useful settler," would undertake to improve the land he was granted, and would take a formal oath of allegiance.

Yet Simcoe's immigration policy did not meet with the complete approval of the authorities in Whitehall. Secretary of State Dundas in particular was doubtful of its wisdom, and in July 1792 warned Simcoe of the difficulties which were bound to arise:

> . . . an ingrafted population (if I may so call it) to a great extent and outrunning (as it must do), all those regulations, laws, usages, and customs, which grow up and go hand in hand with a progressive and regular population, must I conceive in all cases be attended with a want of that regularity, and stability, which all, but particularly Colonial Governments, require. [8]

Simcoe in reply argued with some truth that immigrants from the United States would be far more valuable to Canada than immigrants from Europe. The Americans were, he felt, "allured by the advantages of the British Government, which they have felt, and to which it is my firm and uniform belief, during every period of the late war, the greatest part of the native Colonists were unalterably attached." In the following year he was to point out, more realistically, that "the preference of the British form of government is alleged by some for quitting the States, but the oppression of the Land Jobbers, and the uncertainty of titles, is the more general reason." [9]

Both Simcoe and Dundas were partially right. Dundas was correct in forecasting the problems that were later to arise, basically through the conflict between American and British theories of government. Simcoe was correct in asserting that the development of the province required immigration on a large scale and that from no other source than the United States, at this time, could a large number of useful settlers be drawn. The conflict between their views did not arise from personal idiosyncrasy or faulty logic; it was implicit in the very situation of the colony.

How many immigrants from the United States took advantage of the

land grant policy of Simcoe and his successors is uncertain.[10] Michael
Smith, whose survey of the colony in 1812 is a valuable source of information, states that by that year six out of every ten persons in Upper Canada
were of American birth or descent.[11] One quarter of these (15 per cent of
the total) were Loyalists and their children.[12] The remaining 40 per cent
of the population were Indians, French, and immigrants from Britain. The
total population at the time Smith wrote was probably just over 80,000.[13]
The inhabited part of the province then consisted only of a narrow strip
along the edge of the lakes, with a few inland settlements along Yonge
Street and in the Thames valley. The Loyalists had settled principally
along the north shore of Lake Ontario and in the Niagara district. The
later non-Loyalist American immigrants had settled principally along the
Lake Erie "front." The area between Lake Erie and the River Thames, in
fact, was something very like an American territory under British rule.

This American immigration was at no time up to 1812 opposed by
British policy. The colonial authorities, however, seem to have had little
conception of the social and political problems so created. Even Dundas'
gloomy forebodings were forgotten, and sources of friction allowed to
develop without any clear appreciation of the dangers. Chief among these
problems were the spread of republican ideas, irreconcilable with Simcoe's
ideal of a benevolent autocracy, and the submergence of the original
Loyalist population under a wave of land-hungry settlers who were
Americans in spirit and sympathy, no matter what oath of allegiance
accompanied their grants.[14]

But this immigration policy was by no means Simcoe's only legacy
to Upper Canada, and it represented a source of strain in the society only
because the ideas, hopes, and aspirations which the Americans brought
with them were in conflict with the constitution and social organization of
the colony which he had helped to establish. Early in 1791 he had written
to his friend Sir Joseph Banks, President of the Royal Society:

> I mean to prepare for whatever convulsions may happen in the United
> States, and the method I propose is by establishing a free, honourable
> British Government, and a pure administration of its Laws, which shall
> hold out to the solitary emigrants, and to the several States, advantages
> that the present form of Government doth not and cannot permit them
> to enjoy.[15]

What did this amount to in practice? Simcoe, of course, had to work
within the framework of the Constitutional Act of 1791.[16] That Act established in Upper Canada an elected Legislative Assembly and an appointed
Legislative Council, but made no attempt to define the relationship between
the two. Grenville's dispatches make it clear, however, that the Council was
intended to develop into something analogous to the House of Lords, and
that the creation of a colonial aristocracy was seriously contemplated.[17]
Since an aristocracy of birth was out of the question, an aristocracy of

wealth was to be substituted, and in Upper Canada, where no man was very rich, wealth meant land grants. The Constitutional Act had suggested the policy to be followed in this respect by providing that, of all Crown lands granted, one seventh part was to be reserved for the support of "a Protestant Clergy." The phrase was not elaborated, but subsequent sections made provision for the endowment of Anglican parsonages and rectories in each township and for the appointment of a bishop of the Church of England. The implication was clear that one seventh of all land granted in the province was to be reserved for the benefit of the Church of England and its clergy. And although no mention was made of it in the statute, a similar policy was pursued in the case of Crown Reserves. This policy of reserving lands equal to a further seventh of all grants made was foreshadowed in Dorchester's dispatch to Sydney on June 13, 1787, and its intent made painfully clear.[18] Dorchester wrote:

> These reserved parcels of land will enable His Majesty to reward such of His provincial Servants as may merit the Royal favour, and will also enable the Crown to create and strengthen an aristocracy, of which the best use may be made on this Continent, where all Governments are feeble, and the general condition of things tends to a wild democracy.

The Constitutional Act, in a word, might establish popularly-elected Assemblies and grant to them the nominal control over provincial taxing and spending, but it was clearly intended that these dangerous concessions to democracy should be offset by the power of appointed Councils, the members of which would be drawn from a rich and powerful elite, linked to Britain by ties both of loyalty and interest. This policy rested on the assumption that there would continue to exist in Upper Canada a population which would accept serious limitations upon self-government and a hierarchical social structure in which no serious conflicts of interest and ideology would arise. Only by some such assumption as this can we reconcile the grant of popularly-elected Assemblies with the creation of an executive owing responsibility not to those Assemblies but to the governor and, in some vague sense, to the British Crown, with the establishment of the Church of England, and with the explicit intention to create and subsidize a colonial aristocracy. It was a policy fashioned for Loyalists, not for Americans, and workable only on the assumption that the Loyalists and their descendants would remain the dominant element in the population of Upper Canada. But, as we have seen, American immigration made this assumption less and less valid as the years went by.

No formal attempt was ever made to create the aristocracy of which Simcoe and Dorchester had spoken. But, in a different form, the theory that the social and political life of the colony should be dominated and guided by a privileged elite lingered on and became actuality. There developed an aristocracy of office and privilege, the heart of whose power lay in the appointed Legislative and Executive Councils and in the Church of England. To be sure, the appearance of such an elite was hardly surprising. Communications throughout the colony were poor, newspapers slow in appearing and with limited circulation, roads execrable, and the lakes frozen for half the year. Men who had both the talent and the leisure for politics were scarce. Problems of government, on the other hand, were urgent. Small wonder that there grew up around the lieutenant governor, first at Niagara and later at York (Toronto), a small coterie of officials and advisers, men trained in the law or some other profession, ambitious, often talented, seeking some avenue to recognition and status not open to farmers, storekeepers, and millers. Small wonder, too, that when once the land-granting authority was in their hands they saw little reason to refrain from exercising it to buttress their position and that of their friends and relations. It might not quickly make them rich, for when free land was so readily available only the choicest lots brought a price, but it was a symbol of their power and would benefit their descendants. As John Elmsley, first chief justice, neatly expressed it: "Can lands be in any hands better than in those of the officers of Government, in a country in which the influence of extensive property is so much wanted to give effect to the Laws and keep the turbulent in good order? And in whose hands can they be more safely placed than in ours, who depend so entirely upon the King and the Mother Country?" [19]

Between July 1792 and December 1798, 3654 title deeds for land were issued, conveying in all over one million acres.[20] Not all of this land, of course, went to the Government House clique. Loyalists and their children, when they came of age, received grants of between two and twelve hundred acres, and American immigrants continued to receive in normal cases two hundred acres apiece. Nevertheless, effective limitations on the land-granting activities of the provincial officials were few and abuses frequent.[21] As long as speculation was avoided — and speculation, or the buying of land to sell at a higher price without improvement, was a word applied only to Americans — restrictions were felt to be unnecessary.

Good reasons could be produced to justify this attitude. In the first place, the population was still scanty and miserliness in the distribution of land would hardly encourage immigration. Secondly, as long as tariffs on imports remained of minor importance and had to be shared with Lower Canada, hopes for obtaining revenue to support the civil government of the colony rested upon the possibility of selling or leasing the Crown Reserves. There was no reason for restraint or circumspection here. Thirdly, to clinch these seemingly sound arguments — and here the Simcoe tradition came into its own — did not the welfare and stability of the colony depend upon the maintenance of a privileged class of officials and settlers of proven loyalty? And should not such persons be especially favored in the distribution of the "King's Bounty" in order that rank

might be buttressed by wealth and loyalty by a vested interest in the
status quo? Provincial officers, too, were poorly paid and, unlike merchants
and other businessmen, had little time to spare for money-making. Should
they suffer for that reason? Thus Peter Russell, Simcoe's successor, tactfully took it upon himself to remind the Duke of Portland that

> . . . there are now in this Province a great many individuals (particu-
> larly Merchants) who, having no official duties to discharge nor any
> official rank to support, have devoted their whole time and attention to
> the improvement of their fortunes; and . . . in consequence many of
> them are by purchases on very easy terms in possession of from 20 to
> 50,000 acres of land in it, and, tho' neither from birth, education, nor
> habits of life entitled (as we presume to think) to put themselves on a
> level with us, will eventually leave fortunes to their families consider-
> ably beyond what we can hope for our own.[22]

Generosity to Russell, Elmsley, and the others did not mean speculation,
even though there was small possibility that the thousands of acres granted
could be put under cultivation within the foreseeable future.[23] On the contrary, it insured that those who had achieved the honor of rendering the
Crown good service in peace or war would be enabled to transmit that
honor to their descendants. Loyal subjects did not speculate; they accumulated wealth for their children. And if the man who made the grant not
infrequently wore the same coat as the man who received it, that was
merely an incidental convenience.

It was against this clique that Thorpe, Jackson, and Willcocks, leaders
of Upper Canada's first reform party, fulminated between 1806 and 1812.[24]
With a nice sense of the insult which would cut deepest, they called it a
"shopkeeper aristocracy." It was against the same tight circle of power
and privilege that Robert Gourlay, the Scottish agitator, raged bitterly but
without lasting effect from 1817 until his expulsion from the province two
years later.[25] And it was in opposition to the same monopoly of political
power, now dubbed the "Family Compact," that William Lyon Mackenzie
and his fellow Reformers were to lead the colony into armed rebellion in
1837. Officeholders changed; bureaucrats died, resigned, or returned to
England; lieutenant governors came and went; but the clique remained.
Technically they were the servants and advisers of the lieutenant governor;
practically, since they had the indispensable knowledge and experience of
the affairs of the colony which he lacked, he was their instrument.[26]

The qualifications which were required for admission to the charmed
circle of the Family Compact have largely eluded investigation. Neither
talent, wealth, nor birth seems to have been indispensable. Archdeacon
Strachan, for instance, was the son of an Aberdeenshire quarryman. The
Baldwins, father and son, were as well born and wealthy as any member
of the Compact, yet were in the Reform camp. John Beverley Robinson,
the attorney general, was no abler a politician than Marshall Spring

Bidwell, leader of the moderate Reformers. W. S. Wallace finds only one generalization possible: "All that can be said about the Family Compact is that it was a local oligarchy, composed of men, some well-born, some ill-born, some brilliant, some stupid, whom the caprices of a small provincial society, with a code all its own, had pitchforked into power." [27]

No matter how its members were recruited, the dominance of the Compact over the affairs of Upper Canada in the twenty-odd years after 1815 was very real. It was a dominance attained not by wealth, for few of the leading Tories were rich men, but by the monopoly of certain key positions of social control. In economic life it acted through the government-sponsored Bank of Upper Canada; [28] in politics through the Executive and Legislative Councils; and in religion and education through the Church of England. There were few avenues of ascent in the social structure of Upper Canada which were not substantially controlled by the Family Compact. The Methodist church was one, the Reform party another, and business was coming to be a third. But business, whenever it resorted to the legislature for sanction or assistance — whenever, that is to say, it impinged upon the sphere of political action — had to reckon seriously with the power of the Compact. This was especially true of such an enterprise as the Welland Canal Company, which represented a substantial concentration of capital and raised controversial issues of public policy. Such an enterprise could not hope to succeed without the active support of the Compact; but to secure this support, it had to pay the price which the Compact demanded.

But this was not the only way in which the Simcoe tradition exercised an enduring influence upon the development of Upper Canada. The open-handed granting of land not only buttressed the prestige and influence of the privileged few; it also reserved from settlement large portions of land which, now held for speculative purposes, remained uncleared and unsettled while other areas were being brought under cultivation. Formally, each grant was made on the condition that the land should be cleared and a dwelling erected on it, but there were many ways of circumventing this technicality. In any case, the condition did not apply to the Clergy and Crown Reserves, which in every township withheld two sevenths of the land from settlement. In a sense, the government and the Anglican church were the largest land speculators in Upper Canada.

These uncleared and unsettled sections acted as barriers to settlement, prevented the construction of through roads, forced new settlers into the back areas away from lake transportation, and set before the eyes of every farmer a permanent reminder that by his efforts he was enriching not so much himself and his family, but rather the Church of England and the provincial bureaucracy. What made the grievance more acute was the fact that revenues from Crown Reserves, being part of the Royal prerogative, were spent by the provincial executive without the consent of the Assembly, so that the principal check on arbitrary executive action possessed by the elected branch of the legislature was effectively nullified.

The Clergy Reserves and abuses in land granting ranked high on every Reformer's list of grievances, and it appears probable that they did to some extent stunt the growth of the colony, particularly after 1815. Certainly it was widely believed at the time that this was so. When, late in 1817, Robert Gourlay circulated his famous questionnaire to the townships of Upper Canada, the answers to his last question, "What, in your opinion, retards the improvement of your township in particular, or the province in general . . . ?" were remarkable only for their unanimity. With a monotonous and damning regularity the respondents — usually the most influential men in each township — fastened on the Clergy Reserves and the large tracts of land held by speculators as the most important cause of slow development.

Up to 1810, however, it must be admitted that the economic development of Upper Canada was not unsatisfactory. The Loyalists brought with them the accumulated experience of a century and a half of frontier expansion and, in the early years, received generous support from the British government. Not only did the original Loyalists and their children receive free grants of land; they also obtained without charge full rations for two years and a stock of agricultural implements, while the government-built grist mills ground their wheat free of toll until 1791. The Upper Canada settlements, too, unlike those in Ohio, had no reason to fear the Indians. Beyond all this, markets for surplus agricultural products were readily available, not only for the Loyalists but also for the American immigrants who came after them. The military garrisons at Montreal, Kingston, Niagara, and Detroit provided an excellent and stable market, for after 1785 the government pursued a deliberate policy of subsidization, paying to the garrison contractors the market price for flour in Lower Canada, plus most of the cost of transporting it upriver from Lachine, even although the contractors actually obtained the flour from surrounding settlements in Upper Canada. And, in addition, the fur trade obtained most of its supplies from the Upper Canada settlements, for Michilimackinac and the other western posts seldom produced more than a small proportion of their requirements.[29]

Of more long-run importance than the local garrisons and the fur trade was the growth of an export trade in agricultural products to Montreal and to the United States. Settlements on the American side of the Lakes were few and scattered until the British evacuated the western posts in 1796. When this area did fill up, the new settlements were supplied for several years from farms in Upper Canada, which had on the average a decade of development behind them.[30] This American demand induced high prices and a brisk trade across the Lakes for four or five years after 1796 and, combined with partial crop failures, retarded the development of the export trade in wheat and flour down the St. Lawrence to Montreal, which seems to have begun in 1794.[31] After 1800, however, when the American settlements ceased to be net importers of agricultural produce, this St. Lawrence trade revived and in a few years not only Canadian but also American wheat and flour were finding their way in considerable volume to Montreal. In June 1801, a Queenston merchant reported that at least 5000 barrels of flour were exported to Montreal from the Niagara district alone, "which for the first year," he remarked, "is really very great." [32] In the same year Richard Cartwright estimated that Upper Canada merchants from Kingston westward consigned to Montreal a total of 14,283 barrels of flour of various grades.[33] In 1802 the figure was 11,422.[34]

In the following years this movement of agricultural produce down the St. Lawrence continued in increasing volume. Potash was an important component of the trade, but wheat and flour were its mainstays. The final market for these products was Great Britain, where a succession of bad harvests and, from time to time, the interruption of Baltic supplies, nullified the restrictions of the Corn Laws. The West Indies offered an alternative market, but here American competition was severe. It was in these years after 1800 that Upper Canada was becoming incorporated in the British metropolitan economy. While local demand continued to be important, it was the export trade in wheat and flour that held the key to Upper Canada's development, and it was around this trade that the mercantile organization of the colony grew up.

The basis for the economic life of Upper Canada — the great artery which kept it alive — was in this period and until the coming of the railroads in the 1850's the St. Lawrence River and the Great Lakes. Roads were bad and in many cases impassable except in winter. The river and the lakes, in contrast, provided during the open season a ready means of conveying goods and men. This was the transportation system which enabled Upper Canada to develop and which inspired in the sober merchants of Montreal visions of easy access to the continental hinterland. And for the time it was a transportation system which, in comparison with available alternatives, met the demands on it very adequately. Up to 1825, indeed, the whole of the St. Lawrence and Great Lakes basin, both Canadian and American, was tributary to Montreal, while the North West Company and its fur-trading competitors penetrated still farther west. Only the economies of water transportation made this possible. While other commercial centers of the Atlantic seaboard struggled painfully by land over the barrier of the Appalachians, with New York casting hopeful glances at the valleys of the Hudson and the Mohawk, Montreal enjoyed the benefits of a natural highway into the interior which, though sadly imperfect, was vastly superior to its rivals.

For many decades before the founding of Upper Canada the economies of this great trunk line to the interior had been exploited by the Montreal fur trade, and it was on the model of the fur trade that the export and import trade of Upper Canada was first organized.[35] In several cases, particularly after the rise to dominance of the North West Company, Montreal firms previously interested in the fur trade turned to the trade in Upper Canada wheat and flour, or to the importing of manufactured goods for sale to the new settlements.[36] This shift in their line of business was probably not very difficult. The fur trade had taught them familiarity with the transportation facilities of the river and the lakes. As in the fur trade, they had to provide credit to their agents or correspondents in the interior, though now it was the Upper Canada storekeeper, not the *coureur de bois* or the wintering partner, whose account had to be carried on the books from season to season. And, as in the fur trade, the goods and produce moving to and from the interior had to pass through the wharfs, warehouses, and markets of Montreal. As far as the Montreal houses were concerned, it was merely the substitution of one staple for another. The development of the Upper Canada grain trade meant, in its early years, little change in the business life of Montreal.

In the interior, however, the case was different. Here a new figure became important: the country merchant. Unknown to the fur trade, these merchants played a crucial role in the developing export trade and in the social life of the new settlements of Upper Canada. All of them operated on the basis of Montreal credit, importing goods upriver for sale (or more often barter) to the settlers, and accepting in return such grain, potash, or other products as were available. Many of them owned their own mills and whenever possible, to save transportation costs, they ground the wheat into flour before sending it downriver on *bateaux*, Durham boats, or rafts, for sale through commission merchants in Montreal.

These Upper Canada merchants were in business on their own account, not as partners or agents of Montreal firms. They were, in fact, the only businessmen of whom Upper Canada could boast, and they occupied a rather peculiar position in the social scale. Richard Cartwright and Robert Hamilton, for instance, were both Legislative Councillors and rich men by the standards of the time. Yet Simcoe referred to them as "monopolizing and unprincipled merchants"; they had, he admitted, more wealth than the settlers, but it had been recently acquired and would probably be quickly lost. Hamilton and Cartwright were, as he expressed it, "men who kept but one table" — that is, dined with their servants — and as such dubious candidates for the provincial aristocracy. Yet they could not be altogether ignored. As Simcoe wrote to Dundas:

> Mr. Hamilton is an avowed Republican in his sentiments and altho' the merchants are justly obnoxious to the settlers of this Province, and he is particularly so, yet the ascendancy that he and his friend, Mr. Cartwright, *must acquire,* by being agents for the contract which supplies the

King's Troops with provisions, is of that nature, that there is nothing to prevent them exercising it to the detriment of Government, if they have any particular object to promote, that may gratify their avarice, ambition, or vanity.[37]

To the settlers as well as to the officers of government the merchants, though necessary, were often objects of hostility and suspicion. None of them paid cash for the wheat and flour they purchased; they found it more convenient to issue their own notes, or "bons" as they were called. Currency was very scarce, and these private note issues, though certainly better than no medium of exchange at all, lent themselves to abuse. John McGill, the commissary general, described some of their disadvantages in 1793:

> The nominal money in circulation here . . . is nothing more than notes of hand (or what is termed Bons) on small scrips of paper from 3¾ Sterling to thirty six shillings Sterling issued by people in trade. . . The issuer will not give specie for his own notes unless he receives Nine Dollars for Eight or at the rate of 12½ per Cent discount, though he had perhaps not long before paid those very notes as Cash, to the person who makes the application.[38]

This homemade paper money, which usually circulated only in the immediate neighborhood of the store where it was issued, restricted competition and facilitated the exploitation of the farmer, because it tied him to one local merchant. Not only did the settler bear the risk that his merchant might fail; he also had to accept a considerable loss if he needed currency in a hurry. What it amounted to, in fact, was an elaborate form of truck system.[39] Ordinarily the settler was in debt to the local merchant and could sell his surplus products only to him, at rates of exchange which often seemed arbitrary and unfair. McGill later reported:

> I was lately informed by a very able farmer that supposing flour was sold for 15/ per Cwt. Halifax Currency and to be paid in Merchant's Notes, that he would prefer receiving 12/6 per Cwt. in specie or Government Bills, and that he believed this to be the general sense of the Inhabitants above Niagara.[40]

This chronic indebtedness of the farmer to the merchant was a fruitful source of resentment, especially since many of the merchants accumulated large holdings of land, title to which they had accepted in settlement of bad debts.[41]

But if the farmers could complain of the burden of their debts, so on occasion could the merchants themselves. Just as the farmer was chronically in debt to the local merchant, so was the merchant to Montreal and so indeed was the Montreal importer to his suppliers in Liverpool and London. In good times this system of debts and credits worked tolerably well. On his annual or semiannual trips to Montreal, the Upper Canada merchant would purchase a consignment of goods for the coming season and arrange with the importer the terms on which the account would be met. During the course of the season he would ship consignments of flour, wheat, and potash to Montreal, where they would be disposed of by a commission agent, the proceeds going to satisfy the original debt to the importer who in the meantime had been financing himself by bills drawn on London. In bad times, of course, when harvests were poor or Montreal prices slumped, debts would accumulate and the whole credit system threaten to dissolve into a mass of bankruptcies, mortgages, and prosecutions.[42]

One such country store, that kept by Thomas Cummings at Chippawa, has been described in detail by E. A. Cruikshank.[43] Chippawa was the southern terminus of the Niagara portage, a thriving center of commerce, and Cummings had a first-class location. Nevertheless, at the beginning of 1802 he owed his Montreal correspondents, Messrs. Auldjo, Maitland & Company, the sum of £3643 16s. 9d., plus interest at 6 per cent from April 1, 1802.[44] During the course of that year he increased his indebtedness by £1553 6s. 5d. and received credit for shipments of flour and wheat sent by him to Montreal to the amount of £1186 8s. 8d. Auldjo, Maitland & Company paid the freight, storage, and inspection charges, and deducted them from the proceeds, together with their commission of 2½ per cent on the value of the shipment. To balance his account, Cummings supplemented the proceeds of his consignments whenever possible by remitting bills drawn on the paymaster general at Quebec which he received from the half-pay officers who were among his customers.

An examination of Cummings' accounts calls attention to one of the major handicaps under which all Upper Canada merchants labored: the high costs of transportation to and from the seaboard. As Cruikshank remarks, "While the prices of the articles named seem very moderate, the charges for packing, carterage, river freight, commission, insurance, and other expenses at London and Montreal add forty per cent to the original cost, to which must be added ocean freight, transport from Montreal to La Chine, from La Chine to Kingston, from Kingston to Queenston, and from Queenston to Chippawa, by separate means of conveyance." Similar costs had to be deducted from the final market price of grain exports.

It is clear that these heavy forwarding and handling costs set a limit to the economic development of Upper Canada, lowering as they did the price received by the Upper Canada farmer for his produce at the same time as they raised the price which he had to pay for his imports. But in addition, since these costs were not flexible but had to be borne whether Montreal prices were high or low, whether the harvest was good or bad, they introduced a significant element of rigidity into the chain of debts which linked the Upper Canada producer and merchant to the Montreal market. In times of prosperity the costs of using the St. Lawrence waterway could be borne; but when prices fell they drove the Upper Canada merchant into bankruptcy.

Before 1812 these heavy transport costs do not seem to have been the vital matter which they were later to become. Export surpluses were still relatively small and the economy largely self-sufficient. The Napoleonic Wars meant the practical suspension of the Corn Laws, while the American Embargo and Non-Intercourse Acts between 1807 and 1810 removed an important source of competition. Nevertheless, it is significant that the years in this period during which Upper Canada experienced its greatest prosperity and made its greatest strides forward were precisely those years (1796–1800 and 1812–1815) during which a brisk demand developed in the interior, rather than at Montreal, so that the heavy freight costs of the St. Lawrence outlet no longer had to be met.[45]

The improvement of the St. Lawrence waterway cannot have seemed a particularly urgent problem before 1812. Montreal could dominate its international hinterland around the lower lakes without committing itself to the heavy fixed investments required for the construction of canals. And yet, for men of vision, the nature of the problems which would eventually have to be faced cannot have been obscure. Not forever would the bustling American cities of the Atlantic seaboard be content to see their commercial hinterlands limited by the barrier of the Appalachians. Not forever would Spain block the Mississippi. Not forever would the growing settlements of Ohio and the Western Reserve send their produce to Montreal. And not for many years longer would the North West Company of Montreal live to provide the backbone for the commerce of the St. Lawrence. When these changes took place, Montreal would no longer be able to enjoy without effort its natural monopoly of the trade of the interior.

When the United States and the Canadas found themselves at war in 1812, it was not against Quebec or Montreal, the citadels of British dominion in North America, that the main force of American invasion was directed. It was against the villages and settlements of Upper Canada and in particular against the Niagara frontier between Lakes Erie and Ontario. Was this a major strategic error? Surely not. Whatever the complex of causes — some maritime in nature, some arising from the demands of frontier "expansionists" [46] — which precipitated the outbreak of hostilities, it is not to be questioned that the Niagara peninsula and, to a lesser extent, Detroit, were the keys to the British trunk line of communications to the interior. They were the bottlenecks through which passed the trade of the Great Lakes. If the United States could control these two points — Niagara alone would suffice, if firmly held — British control of the interior, in peace and in war, would be at an end.[47]

This had been clearly foreseen by Simcoe. When he first came to Upper Canada he stated categorically that the province was indefensible if the posts in American territory then held by the British (Niagara, Oswego, and Detroit) were given up. With the signing of Jay's Treaty these posts were evacuated. Simcoe immediately turned his attention to the next best thing:

roads which, by opening up communications over land, would by-pass the two critical areas. Dundas Street was planned to by-pass Niagara and Yonge Street to by-pass Detroit. These roads, of course, facilitated the process of settlement, but their prime purpose was strategic, as indeed was his choice of London on the River La Tranche as the new provincial capital. Very shortly after his arrival he wrote with enthusiasm to Dundas:

> I am happy to have found in the Surveyor's office an actual survey of the River *La Tranche*. It answers my most sanguine expectations & I have but little doubt but that its communication with the *Ontario & Erie* will be found practicable, the whole forming a route which in *all* respects may annihilate the political consequences of Niagara and Lake Erie.[48]

When, as Simcoe had anticipated, war did come, both Niagara and Detroit were successfully defended; but mediocre American generalship and poor support from federal and state governments had more to do with this than any of Simcoe's roads. It was a minor miracle which no one had any right to expect, and it did not mean that the danger had vanished. If American command of the lakes and the territory tributary to the lakes was not to be secured by war, had not peace more subtle weapons?

It is probably more significant than is commonly recognized that the legislators of New York State did not decide to construct their Great Western Canal to Lake Erie, rather than to Lake Ontario, until after the conclusion of the War of 1812. That the Great Lakes could and should be connected with the Atlantic by way of the Hudson and Mohawk rivers was generally agreed upon and had been so for some considerable time. But the question of the route remained open, and in particular the question of whether the projected canal should be cut to Lake Ontario or to Lake Erie. There was much to be said for the Ontario route: it was shorter, and more familiar to travelers and traders; greater advantage could be taken of natural waterways; and it would probably be much cheaper. The Erie route, on the other hand, was long and a far greater length of artificial navigation would be necessary. What was the sense of making this extended cutting south of Lake Ontario when the lake itself was available and could accommodate all the traffic which was then or was ever likely to be forthcoming?

For over three decades this question remained unsettled. According to Elkanah Watson, believed by some to be the original projector of the Erie Canal, up to 1798 "the utmost stretch of our views was to follow nature's canal, and to remove natural or artificial obstructions; but we never entertained the most distant conception of a canal from Lake Erie to the Hudson. We should not have considered it much more extravagant to have suggested the possibility of a canal to the moon." [49] The first serious advocacy of the Erie route came with Jesse Hawley's essays on internal navigation in 1807, the appointment of James Geddes as surveyor in 1808, and the famous report of the seven commissioners, of which De Witt Clinton was one, in 1811.[50] But still no final decision was taken. The war held up progress; the Supply Bill of 1814 annulled the power of the canal commissioners to borrow money on the credit of the state; and Governor Tompkins, Clinton's political rival, announced himself more in favor of roads than canals and, if canals were to be built, more in favor of the Lake Ontario than the Lake Erie route.[51] At the end of the war in 1815 New York was still a long way from the Great Lakes.

The first spadeful of earth on the Erie Canal was turned on July 4, 1817 — less than two years after the end of the war. What brought about this sudden change in sentiment? What new factor was introduced into the situation which put an end to debate and decided the matter in favor of the Lake Erie route? The immediate cause is obvious: the publication early in 1816 of the famous "Memorial of the Citizens of New York," written by De Witt Clinton.[52] But, as an examination of the arguments used in that memorial suggests, the fundamental consideration which tipped the scales in favor of the Erie route was none other than the recognition that, since armed aggression against Upper Canada had failed, Montreal's dominance of Lake Ontario would have to be accepted. There would be no purpose in cutting a canal from the Mohawk River to Lake Ontario unless a canal were also cut across the Niagara peninsula to connect Lake Ontario with Lake Erie. But, supposing such a canal were built, would it not benefit Montreal more than it did New York? Thus Clinton argued:

> The most serious objection against the Ontario route is, that it will inevitably enrich the territory of a foreign power, at the expense of the United States. If a canal is cut around the falls of Niagara, and no countervailing or counteracting system is adopted in relation to Lake Erie, the commerce of the west is lost to us for ever.[53]

The supporters of the Erie route, in short, argued as follows: if a cargo of western produce was once afloat on Lake Ontario, it would certainly go to Montreal rather than to New York. Even if prices were slightly higher in New York, a cargo from the western states, once it reached Lake Ontario, could just as easily go to Prescott or Ogdensburg, only one hundred and twenty miles from Montreal, as it could to Oswego, more than three times that distance from New York. Further, produce could go from Prescott to Montreal by way of the St. Lawrence in thirty hours, while from Oswego to New York took at least eight days.[54] Even if these factors of time and distance were discounted, the merchants of New York and Albany who were the chief supporters of the canal scheme had no wish even to run the risk of facilitating Montreal's communications with the interior in the attempt to improve their own. Would it not be far safer to by-pass Lake Ontario altogether, run the New York canal direct to Lake Erie, and leave the Niagara barrier as an obstacle in the British route to the interior, but not in the American?

The alternative had clear advantages. By tapping the flow of western produce beyond Niagara, on the lake where it was first shipped, Montreal's supremacy on Lake Ontario could be reduced to an empty boast. It was the territory tributary to Lake Erie which was the prize of the future. Even before the Erie Canal was finished, a comparison of freight rates suggested the profound effects it would produce. De Witt Clinton stated in 1819:

> At the present period a ton of commodities can be conveyed from Buffalo to Albany, by land, for one hundred dollars, and to Montreal, principally by water, for twenty-five. . . When the great western canal is finished, the expense of transportation from Buffalo to Albany, will not exceed ten dollars a ton. Almost the whole of the ascending trade of the west, will be derived from the city of New York, and a great portion of the descending products will accumulate in that important depot.[55]

These expectations, and others less modest, were amply to be fulfilled.

In the long-range commercial strategy of New York State which underlay the building of the Erie Canal, the Niagara barrier played a vital role. The fact that there could be no direct communication by water between Lake Ontario and Lake Erie was of basic importance in this peacetime metropolitan rivalry, just as it had been in the campaigns of the War of 1812. What decided the New York legislators in favor of the Lake Erie route was not the fact that they could not cut a canal across the Niagara barrier, but rather that they did not choose to do so. They wished it to remain a barrier, because they could circumvent it by means of the Erie Canal whereas Montreal could not. Once the Erie Canal was completed it would not, they believed, be of very much importance whether or not the British government or any other party built a Niagara canal. One New York propagandist argued in 1820 that

> . . . even if there was a canal cut round the falls of Niagara by the British government, it would be less expensive to take produce to New York, through the medium of the Western canal, from the mouth of Lake Erie, than from any point on the Niagara river to the city of Montreal. The facilities of returning from the respective places to the lake country will bear no comparison. The Hudson and the canal will afford a navigation that cannot be equalled by the St. Lawrence, with its rapids, dangers, and obstructions. Besides, the St. Lawrence is closed by the intensities of climate, about seven months in the year. The harbour of New York is open at all seasons, and the Hudson and the canals will be navigable two and perhaps three months longer than the St. Lawrence, and lead to a more extensive market.[56]

With these comforting reflections the fear of potential competition was assuaged. Nevertheless, if Montreal was ever to meet the challenge of the Erie Canal, a canal round the falls of Niagara would certainly be a prime requisite.

The Erie Canal, finally completed in 1825, succeeded brilliantly in achieving what military force had failed to achieve: the destruction of

Montreal's commercial empire around the lower lakes. No longer was western New York tributary to Montreal. No longer were Albany legislators reminded of "the well-known fact, that merchandize from Montreal has been sold to an alarming extent on our borders for fifteen per cent. below the New York prices." No longer did the steadily expanding exports of the Midwest have to find their way over the Niagara portage, across Lake Ontario, and down the rapids of the St. Lawrence. The Appalachian barrier had been overcome, and Montreal's commercial supremacy, based as it had been on a monopoly of the only natural water route (save the Mississippi) around that barrier, was at an end.

It was never to be regained. Not until 1848 was the canalization of the St. Lawrence completed, and by that date New York was building railroads. This is not the place to recapitulate D. G. Creighton's masterly analysis of the struggles of the Montreal mercantile community to rebuild their lost commercial empire.[57] Suffice it to say that the time for action was not after but before 1825, for after the Erie had been completed the trade of the West was already lost and its recovery necessarily an uphill battle with every advantage in favor of the New York route. Admittedly in 1825, after much financial difficulty, the Lachine Canal was completed, but this was little more than a token response, negligible in comparison with what was required.

Perhaps the major difficulty was that the task of improving the St. Lawrence route required coöperation between the two provinces, Upper and Lower Canada. For political reasons this was difficult to achieve. The French-dominated Assembly of Lower Canada was completely out of sympathy with the aspirations of the English mercantile community. The merchants themselves were not rich men, and those that made profits often remitted them to England for investment or purchased seigniories. The depression which began in 1819 caused severe financial stringency, and the disappearance of the North West Company and with it the St. Lawrence fur trade in 1821 was a serious blow. The timber trade, with its peculiar transportation requirements and its highly speculative and uncertain profits, did not encourage interest in canals. The British government, for its part, after assisting in the financing of the Lachine Canal, confined its energies and expenditure to the improvement of the Rideau, a project military rather than commercial in nature and a poor substitute for the canalization of the St. Lawrence which alone would have enabled Montreal to compete on something like equal terms with Buffalo, Albany, and New York. In sum, little was done, and the businessmen of Lower Canada, absorbed in their political squabbles with the French, quieted their consciences by reflecting that the St. Lawrence was "not placed there by the Great Maker for mere ornament" [58] and that the trade of the West would, in due season, return to its "natural" channel. And so the opportunity was allowed to pass.

The story which we are to tell in the pages which follow takes place in Upper Canada, not in Montreal. It is, in essence, the story of how Upper Canada met the challenge of the Erie Canal. That a reaction of some kind would occur was to be expected, for Upper Canada included the Niagara peninsula which, as we have seen, figured largely in the calculations of the New York canal-builders. Further, while the Erie Canal unified the western and eastern sections of New York State, it threatened to split the western and eastern sections of Upper Canada, for western Upper Canada, bordering Lake Erie, was certain to feel the pull of Buffalo and the New York market as soon as the canal was opened. This was already the part of the province most American in character, and commercial dependence on an American transportation route was certain to have political consequences. And yet, even if these considerations did suggest that Upper Canada would play a major role in the attempt to recapture for the St. Lawrence the trade of the West, was it to be expected that this inland province, with its population in 1824 of less than 150,000, would perform that role effectively? How well-equipped was Upper Canada, in terms of resources and organization, to embark on a program of canal construction?

From the point of view of economic resources, Upper Canada was well supplied with only one item: land. Capital was extremely scarce.[59] What income could be spared from consumption was ordinarily devoted to land purchase and agricultural improvements. The province had no seaport, and thus was deprived of the mercantile wealth which in other places proved a fruitful source of investible funds. Montreal merchants rarely invested in Upper Canada, except when they had to accept title to land or buildings in settlement of commercial debts. There were no banks until after 1815, and even then for many years the Bank of Upper Canada, a semigovernmental institution deriving its profits from the discounting of commercial and accommodation paper, not from long-term loans, dominated the financial scene. There were no joint stock companies until the early bank charters. Not until 1822 did Upper Canada have a public debt, and not until 1834 did the province float a loan in the London capital market.

Labor resources were more plentiful. There was probably a considerable volume of disguised unemployment in agriculture, forming a reserve which could be drawn on for public works. In addition, immigration could be depended upon to supplement the natural increase of the population. After 1815 a serious attempt was made by the provincial authorities to prevent Americans from settling in Upper Canada. Although it was difficult to distinguish an American from a Canadian once he had crossed the border, this attempt to shut out American immigration does appear to have diverted a considerable portion of the American westward movement away from Upper Canada and toward Ohio. Immigration from Britain was expected to compensate for the loss of American settlers, and to a certain extent did so, but the great increase in immigration from Britain did not begin until 1826, so that for approximately a decade the rate of increase of Upper Canada's labor force was less than might otherwise have obtained.[60] Whether immigrants from Britain remained in Canada or drifted south to the United States depended largely on the terms on which land could be purchased and on the employment opportunities available. On the whole, there do not seem to have been many cases in this period in which labor rather than capital was the limiting factor in development. One writer has concluded that "it was capital that set the pace. When capital was found for development, a commensurate labour supply was not far behind, if it was not already there." [61]

We have, then, to think of Upper Canada as an economy in which agriculture was still by far the predominant form of economic activity, an economy highly vulnerable to the price fluctuations of a few staple exports, with a rudimentary banking system and no large reserves of disposable wealth. The country merchant was still the typical if not the only variety of businessman with which the society was familiar. Experience in the promotion, management, and financing of large-scale business organizations was negligible.

But in many other respects Upper Canada entered upon the years after 1815 ill-prepared for the tasks which it was to face. These were the years when new theories of colonial government were arising to challenge the conception of a benevolent paternalism which was the legacy of Simcoe and his successors, when men faced and solved in principle if not yet in practice the problem of how colonies could govern themselves and yet retain allegiance in a wider empire. And these were the years, too, when the two Canadian provinces, still divided politically and yet inextricably linked together by economic interest, were searching for their justification and reason for being amid the crumbling ruins of the old system of imperial trade. To the necessity for solving these problems the ever-present threat and challenge of the young American republic to the south gave urgency. It was the catalytic quality of American ideas, reinforced by conceptions of personal liberty and self-government emanating from France and from Britain itself, which precipitated change and turned friction into open conflict. And it was the example of American ideas and the necessity for counteracting the threat of American expansion which led men, despite their inexperience and the paucity of their resources, to look to their interests and take up the work which needed to be done.

Such was the society in which, in the years after 1815, certain men took it upon themselves to undertake the construction of a canal across the Niagara peninsula. How they did so, who they were, and to what extent they succeeded, will be told in the chapters which follow.

CHAPTER TWO

PROMOTION

IN THIS CHAPTER WE SHALL BE CONCERNED WITH THE PROMOTION of the Welland Canal Company, which is to say with the events leading up to the securing of a charter from the legislature and the mobilizing of sufficient capital to commence construction. It is both natural and convenient to begin by introducing the man to whom tradition accords the chief credit for the work, namely William Hamilton Merritt. Our story begins, then, in March 1815, at the conclusion of the War of 1812, when Merritt returned to his home in Upper Canada from the prisoner-of-war camp in Massachusetts where he had been detained since his capture at the battle of Lundy's Lane eight months before. Born in the United States in 1793, Merritt had first come to Canada at the age of three with his father, Thomas Merritt, who had decided to settle in British territory.[1] Before the Revolution the Merritts had been a closely-knit clan of freehold farmers in Westchester County, New York. Thomas Merritt and his brothers had taken the king's side in the revolutionary fighting, and now in 1815 there were two main Loyalist branches of the family in the British North American colonies, one in Upper Canada, the other in New Brunswick.

Before joining the militia in 1812 William Hamilton Merritt had worked for a while in a local store in the village of St. Catharines, sometimes called Shipman's Corners, in the Niagara district. His commercial experience was, however, slight. As he later confessed in the privacy of his journal, "I understood no branch of business in which I was engaged, having been brought up without any fixed object in view of earning a livelihood."[2] Nevertheless, immediately the war was over, he plunged energetically into business, impressed perhaps with the newly-acquired responsibility of supporting a wife who was the daughter of a New York senator.[3] First he arranged for the construction of a large house and general store in St. Catharines. Shortly thereafter he bought a farm and a mill site on Twelve Mile Creek, a small stream which adjoined his father's property, and there built a milldam, a sawmill, a flour mill with three run of stones, a distillery, a potashery, a cooper shop, and a smithy, not to mention five dwelling houses for the accommodation of his employees. About the same time he began drilling for salt, sinking two shafts to tap a spring under his property. In September 1816, when his sister married a certain Charles Ingersoll who had been his subordinate officer during the war, Merritt took his brother-in-law into partnership and moved his store into his new partner's house.[4]

By the end of 1816 the firm of Merritt and Ingersoll could boast extensive property and a well-integrated range of business activities. For this achievement most of the credit was due to Merritt, who in these two years displayed for the first time the driving energy, impatience, and enthusiasm which were to be the most striking characteristics of his subsequent career.

Securely founded as the young partnership might appear, it had its weak points. Merritt and Ingersoll had discounted future risks very heavily, and the evidence of their optimism hung over them in the form of debts and liabilities. For the house and store in St. Catharines (now unnecessarily large since the business had been transferred to Ingersoll's establishment) Merritt had incurred a debt of $1250. The farm and mill site had originally been part of the estate of Robert Hamilton, first and most influential of the Niagara merchants, and it was still encumbered by a debt to Hamilton's executors. In purchasing the property Merritt gave bond that he would pay up to $1000 in satisfaction of the debt, the whole transaction ultimately costing him $4000.[5] In taking his brother-in-law into partnership Merritt gained the assistance of a wartime comrade whom he could trust and whose capacity he knew, but it does not appear that Ingersoll contributed any financial resources beyond the use of his house. The mills, distillery, and other ventures were valuable ancillaries to the store business but they were all built on borrowed money, supplied principally by Merritt's father and father-in-law. Only highly optimistic estimates of future earning capacity could justify such heavy liabilities.

Apart from these relatively long-term investments, Merritt required credit to buy goods for his store. During 1815, before entering the partnership with Ingersoll, he traveled to Montreal, Quebec, New York, Albany, and Utica, making arrangements for credit in each place and ordering consignments of goods. His purchases were extensive, amounting in all to just under $6640. Since his house was not yet completed, Merritt divided his consignments into small parcels and offered them for sale at St. Catharines, Queenston, and the naval station on Grand River, all in the Niagara peninsula. This first venture, coming as it did in time to reap the full benefit of high prices and inflated postwar demand, appears to have been successful.[6]

There was nothing novel or original about this store business, although the scale on which Merritt planned to operate was perhaps exceptional. He was merely following the example of many other upcountry merchants in Canada and throughout North America, Montreal being for him what Boston, New York, Philadelphia, Baltimore, and similar seaports were for others.[7] It was a system which, so far as Upper Canada was concerned, had not altered materially since 1797, when Richard Cartwright, a merchant of Kingston, had written to Davison & Company of London to explain why he could not deal with them directly:

> Not having a seaport in our Province, it would be impossible or extremely inconvenient for any person here to import goods except through the medium of a Montreal house. . . The mode usually practised is this: the merchant sends his order for English goods to his correspondent at Montreal, who imports them from London, guarantees the payment of them there, and receives and forwards them to this country for a commission of five per cent on the amount of the English invoice. The payments are all made by the Upper Canada merchant in Montreal, and there is no direct communication whatever between him and the shipper in London. . . This mode of business seems necessarily to be imposed on us by our inland situation.[8]

Storekeeping was a not inappropriate choice of occupation for a young man like Merritt — not much inclined to farming, without sufficient influence to obtain employment in the colonial bureaucracy, and lacking the education to equip him for a profession. It was generally thought to be highly profitable. As late as 1844 John Langton asserted that he knew of no money-making business in Upper Canada other than the law, storekeeping, tavern-keeping, and horse-dealing. "Store-keeping," he wrote, "is decidedly the most money-making and is carried on with very little capital, but it appears to me that those who make it pay are invariably those who have started with next to nothing and have gradually crept up in the world, increasing their business as their capital, custom, and experience increased."[9] A knowledge of simple bookkeeping and a healthy fear of the consequences of "over-trading" were more important qualifications than formal education, political influence, or high social position.

From the economic point of view, the strength of Merritt's position lay in the integration of his store with the manufacturing establishments which he was erecting on Twelve Mile Creek. The water power of the Creek was the key to his plans and aspirations. It was on the proceeds of these enterprises — the mills, distillery, and the rest — that he was mainly relying to meet his notes as they fell due, to maintain his credit standing in Montreal, and to pay off the local debts incurred at St. Catharines. Especially important was the gristmill, which would enable him to send consignments of flour, less bulky and more valuable than wheat, down the St. Lawrence to the Montreal market. There it would be disposed of by the commission agents with whom he had established regular correspondence, Messrs. Armour and Davies. The proceeds of these consignments, supplemented from time to time by such government bills as he might receive in trade from half-pay officers, pensioners, and the like, would, assuming remunerative prices, suffice to pay off his debts and maintain amicable relations with his wholesalers. Such at least was the system on which Merritt proposed to do business and which gave point to the closely-related enterprises he was building around the water power of Twelve Mile Creek.

Merritt had, however, entered upon his business career at a time when the effects of inflationary war finance between 1812 and 1815 were still being felt. War expenditures for the supply of troops in Upper Canada had created a situation which was highly abnormal and which dissipated itself by 1818. His heavy investments and the extended scale on which he planned to operate were not to prove justified outside the immediate economic context which inspired them.

Merritt's energies during these years were not completely taken up by his store and his mills. Not only did he take his initial steps in political activity in support of Robert Gourlay, the intransigent Scottish agitator whose brief sojourn in Upper Canada marked the beginning of organized opposition to the government, but also, and more important, in 1818 he showed the first signs of interests in what was to prove his lifelong obsession: waterway improvements.

At the close of the summer of 1818, when Merritt returned from his annual purchasing trip to Montreal, he found himself confronted with a problem of some seriousness in connection with his flour and saw mills on Twelve Mile Creek. With the cutting of timber and clearing of land which had accompanied the settlement of the Niagara peninsula, the flow of water in the Creek had diminished and its seasonal fluctuations become more extreme. There was either too much water or too little, sudden freshets in the spring, a mere trickle in the summer. An unexpected flood might destroy the milldam, a summer drought might dry up the stream, halt the mill wheels, and make it impossible for Merritt to bring up by boat the supplies needed for his store. The problem was especially acute at the end of a hot, dry summer such as that which had just passed, and it was not confined to Merritt. There were other millers on Twelve Mile Creek — George Keefer, John DeCew, and others — who faced the same difficulty of supplementing and regulating the water supply on which their livelihood depended. Merritt talked the matter over with the other millers, borrowed a water level, and on September 18, 1818, proceeded with their help to survey the course of Twelve Mile Creek and in particular to estimate the height of a certain ridge of high ground which separated the headwaters of the creek from the Chippawa or Welland River. The field notes taken on this occasion have been preserved.[10] Merritt estimated the height of the ridge at thirty feet, which was approximately half the correct elevation.

What Merritt and his friends intended to do at this point is quite clear: they hoped to dig a cutting from the Welland River to the headwaters of the creek, thus remedying the lack of water which was restricting the working of their mills. To say that they were planning a canal would be an exaggeration; what they had in mind was something not much larger than an irrigation ditch. But it required little imagination to discern the far-reaching implications of the scheme.

Lake Ontario and Lake Erie are separated by the Niagara peninsula, a neck of land of some twenty-five miles in width. Lake Erie is about three hundred feet higher above sea level than Lake Ontario, to which it is connected by the Niagara River, with the famous falls of Niagara marking the difference in level. The problem of constructing a navigable waterway between the two lakes is essentially a matter of surmounting this difference in level — of accomplishing by means of locks and cuttings, one might almost say, what the falls of Niagara accomplish in one magnificent leap.[11]

Along the length of the Niagara peninsula, from east to west, there runs, roughly parallel to the shore of Lake Ontario, a geological formation popularly known as "the Mountain." The name is misleading, for the formation is not a mountain but an escarpment between two plateaus. Probably in some remote age it formed the shore of the lake. This escarpment stretches the whole length of the peninsula, approximating in some places to a rocky cliff, crosses the Niagara ravine at Queenston and Lewiston, the northern termini of the Canadian and American portages, and continues into American territory.[12]

Along the northern margin of the peninsula, between the foot of the escarpment and the shore of Lake Ontario, lies the first of our two plateaus, a narrow coastal strip of highly fertile land. Along the top of the escarpment, and forming as it were the spine of the peninsula, there runs a ridge, about sixty feet high and two miles across. This was the ridge which Merritt and his friends had surveyed. South of this ridge and approximately parallel to it runs the Welland or Chippawa River, which enters the Niagara River above the falls. Between the Welland River and Lake Erie lies the second of our plateaus, a stretch of flat, swampy land very little above the level of the lake. The Welland is a slow, deep stream with an average gradient of about two and one-half feet per mile throughout its length and navigable by boats drawing up to twelve feet of water for a distance of some thirty miles from its mouth. For our purposes, then, the chief topographical features of the peninsula are the Lake Ontario plateau, the escarpment, the ridge, the Welland River, and the Lake Erie plateau. Each of these may be visualized without very great error as running roughly parallel to the others.

Flowing down the escarpment and across the coastal strip into Lake Ontario were and are a number of small creeks, popularly known by the approximate distances of their mouths from the mouth of the Niagara River. Twelve Mile Creek, the locus of Merritt's activities, was one of these. There was nothing particularly distinctive about it, except perhaps the fact that near the village of St. Catharines it forked into two main branches, the eastward of which descended the escarpment directly, while the westward followed a more leisurely course from DeCew Falls, three miles southwest of the village. Twelve Mile Creek had its source near a place now known as Allanburgh. From Allanburgh due south across the ridge to the Welland River the distance was only about two and a half miles.

The escarpment and these few miles of high ground between Allanburgh and the Welland River represented the only major obstacles to a continuous water communication between Lake Erie and Lake Ontario. To render this communication navigable even by small boats was, of course, no small problem, but in its bare essentials the idea was very simple. The Niagara River was navigable from Lake Erie to the mouth of the Welland; the Welland was navigable from its junction with the Niagara to any point less than thirty miles upstream; Twelve Mile Creek required only enlargement and deepening to be navigable from Lake Ontario to the foot of the escarpment. Something would have to be done about the ascent of the escarpment, for the ravine which the main branch of the creek had cut for itself was by no means suitable in its natural state for the passage of boats. But some simple expedient — perhaps a wooden slide or "railway" such as the fur-traders had used on the Lewiston portage for their *bateaux* — would overcome this difficulty. Then only the ridge would remain to separate the two watercourses. A tunnel or deep cutting would certainly be required for this section, for it would form the summit level of the canal and therefore could not be permitted to rise above the level of the water supply, or in other words the Welland River.

Precisely when and by whom the possibilities which lay behind Merritt's crude and amateurish survey were first realized is a matter for conjecture. There is no evidence on the point, nor perhaps is it of much importance. By the fourteenth of October, when the survey and plans were presented at a public meeting in Niagara, the project had already grown beyond its original bounds. From a ditch to convey water, it had become a canal to carry boats. And as the project became more concrete and its feasibility more apparent, so did opposition begin to show itself. The coöperation of the farmers, millers, and merchants of the St. Catharines area could be taken for granted. Not so the support of Niagara and Queenston which, if Merritt got his way as to the route to be followed, would be by-passed and the portage which was the backbone of their business life ruined. Niagara boasted two newspapers, it was the principal source of local capital, and it had influence in the legislature. Its good will could not lightly be sacrificed.[13]

It was perhaps fortunate that Merritt's knowledge of surveying was imperfect and the instruments available to him inadequate, for had the height of the ridge been correctly estimated the project might well have been abandoned after the first surveys. It may have been this error which convinced Merritt and his friends that a canal was practicable. The first petition to the legislature, dated October 14, 1818, reflected the optimism which characterized their approach to the problem:

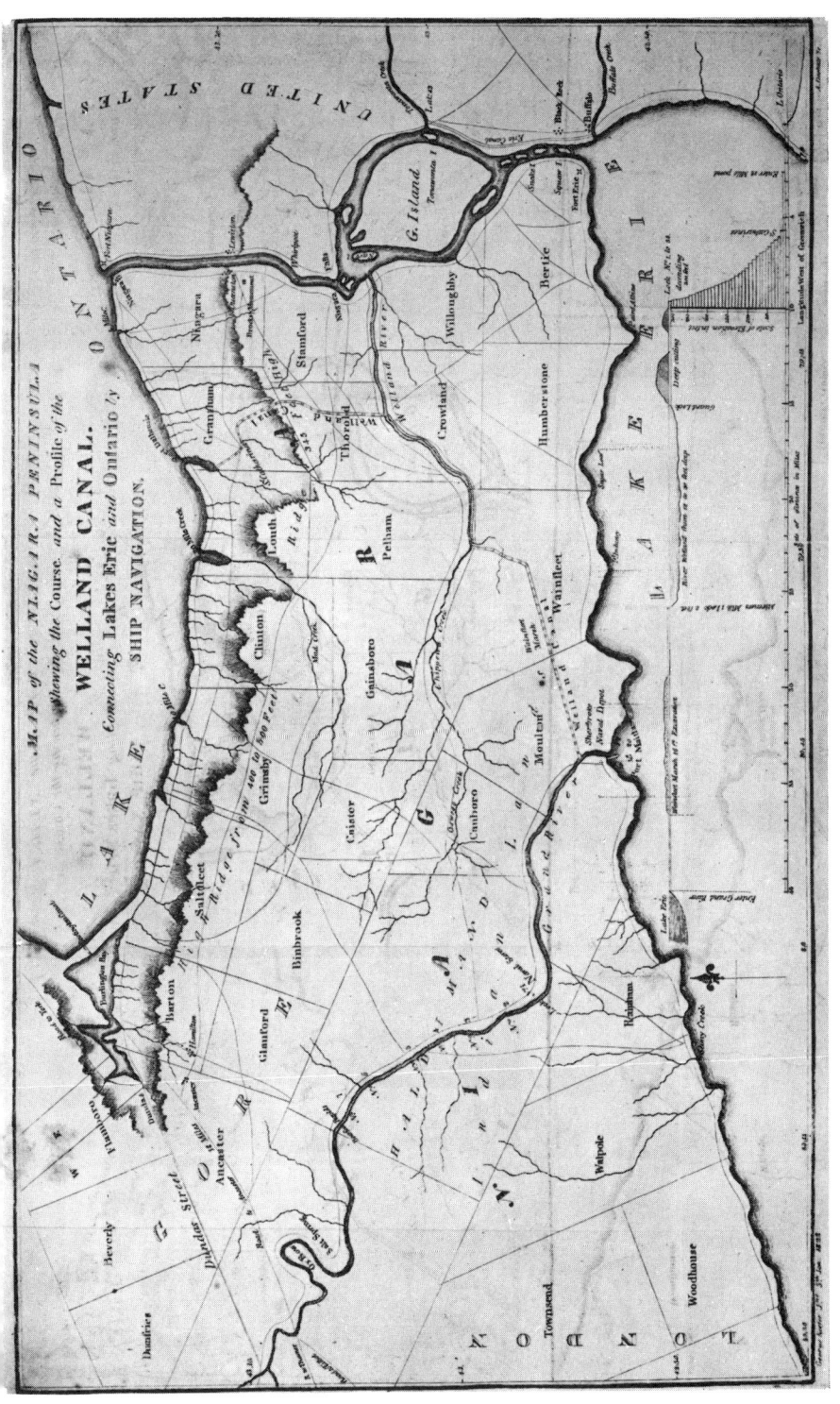

THE WELLAND CANAL
as planned in 1824 and 1825

Source: *American Journal of Science and Arts* (July 1828)

Your Petitioners, viewing the great benefits these provinces will derive from having a Canal made between Lakes Erie and Ontario, have examined the Report on levelling the land between Chippewa [sic] and the source of the Twelve Mile Creek, and have every reason to believe that a communication can be effected at a trifling expense, from the accompanying plan which will be submitted to Your Honorable Body. From the source of the Twelve Mile Creek where the excavation will end, to the brow of the Mountain at Captain Du Coo's [sic] is a gentle descent, not a lock will be necessary; after descending the Falls it will be necessary to make locks to pass four or five Milldams, and the navigation will be complete for boats to Lake Ontario.

The grand object of the American people appears to be opening a navigation with Lake Erie, which design our canal, if effected soon, would counteract; and take down the whole of the produce from the Western country.

Your Petitioners therefore beg that you will appoint some scientific men to view the country between Chippewa [sic] and Lake Ontario, and adopt such measures for carrying the above objects into effect as you in your wisdom may deem meet.[14]

Several points may be noted about this petition. In the first place the objective of the proposed canal was explicitly stated to be to capture the trade of the American Midwest and of western Upper Canada, and thus to counteract the anticipated effects of the Erie Canal, then under construction. Secondly, the petitioners did not request incorporation as a chartered company, nor give any indication that they proposed to undertake construction themselves. They asked merely for the appointment of official surveyors and some expression of legislative interest. And thirdly, the petition was submitted, not over the signatures of Merritt and his neighbors alone, but as supported by men of influence throughout the Niagara district. Merritt did not make himself conspicuous.[15]

The petition, it will be observed, specified Merritt's Twelve Mile Creek route. Opposition in the Niagara press appeared at once. On October 29, Andrew Heron, editor of the *Gleaner,* expressed his strong disapproval:

If the intention is to bring the canal down the mountain in the channel of the 12 Mile Creek, we consider that impracticable as the great freshets that come down that stream collected on the high lands would impede the navigation at times and injure the locks. It would also be very difficult to form a harbour on the banks of the lake even for boats, the great body of loose sand would render it very difficult upon a large plan. We are decidedly of opinion that the canal should come into the Niagara river, where every vessel would be sure of a good harbour and a lock could be constructed to receive vessels of 100 tons burthen. . . Whatever is done we hope it will be done on a large plan; paltry improvements are only throwing away money.[16]

In the legislature, the petition was referred as a "matter of great National Importance" to a select committee of four members, who reported themselves in favor of the project, but implied in their statement that it should be handled by a private company. "It is the opinion of Your Committee," they reported,

> . . . that a canal cut agreeably to the plan proposed by the Petitioners alluded to would be of great benefit to the Commercial Interests of the Province, and ought to be encouraged by every means of furtherance by Your Honorable House.
>
> And Your Committee are further of opinion that should any number of persons be disposed to associate themselves for the purpose of carrying such a project into execution, it would comport with the true interests of this Province to give to such an incorporated body the authority and sanction of law, and to provide for their obtaining the use of such lands as may be required for the cutting of the said canal in a manner similar to that already pointed out by the Statute for the improvement and altering of Highways and Roads throughout the Province.[17]

And there, for the moment, the matter rested.

We have already observed that Merritt's scheme called for no great originality of conception. It is equally important to note that it fell upon receptive ears. Waterway improvement schemes were at this time being discussed in the highest quarters, and had been under active consideration since the close of the war. The strain on military communications and lines of supply occasioned by the American attack on Upper Canada had called attention in no uncertain manner to the limitations of the St. Lawrence River in its unimproved condition. Not only was it highly vulnerable, forming as it did for a considerable distance the international boundary, but it was of limited capacity, interrupted by rapids, slow, and expensive. The cost of transport from Montreal to Kingston was as high as fifty-four shillings per hundredweight, while to take a 24-pounder gun from Quebec to Amherstburg cost £600.[18] The danger that, in the event of renewed hostilities, the line of supply might be cut completely was perhaps of greater weight with the colonial authorities than considerations of cost, but the fact remained that during the winter of 1814–15 the contractors for the transport of government stores between Montreal and Kingston had cleared a net profit of £30,000.[19] Considerations of strategy and economy, therefore, combined to suggest the need for an alternative or improved route. In 1815 a certain Lieutenant Jebb was detailed to investigate the possibility of constructing a water communication between Montreal and Kingston by way of the Ottawa and Rideau rivers. With the end of the war his report was temporarily shelved. It contained the first survey of the route of the Rideau Canal, the construction of which was begun by the British government in 1827.

Wartime experience likewise directed attention, though with somewhat less urgency, to the desirability of a canal across the Niagara peninsula. It was the Niagara barrier which had made necessary the maintenance of separate fleets on Lakes Ontario and Erie, and command of the lakes had shown itself to be indispensable to successful operations on land. The two portage roads — one on the Canadian and one on the American side — were even more obvious bottlenecks in the through route than the St. Lawrence rapids and no less certain to be put out of action in the event of war. As early as 1799 Robert Hamilton, intimately connected as he was with the business of the Niagara portage, had petitioned the legislature for permission to construct a canal, but his bill had provoked wide opposition and was dropped. With Hamilton's death in 1809, nothing further was done.[20] During the war the lack of such a canal necessitated the transport of supplies for the Detroit frontier overland from the head of Lake Ontario to the Grand River and thence to Oxford on the Thames.[21] Naval operations on the lakes and the difficulties of land transportation strikingly demonstrated the potential military value of a Niagara canal. But at the same time the vulnerability of the Niagara peninsula to American attack impressed itself forcibly on military minds. This conflict between defense and convenience was not to be easily resolved.

But interest in canal construction was not confined to the imperial strategists. It was also a matter of immediate importance to the agriculturalists and merchants of the two Canadas. Almost every visitor to Upper Canada in the ten years after 1815 commented upon the benefits which canals would bring, and the apparent ease with which they could be constructed. Widespread local interest in the subject reflected itself in numerous expressions of legislative concern, but little effective action. In February 1817 Lieutenant Governor Gore commended the provincial legislature for the liberal appropriations made for road construction, adding that "the water communication of the River St. Lawrence below Prescott is also deserving of your serious consideration." The legislature responded with a small appropriation for a preliminary survey. In the same session one Adam Dixon, a merchant of Cornwall, requested permission to construct locks at Moulinette and Mille Roches as a means of "facilitating the intercourse between the two provinces, particularly at a time when in a neighbouring country every effort is made at internal improvements for the purpose of diverting into new channels that trade which we have hitherto enjoyed." His petition was backed by twelve merchants of Upper Canada and no less than seventeen Montreal firms, but was rejected on the ground that other individuals had already begun the work.[22] In the session of 1818 a joint address of the two houses of the legislature declared the improvement of the St. Lawrence to be a subject of the first importance and expressed a "desire that concurrent means may be adopted by both Provinces for effecting so desirable an object on liberal and united principles."[23] Meanwhile the legislature of Lower Canada had voted £500 for navigation improvements. Commissioners appointed by each province declared in a joint report submitted in October 1818 that the improvement of internal navigation was essential to the prosperity of both provinces in time of peace and to their security in time of war, and went on to argue that:

> To secure to these Provinces the advantages of the Trade they already
> possess, it is urgent that no time should be lost in forwarding the work
> necessary to facilitate such water communication before the United
> States may have completed their grand Canal from Lake Erie to the Hud-
> son River, in the State of New York; which canal when so completed will
> carry to New York the numerous and precious cargoes which would
> continue to be exported by the Province of Quebec, if both Canadas
> availed themselves of the means they have to carry the same at a smaller
> expense and in a shorter time by the natural outlet of the St. Lawrence.[24]

If reports and resolutions alone could have built canals, Upper Canada
would have had no need to fear the competition of "Clinton's ditch."
Public interest in the matter was no less in Upper Canada than in New York.
But more was necessary than awareness of the problem and confidence
that it could be solved. Effective action demanded agreement on such basic
questions as who should build the canals, where, when, and at whose
expense.

For a while it looked as if something would be done. On November 18,
1818, a joint address of both houses of the Upper Canada legislature was
adopted praying for an appropriation of the waste lands of the Crown "for
the purpose of improving the navigation of the River St. Lawrence and for
cutting canals through this province." At the same time an act was passed
appropriating £2000 to defray the costs of surveys.[25] And then suddenly the
wheels of government ground to a stop. Quite unexpectedly and through
no fault of its own, Upper Canada found itself deprived of its principal
source of public revenue. A political crisis in Lower Canada had blocked
the passage of the usual bill for the appointment of commissioners to
negotiate with Upper Canada over the division of the customs revenues.
These duties, collected in Lower Canada and divided between the provinces
by arbitration, had always been a fruitful source of contention. Usually
some modus vivendi had been found, but now in 1819 the squabbles of the
Lower Canada Assembly with the governor and his Councils had culminated
in complete deadlock.

The repercussions on the finances of the upper province were immediate
and serious. In the summer of 1819 Robert Nichol, chairman of the select
committee on the public accounts, submitted a report to the Assembly which
showed a deficit of £16,600 to be covered by new taxation. Nichol had been
quartermaster general of militia during the war; probably no man in the
province had a more intimate personal knowledge of the difficulties at-
tending the transport of supplies to and from Montreal than he. Nevertheless he felt bound to recommend to the Assembly that "of the above
deficiency the sum for the survey of the River St. Lawrence may not be
called for, and with a view of relieving the Provincial Revenue from the
present pressure, it might be desirable to address His Excellency, the Lieu-

tenant Governor, requesting him to suspend the operations of the Bill until the funds are provided to meet the expense." [26] For the next two years all legislative action in connection with the improvement of internal navigation was halted.

This breakdown in continuity of development was in essence a consequence of the limitations of that cornerstone of the Canadian constitution, the Act of 1791. The conflict between autocratic government based on Crown revenues from land and democratic aspirations imported from the United States, France, and Ireland and based on revenues from trade, reached its climax first in Lower Canada, but had serious repercussions upon Upper Canada with its more homogeneous population and greater preoccupation with public expenditures for developmental purposes. The upper province, dependent for the greater part of its public revenue on import duties levied at the only place where trade was sufficiently concentrated and regular to be taxed, and denied by its lack of a seaport the capital accumulations in private hands which might have rendered dependence on legislative action less essential, was vulnerable not only to political disunity within its own borders, but also to the deep-rooted conflicts of Lower Canada. The limitations of a constitution based on land ownership and on an executive owning responsibility only to the British parliament and the colonial office received their first practical demonstration in 1819. Many years were to pass before these limitations were recognized and attempts made to remedy them. In the meantime petitions remained unanswered and waterways unimproved.

Meanwhile Merritt's affairs had taken a sudden turn for the worse, as had those of the economy as a whole. The first few years after the conclusion of the War of 1812 had been a period of considerable prosperity for Upper Canada. These good years now abruptly ended, as agricultural prices slumped and credit evaporated. The prime cause of the brief period of postwar prosperity had lain in the existence of a large local market which nullified the effects of an inland situation and high costs of access to the sea. Before the war such a market had been provided by military garrisons, by such public works as the government undertook, and by the American settlements which were developing around the south side of the lakes.[27] During the war it had been provided by military purchases within the colony. The military commissariat spent freely, for the regular troops and the militia had to be fed and, thanks to the openhanded issue of Army Bills by government agents at Montreal and Niagara, there was no shortage of currency. By February 1815 there was a total of £1.3 million of these bills in circulation.[28]

The short-run effect of the war, then, was highly stimulating. Insofar as an agrarian economy, only one stage removed from barter, can experience an inflation, Upper Canada did. Suddenly it became easy to make money.

But the long-run effects were less happy. After 1815 local markets dwindled sharply. The American settlements were now competitors, not customers. Army Bill currency was rapidly called in and converted into bills on London which were remitted in payment for imports, thus exercising a highly deflationary influence.[29] This was accentuated by heavy imports of livestock from the United States for the restocking of Canadian farms between 1815 and 1817, apparent in numerous complaints that precious specie was disappearing across the border and not returning. Meanwhile in Britain the Corn Law of 1815 closed the ports to colonial wheat until the British price rose above 67s. a quarter.[30] An excellent British harvest in 1820 brought the price well below this figure. With the demobilization of the militia, agricultural labor was released for employment, and increased Canadian production, when the British ports were closed, glutted the Montreal market and brought catastrophic price falls. Deep depression in the United States after 1819 completed the picture. Between 1819 and 1822 the Upper Canada price of wheat fell from about one dollar a bushel to fifty cents. Livestock prices were reduced by about one half and real-estate values by a greater percentage.[31] This downward trend of agricultural prices accentuated the burden of the farmer's indebtedness to the local merchant and of the latter's debts to Montreal. By 1821 an informed observer could write:

> Most of the merchants have very large outstanding debts, which, if collected by means of suits, would ruin two-thirds of the farmers in the Province; and should the Montreal wholesale dealers have recourse to similar measures, many of their correspondents would become insolvent likewise.[32]

Upper Canada after 1815 faced for the first time the challenge of competition in export markets. Agricultural distress from 1817 onward, which seems to have been particularly severe in the war-ravaged Niagara district, and agitation for the improvement of the St. Lawrence navigation, originating partly in the same locality, were symptomatic of the new situation.[33] A select committee of the Assembly reporting in 1821 summarized the problem succinctly: "The great and indeed only efficient measure by which . . . a permanent relief can be afforded to the commerce of Upper Canada, and the safe, easy, expeditious and economical exportation of our staples to the markets to which we have access can be secured, is the improvement of our inland navigation." [34]

Transportation improvements and agricultural recovery were alike slow in arriving. In the interim, Merritt's attention and energies were too fully occupied with immediate problems of survival and solvency to permit further progress with his canal scheme. By the end of 1816 the firm of Merritt and Ingersoll had local debts to the amount of $8400, mostly incurred for the purchase of property in the neighborhood of St. Catharines. By 1819, in addition to these liabilities, they had trade debts amounting to more than $6400. Messrs. Armour and Davies, their Montreal agents, obtained judgment against them for a debt of $1307, and the house and mills as well as Ingersoll's lands in western Upper Canada were mortgaged as security for payment. Other creditors were less fortunate. Merritt's saltworks, too, proved difficult to exploit; rock drilling was necessary and the lining of the shaft to prevent the entry of fresh water was an unlooked-for expense. Not until January 1818 was brine obtained in strength and volume sufficient to make boiling commercially practicable. Four years after his entry into business, then, Merritt was bankrupt, a situation with which he was to become increasingly familiar.[35]

Whether the circumstances of Merritt's first introduction to the hazards of business life, and in particular his early education in the gentle art of paying old debts with new, had any influence upon his subsequent career is a matter for conjecture. One thing is clear: namely that when in 1823 Merritt was freed at last by the aid of his relatives from the more pressing of his debts and could turn his attention once again to the canal project set aside five years before, the tactics he used were strikingly at variance with those adopted in 1818. The petition of 1818 had been framed in terms of government construction; Merritt and his friends had given no indication that they contemplated building the canal themselves. Now at the end of 1823 a different and bolder approach was used. What Merritt wanted now was a private company.

The explanation for this new strategy is not far to seek. Although no progress in actual canal construction had been made in the five years' interval, the government had not been entirely idle. Surveys had been made and plans drawn up. A Niagara canal of some sort was almost certain to be begun within the next few years. The trouble was that the canal which the government proposed to build did not suit Merritt's book at all. For one thing, if the plans were adhered to, it would not run through Twelve Mile Creek.

A select committee of the Assembly, reporting in 1821, had strongly recommended that an immediate start be made with canal construction.[36] Imperial aid was relied upon, and the technical difficulties discounted. Data from the reports of the New York canal commissioners were used to obtain a "tolerably correct estimate" of the costs involved. Acting on these recommendations, the legislature had appointed three canal commissioners, and the Clowes brothers, Samuel and James, who had something of a reputation as land surveyors, had been hired as engineers. The next two years were occupied with surveys and exploration. In 1823 three reports were submitted, one dealing with the Niagara project, one with the Kingston–Ottawa route, and one with a proposed cutting between Lake Ontario and Burlington Bay.[37]

These reports are extremely interesting, not because they had any very important direct consequences but as showing what may be called the official view of how the improvement of internal navigation should be carried out. The select committee of 1821 had recommended that "a work of this description should not be on an exposed frontier, but should be, wherever circumstances admit of it, inland." With this advice, reflecting as it did the almost obsessive fear of American invasion which characterized official policy in this period, the canal commissioners heartily concurred. The consequence was that for the Niagara project they recommended a canal sixty-two miles long, from Burlington Bay to Grand River, the summit level of which was to be supplied by a feeder which ran through a three-mile tunnel. If they had been called upon to map out the most roundabout, expensive, and technically difficult route imaginable, they could hardly have done a better job. But no one could deny that such a canal would not be on an exposed frontier. A similar bias inspired their recommendations for a route from Lake Ontario to tidewater. No use was to be made of the St. Lawrence River above Montreal. Instead they recommended the Kingston–Ottawa–Lachine route which was later adopted by the British government for the Rideau Canal — 218 miles in length as against 170 by the St. Lawrence, and requiring a total lockage of 509 feet, compared with 216½ by the river route.[38] But, once again, it was not on an exposed frontier.

The reasons for this curious antipathy to the shortest distance between two points are sufficiently obvious. Military considerations were of prime importance, the convenience of commerce secondary. The canals were to be built by government organizations, not by private corporations concerned with economy and profits. Their justification was to be found, not in commercial advantage, but in the security of the province. The assumption seems to have been that, once the canals were built, the trade would pass through them, and if the routes chosen were a little longer, a little more roundabout, a little more expensive, that was not of much significance.

The abandonment of the St. Lawrence route was, however, of vital long-run importance, and illustrates the defensive strategy which underlay government policy. As Stacey has pointed out, every British officer who considered Canadian defence problems in the decade 1815–25 reported that a water communication with the Great Lakes independent of the St. Lawrence was a fundamental requirement.[39] If Montreal were to be attacked by an invading American force, that force would come by one of two routes: down the St. Lawrence, or down the Champlain–Richelieu valley. On both these routes, the rapids which were a hazard to commerce were a positive asset from the point of view of defence. To circumvent them would only make invasion easier — a point of view admirably expressed in Sir J. S. Smyth's comment to General Mann: "It does not appear to me that Lt. Col. By has taken a judicious view of the military features of defences in Canada by proposing to improve the navigation of the River from Lake Champlain to the St. Lawrence. If he could add to the impediments, it would, in my opinion, be more advantageous to His Majesty's Service." [40]

Less obviously detrimental to the interests of trade was the official Niagara route. Both Burlington Bay and Grand River had admirable harbors, and probably a government canal along the route recommended by the Clowes brothers, if it could have been built, would have served for the time being. But Hamilton Merritt could hardly be expected to think so. The problems which had first suggested a canal to his mind were still present: the erratic water supply of Twelve Mile Creek, the difficulty of bringing up supplies from the lake shore, the failing power for his mills. Whatever could be said in favor of the government route, it did not pass through Twelve Mile Creek. Nor would it bring that rise in property values on which Merritt was counting to reward him for his labors.

This report on the Erie–Ontario canal was tabled in February, 1823. In the same month Merritt took up once again, in a series of public meetings, the Twelve Mile Creek project. Local support was at first hesitant, but by April sufficient funds had been collected in St. Catharines and Niagara to set about obtaining a survey which would be somewhat more reliable than that initially provided by Merritt and his friends. An engineer named Hiram Tibbet was at this time surveying the line for a similar canal on the American side.[41] Merritt engaged him as soon as his contract expired in May. By the tenth of that month Tibbet had completed his survey and submitted his report.[42]

On March 9, Merritt had written to his wife: "The waters of the Chip[pawa] Cr. will be down the Twelve in two years from this time as certain as fate . . . by a correct calculation $10,000 will accomplish the excavation of the ground." [43] Tibbet's figures were higher than this, but certainly they were optimistic enough. For a canal large enough to pass boats of from twenty to forty tons and drawing four feet of water, he estimated a total cost of about $34,500. If locks were to be used for the descent of the escarpment, instead of the "railroad" of the original plan, he surmised that the cost would be increased by some $20,000. He also proposed a deep cutting from the Welland instead of the proposed tunnel. In general, he confirmed what Merritt and his friends had believed since 1818: that a canal could be constructed cheaply and quickly and that the best route was from the Welland to one of the branches of Twelve Mile Creek.

If Merritt wanted a report which would impress the unsophisticated, this was it. Tibbet was either an incompetent surveyor or his report was "designed to meet the needs of men who desired not advice but corroboration." [44] The fact was that both legislative approval and popular support were necessary if the Clowes route was to be abandoned; to obtain them Merritt needed a report which did not dwell on difficulties. Tibbet was probably well aware that any figures he provided would not be scrutinized with an experienced or overcritical eye.

It is interesting to speculate what would have happened if an American Niagara canal such as that on which Tibbet is said to have been engaged had been completed before the Welland. Certainly many years would have elapsed before the volume of traffic would have justified duplication on the Canadian side. Yet it is clear that, with the only communication between Lakes Erie and Ontario passing through American territory, the high strategy of the imperial planners who built the Rideau with such careful attention to the threat of American attack would have made little sense. The western peninsula of Upper Canada would have been well-nigh indefensible, and the trade of the Midwest would have passed down to Montreal only on American suffrance. In point of fact, this was only one of several projects for an American Niagara canal which were to appear during the next two decades. None of them came to fruition, in the first place because the Welland was already under construction, and secondly because of the opposition of the Buffalo forwarding houses, who were by no means enthusiastic over the prospect of a substantial portion of their trade being diverted through Lake Ontario and thence to Montreal or Oswego.[45] Nevertheless, just as the Erie Canal acted as the spur to Canadian canals generally, so the prospect of an American canal between Lakes Erie and Ontario made it urgent that a Canadian canal between the lakes should be completed, not some time in the remote future, but soon.

It was in this spirit of urgency that Merritt formally introduced his project to the lieutenant governor on June 2, 1823. He requested no legislative assistance beyond a charter. The canal, as he proposed it should be built, was to run from Lake Ontario to the Welland River; from there a branch was to strike across country to the Grand River estuary, thus giving a second entrance on Lake Erie. Its dimensions were to be the same as the canals in New York State, that is to say, with a depth of four feet. For this purpose, what was necessary was a chartered company with an authorized capital of £25,000. Once a charter was obtained, local subscriptions would, he asserted, suffice to raise most of the money.

> A general meeting of the inhabitants of this district will take place to appoint Agents in Quebec, Montreal, Kingston, York, Niagara, Amherstburg, and every other town and township above and below . . . in order that as soon as the returns reach us (if favorable) that we may make preparations to commence the 1st day of May next and thus facilitate the work one year — we can finish the first cut next season and compleat the whole in two years.

Capitalists in Montreal and Quebec, rather than in Great Britain or the United States, would supplement local resources:

> This is a work of such magnitude compared with the slender means of this part of the country, that every exertion must be made to obtain

capital from Lower Canada. We are therefore anxious to publish our
proceedings and give them an extensive circulation. The people of
Lewiston in [the] State of New York have an Act already passed that
effects the same object, and depends on a great portion of their means
from Montreal, which an early knowledge of our intentions will counteract.[46]

If it were necessary or desirable to estimate when the Welland Canal
project first emerged as a concrete plan of action, then this letter to the
lieutenant governor might well be taken as setting the date. Before this
date, Merritt could have withdrawn at any time without loss of face or
self-respect. After it, he was committed to the project and personally identified with it, for good or ill. It is worth while, therefore, to pause and note
the spirit of optimism and easy confidence with which the project was put
forward, and to observe, too, how little reasonable basis there was for any
such sentiments. In the first place, the canal as projected at this time was
wrongly conceived. A depth of only four feet was all right for the Erie,
which was a barge canal; it was all wrong for the Welland which, if it was
to have any commercial value at all, had to be sufficiently large to accommodate the schooners and other vessels then navigating the lakes. But this
fundamental difference between the two types of artificial waterway was
completely ignored at this time. In the second place, even on the assumption that a four-foot canal would be adequate, there appears to have been
no real attempt made to discover whether in fact Merritt's Twelve Mile
Creek route was the best available. It was a practicable route, certainly,
but not the only one. Merritt insisted upon it, and carried his associates
with him, not because he had surveyed others and judged them less suitable, but because it passed through his property. The consequence was considerable local opposition and, as events turned out, loss of political and
financial support from the mercantile community in Niagara. Beyond all
this, it is quite clear that both time and money costs were vastly under-
estimated. The belief that a company with an authorized capital of only
£25,000 would have sufficient financial resources to complete the work dem-
onstrates not merely optimism and overconfidence, but also ignorance and
inexperience.

For these and other inadequacies in the project we must not hold
Merritt blameworthy in a personal sense. There is nothing here analogous
to the unscrupulous promoter circulating a fraudulent prospectus. Merritt
was sincere, in the sense that he was as misinformed as anybody else.[47]
Many thought him mistaken, but none believed him dishonest. Some of
the errors in planning, such as the matter of the dimensions and (to a
certain extent) the capitalization, were to be corrected as persons of greater
experience and talent became involved in the enterprise. Others, unfortunately, such as the substantial underestimation of time and money costs,
were to persist right through the history of the Company. But, if we take a

broad view of the circumstances in which the canal project was born and brought to maturity, it is this atmosphere of high hopes and inflated expectations which stands out as the strategic factor. Had more rational and informed estimates of future costs and earnings been available, no private corporation would have undertaken to build the canal at this time.

The fact that Merritt was not alone in his delusions is adequately demonstrated by the ease with which his proposals were accepted. The petition for a charter of incorporation was presented to the legislature on November 11, 1823, when the session of parliament opened. No serious opposition was encountered, and the act chartering the Company received the lieutenant governor's assent on January 19, 1824.[48] The lack of opposition, and even of serious discussion, is all the more remarkable when we remember that the government had already spent no small sums of money and gone to considerable trouble in preparation for undertaking the work itself. Why were these plans and the officially sponsored route now so readily set aside? Perhaps the simplest explanation is also the most accurate: government construction would have entailed a serious burden on the slender financial resources of the provincial legislature. Construction by a private company, on the other hand, held out at least the promise that the work would be carried through without expense to the province. In 1823, we must recall, the very extensive grants and loans which the Company was later to receive from the provincial treasury were not even contemplated.[49]

This first charter was to be radically amended in the following year. Nevertheless, a few of its provisions deserve mention. The authorized capital was set at £40,000 currency (in contrast to Merritt's original figure of £25,000) divided into 3200 shares of common stock of a par value of £12 10s. 0d. each. Stock voting power was on a graduated scale, so that the number of votes did not increase in direct proportion to the number of shares held.[50] Provision was made for eventual government purchase: the Crown could assume possession of the canal after thirty years upon paying to the stockholders the amount of their shares plus 25 per cent. This was little more than a convention, common at this time in charters which granted semi-monopolistic powers to a corporation, although one stockholder was later to assert that it diminished the marketability of the shares.[51] Authority was given to the Company to appropriate land for the canal, towpaths, and so on, and to supply water power to mills; but full compensation for all property taken over or damage done was to be allotted by an independent board of arbitration. No route was specified in the charter. The view seems to have been that this was a matter to be decided by the persons who invested in the Company, and the Niagara interests appear to have believed that their best plan was to hold their fire.

The charter also named eight persons as provisional directors of the Company:[52] George Keefer, Thomas Merritt, George Adams, William Chisholm, Paul Shipman, John DeCew, Joseph Smith, and William Hamilton Merritt. These individuals may be taken as the entrepreneurial group responsible for the project at this time, and a few biographical details may be of interest.

Except perhaps for Smith, of whom nothing appears to be known, they were all personal friends of the Merritt family and all owned property in the Twelve Mile Creek area, neither Toronto nor Niagara being represented. The two Merritts, Shipman, Chisholm, and Adams were from St. Catharines. Shipman had for many years owned a tavern at the crossroads where the Niagara–Burlington Bay road crossed Twelve Mile Creek, and the town which later became St. Catharines had originally been known as Shipman's Corners. Chisholm owned the local store in the village. Adams was apparently the brother of the Thomas Adams whose farm and mill Merritt had purchased in 1815; he owned a mill lower down the Creek.

DeCew and Keefer were millers in Thorold, farther up the Creek. John DeCew (sometimes spelled De Cou or De Coe) owned the mills at what are still known as DeCew Falls, now a hydroelectric installation, where the west branch of the Creek descends the escarpment. He was descended from a French Huguenot family which had emigrated to Pennsylvania in 1685. One branch at least had settled in Upper Canada before 1790 as Loyalists. John DeCew had served in the militia during the war; his mills were large and his influence not inconsiderable.[53]

George Keefer, who later became first president of the Company, was also a Loyalist.[54] Born in New Jersey in 1773, he married during his eighty-five years of life three wives and had fifteen children, founding a family of some importance in Canadian history. By trade he was originally a cabinetmaker, but when in 1790 he came to Upper Canada with his brother Jacob he turned to occupations more suitable to a frontier economy. Settling on a six-hundred-acre farm near Thorold, he entered business as a storekeeper and built two sawmills and a flour mill. Later he became a magistrate and in 1815 a captain of militia. From time to time he did odd jobs of surveying, for crude leveling was an art of which every miller had to know something.

The close parallel between the histories of the Keefer and the Merritt families is interesting. That George Keefer and Thomas Merritt subscribed jointly to a New York newspaper is only one example of the close relations which existed between two families of similar origin and occupations. George Keefer's famous twelfth son, Thomas Coltrin Keefer, was later to play a major role in the development of Canadian transportation.

These eight provisional directors made up a remarkably homogeneous group. They were all (again with the possible exception of Smith) businessmen of the St. Catharines–Thorold area — merchants, millers, tavern keepers. With the exception of W. H. Merritt they were all first generation Loyalists, not later British or American immigrants. They all had military experience, either in the Revolution or during the War of 1812 or both.

W. H. Merritt was the only second generation Loyalist, and the only one who could be called a young man. Thomas Merritt, his father, was at this time sixty-five, DeCew fifty-eight, Keefer fifty-one, Shipman, Adams, and Chisholm around the same age. Hamilton Merritt was thirty-one.

With the chartering of the Company the first hurdle was passed. The second promised to be more difficult. Securing legislative permission to form a company was one thing; building up an organization, securing the financial resources, and mobilizing the technical skills which alone could enable the Company to begin operations was quite another. The most urgent problem was clearly the raising of money, and it was to this problem that the provisional directors first turned their attention.

It is no great exaggeration to say that in this period the Welland Canal Company was Hamilton Merritt, plus a charter, plus a handful of family friends, plus a collection of rather ill-defined but uniformly optimistic expectations, and very little else. Merritt was the moving spirit behind the whole affair, the man who made sure that what needed to be done was done. In concrete terms what this meant was that he spent more time on Company business than any of the others and was more prominently associated with its affairs in the public eye. Early in January he opened the campaign for local subscriptions by writing a long letter to the Niagara *Gleaner* in which he spelled out the cost estimates in detail and appealed to the people of Niagara and the farmers of the neighborhood to take as many shares as their means would permit.[55] The thorny question of whether Niagara or Twelve Mile Creek should be the Ontario terminus was glossed over delicately:

> I forbear making any remarks on the route to Niagara. After it is levelled by a competent engineer it will be a subject for discussion. . . Most of you say, in case the Canal terminates at the mouth of the Twelve Mile Creek, it will be prejudicial to the interests of Niagara. This is not only a narrow-minded, but I conceive a very erroneous idea of the subject. Drawing a population to this and other situations on the Canal for manufacturing purposes will not lessen yours but . . . be a means of increasing it and enhancing the value of every man's property between the two places.

Cost estimates were handled in the usual confident manner. For the railway Merritt suggested a figure of from three to five thousand dollars, and for the remainder of the work, including locks, excavation, and towpath, a total of $37,350. "Taking the whole route together, nature never presented fewer obstacles, not an aqueduct, extra embankment, or other artificial section except the Railway in the whole distance. . . Were we supported by individuals from a distance we could accomplish this much of ourselves the ensuing summer, and finish the remainder to Lake Ontario the year following."

These hopeful sentiments were not for public consumption alone. On January 11, 1824, Merritt wrote to his father-in-law:

> We intend sending an Agent to Montreal shortly to obtain subscriptions for stock & if we get it taken up the first cut will be finished the present year. I think it will be one of the best speculations offered in the Western Country, at the same time will not embark in it more than the amount of my Mills, and probably $200, and near one Year of my time to carry it into operation. I consider that I will be richly paid in the enhanced value of my property — in case I meet with no other consideration.[56]

It is interesting to note that Merritt at this time regarded the canal as essentially a limited commitment. If the space devoted to it in his letter is any guide, he regarded it as of less importance than a new copper tube to line his salt spring.

On the last day of January a meeting was held at Niagara to organize the Company. A board of managers was formed to act on behalf of the petitioners, and Merritt was appointed general agent, his first task being to obtain subscriptions for stock in Upper and Lower Canada. This occupied him for the next two months.

The capitalists to whom Merritt looked for the disposal of the greater part of his stock were the merchants of Montreal and Quebec. But Merritt went first to York (Toronto), not to Montreal. A few subscriptions might be obtained there, but his real purpose was to get informal sanction for his mission from the members of the colonial executive. Influential names at the head of the subscription list were urgently required; as Merritt put it, "my success in Lower Canada will wholly depend on the respectable countenance I may receive here." [57] His first contact was with an influential member of the Legislative Council, the Hon. John Henry Dunn, who promised to buy stock and — more important — to become president of the Company. The attorney general, the Hon. John Beverley Robinson, also promised his support. At Dunn's suggestion, Merritt wrote to the lieutenant governor, Sir Peregrine Maitland, asking him to head the subscription list "as it will at once insure the success of my mission." [58] Other members of the Tory clique which was shortly afterwards to be known as the Family Compact gave him their unofficial blessing. Only then did Merritt set out for Montreal, stopping on the way at Kingston, Cornwall, Prescott, and every other place where financial support might be obtained. His tactics were the same in each place: private meetings with the leading citizens, informal conversations, explanations, and arguments.[59]

In Montreal and Quebec slightly different methods were used. His business correspondent, George Davies, and Horatio Gates, president of the Bank of Montreal, undertook to canvass Montreal on his behalf, and in Quebec a personal friend, the Hon. James Irvin of the firm of Irvin, McNought & Company performed a similar office. Public meetings were held in both cities, that in Quebec being under the auspices of the Board of Trade. The governor general, Lord Dalhousie, expressed interest in the project, purchased a few shares, and promised to bring up the question of financial assistance with the British government.

"I cannot say I am any nearer the day of departure than before," Merritt wrote to his wife from Quebec.

> . . . They will do nothing after I leave, and it would be rather foreign to leave the business half done, now I am on the spot. I have the satisfaction to say that I will succeed in my object, although it is slow, hard work; everybody wishes the undertaking well, but when it comes to the needfull, they keep their hands from paper.[60]

Two days later he wrote to the provincial secretary in Upper Canada to make his first request for financial assistance from the legislature:

> The greatest drawback to the undertaking is that His Majesty's Government in U.C. have not taken any shares, & it never occurred to me to memorial His Excellency, Sir Peregrine Maitland, to recommend the measure to the favorable consideration of His Majesty's Government. I am fully aware . . . he is favorably disposed to the undertaking. May I beg you will represent to him that a small sum, say £2,500, from the Government will insure the success of the enterprise the present year. . . Government taking shares would induce many to do so that are now backward.[61]

For Merritt to assert that it had "never occurred" to him to request a government purchase of stock was calculated ingenuousness. The fact was that Lower Canada subscriptions had not reached the anticipated figure, as we shall see later. Further, evidence of support from Montreal and Quebec capitalists was a prerequisite to an appeal for aid to the government of Upper Canada, just as evidence of approval from the Toronto clique had been essential to his Lower Canada appeal. To seek government aid before doing all he could to tap private sources would be to invite failure.

Back at St. Catharines, new surveys were made by the Clowes brothers and by Francis Hall, an English engineer trained under Rennie.[62] A board meeting was held on May 15, at which it was decided that no work should be put under contract until all the stock was subscribed and complete surveys and estimates made available. Dunn was not present at this meeting, but was elected president. Two weeks later he refused to accept the office, pointing out that:

> The situation which I have the honour to hold in the Province leaves it quite out of my power to give any personal attention to the object. My duty requires my constant presence at York — this together with my want of experience in filling such an office, renders me under the necessity of requesting you will be pleased to find some other more disposable and fit person as your President.[63]

Dunn's refusal to act as president was a serious setback, which his simultaneous offer to double his subscription did little to offset. He was universally respected, wielded extensive influence in the Legislative Council, and was one of the few men in high official positions who had not publicly committed themselves to either the Tory or the Reform party. His reasons for refusal were plausible, but if he believed they were sufficient he was deceiving himself, for he was later to hold the presidency for many years without apparent embarrassment to his government office. But, serious as was the loss of such a man in a personal sense, equally ominous were the implications of his withdrawal. Did it mean that the Toronto clique had decided after all to withhold their support? Something like this certainly seems to have been the case, for Dunn's objections quickly vanished in the year following, when amendments to the charter practically converted the Company's directorate into a Family Compact monopoly.

But Dunn's withdrawal was not the only ominous portent which appeared at this time — ominous, that is, to Merritt and his friends at St. Catharines. The new surveys run by Hall and the Clowes brothers told a story rather different from Tibbet's early appraisal. These surveys were the first to cover the whole route from Lake Ontario to the Welland and from there to Grand River, and they were the first to include estimates both for the original Twelve Mile Creek route and for the alternative route to Niagara. It became clear that from the point of view of construction costs there was little to choose between them. That to Niagara would cost about £2000 more, but on the other hand it could be made more durable and there would be no need to build a harbor. These findings made it very difficult to resist the continued pressure of the Niagara merchants, expressed in newspapers, public meetings, and legislative debates. It began to look as if the vested interests of Niagara might prove too strong for Merritt and his friends on Twelve Mile Creek.

Finance, however, was already emerging as the major problem. Analysis of the subscriptions up to this date discloses that the stock of the Company was far from completely taken up.[64] A total of 483 subscriptions had been promised in St. Catharines, Niagara, York, and other places in Upper Canada, making £6037 10s. 0d.[65] The 171 shares sold at Niagara were practically, if not formally, conditional upon the adoption of that town as terminus. Merritt's trip to Montreal and Quebec had brought the total to £12,500, compared with an authorized capital of £40,000. Clearly Canadian capital was inadequate for the task, even on the limited scale then proposed. Other sources would have to be tapped.

Two possibilities presented themselves: the provincial government, and private investors in the United States. Merritt's request for a purchase of stock by the government of Upper Canada had so far produced no results, but the completion of the surveys opened up a new possibility, namely land grants. The branch of the canal from the Welland to Grand River would pass through an extensive swamp, known as the Cranberry Marsh, containing about 13,000 acres of land which was in its present state of no use to anyone and "a great injury to the neighborhood from the unhealthy vapours that proceed from these stagnant waters in the summer, and being a harbour for wolves and other beasts of prey." [66] The elevation of this swamp was about ten feet higher than the Welland, so that it would be easy and perhaps necessary for the Company to drain it. A clearer case for a land grant could hardly be found. With a sizeable grant to its name, the Company would have something more tangible than hopes and promises to attract investors.

Accordingly, early in August 1824 a petition was presented to Lieutenant Governor Maitland in which the directors stated that they had found "the greatest difficulty in getting the remainder of the stock subscribed, from the supposed magnitude of the undertaking and the extreme scarcity of money." They therefore prayed for a grant of "all the waste lands of the Crown now in the Township of Wainfleet [that is, the marsh referred to above] or any other Your Excellency may please to recommend." [67] This petition was to have important consequences, for Maitland could hardly make such a large grant on his own responsibility. The question, therefore, was referred back to London; this brought the Welland Canal Company for the first time into conflict with colonial defence policy.

Petitions to the lieutenant governor were slow in bearing fruit; more immediately helpful would be American capital. On December 6, therefore, the directors instructed Merritt to proceed to New York to see if stock could be sold there. He arrived on the twenty-fourth and was immediately successful. If an "extreme scarcity of money" had really proved an obstacle in Montreal, New York was a very different story. Speculative activity was running at a high level in these months. The man Merritt chiefly succeeded in interesting was engaged in what was probably the most speculative business of all: lotteries.

John Barentse Yates was a senior partner in the firm of Yates and McIntyre, probably the largest firm of lottery managers in the United States at this time.[68] Lottery managers were the aristocracy of the gambling world. They took over the management of the lottery from the institution to which it had been granted by the legislature, sold the tickets to dealers (usually at a premium), and organized the successive drawings. Nominally they operated on a commission basis, deducting from the amount of the prizes between 10 and 25 per cent over and above the amount retained for the benefit of the original grantees. Practically, there were many opportunities for profit beyond this percentage. To judge from the anti-lottery pamphlets which form the most accessible source material for the study of this type of business, lottery managers made immense profits, but there are good reasons for doubting the accuracy of such statements. The whole system seems to have been shot through with fraud

and deception. Nevertheless, in this period at least, it was quite a respectable business and lottery managers occupied positions of some prestige in
the financial community.

As John B. Yates will play a role in the story of the Welland Canal
Company second in importance only to that of Merritt, some analysis of
his motives for becoming involved with the Company is clearly called for.
There were, of course, certain features of the project likely to make an
immediate appeal to American investors, particularly in New York State.
A canal cut across the Niagara peninsula would open up the possibility of
direct shipments between ports on Lake Ontario and ports on Lake Erie.
If this was important for Montreal, it was no less so for New York and
Albany, particularly in view of the fact that a side-cutting from Syracuse
on the Erie Canal to Oswego on Lake Ontario was already planned and
would shortly be completed. The completion of this Oswego Canal, together with the Welland, would open up an alternative route from the
Hudson River to the west — and one which promised to be both cheaper
and faster than the Erie. Schooners on the Lakes could make better time
and carry larger cargoes than barges on the Erie. A cargo loaded on a
lake vessel at, say, Cleveland, would reach Syracuse considerably earlier
by way of Lake Erie, the Welland, Lake Ontario, and the Oswego than it
would via Buffalo and the long western section of the Erie.

There were good reasons, too, why Yates in particular should take
more than a passing interest in the project. He had friends in Canada, he
had served on the Niagara frontier during the War of 1812, and he owned
property in the village of Chittenango, near the proposed junction point
of the Oswego and Erie Canals. The Welland Canal project was more to
him than a line on a map or a phrase in a prospectus; he knew the country
and its prospects. But more than this was involved. The financial arrangements characteristic of the lottery business were such that lottery managers
not infrequently found themselves with substantial sums of money lying
idle on their hands. Receipts from the sale of tickets were paid in regularly,
while disbursements for prizes and contractual payments to beneficiaries
fell due only at stated intervals. The possibility therefore arose of putting
these idle balances to profitable use. This is why we find lottery firms,
particularly after 1820, branching out into loan contracting and stock
speculation;[69] and this is probably one of the reasons why Yates decided
to back the Welland Canal project.

It may be well to point out, however, that a lottery business was in
reality a most unsuitable basis for ventures in the field of loan contracting.
True, there were idle balances to be used; but these balances were essentially temporary and short-lived. They would have served admirably for
use in a call-loan market, had one existed, but they could not safely be
used to finance long-term investment. This meant that if the loan could
be handled as a "quick in–quick out" transaction, trouble might be

avoided; but if there was delay in disposing of the loan to final investors the consequences were likely to be serious. Add to this the fact that the market for lottery tickets in this period was steadily declining, and it will be obvious that on a correct view of the situation Yates would have been well advised to steer clear of any investment which threatened to freeze his resources.

Yates took no such view of the matter. Purchases of Welland Canal stock would, he believed, not only prove a profitable investment in the long run, but also appreciate in capital value in the immediate future, so that the shares could be sold off gradually at a premium to final investors. Accordingly he took the lead in forming a "list" of subscribers (eight in all) who between them undertook to purchase most of the shares which Merritt had to dispose of, Yates himself purchasing the largest single amount, some six hundred shares.[70] In addition, Merritt entered into an arrangement with Alfred Hovey, of the firm of Hovey & Ward, canal contractors of Montezuma, New York, by which the latter became a stock-holder to the extent of two hundred shares. Hovey and Ward were later employed on the canal, and it is probable that this "purchase" of stock was actually a kind of retainer.

It seems undeniable that without this influx of capital from the United States the Welland Canal Company would soon have gone out of existence. The eagerness with which these New York investors seized upon the project contrasts sharply with the hesitancy of the Montreal merchants. In part this contrast is probably to be explained by an early awareness of what later proved to be the case — namely that in the short run at least the Welland was more of a link in American than in Canadian transportation routes. But in part it was undoubtedly due to the success of the Erie Canal which, though not yet completed, had engendered in the businessmen of New York and Albany a feeling of confidence in the ability of canal projects to pay their way and yield a profit. Compared to the Erie, the Welland project must have seemed a work of relatively small size and little risk. It was to be only twenty-eight miles long, in contrast to the Erie's three hundred and sixty, and no unusual engineering difficulties were anticipated. The fact that it was to be undertaken by a private corporation and not by a legislative body must have made it seem an unusually attractive proposition for the speculative investor. But we should note, too, in all fairness to Merritt and his Upper Canada associates, that Yates and his fellow investors in New York would hardly have backed the project so whole-heartedly had it not, at least on the surface, borne all the appearances of a sound proposition. These Albany and New York businessmen were something very different from the inexperienced farmers and officials of St. Catharines and York. They were men who knew something about canals and trade routes and who had many other ways of investing their money. The fact that in later years they were to regret that they had ever heard of the Welland Canal only emphasizes that in the beginning the project was sufficiently sound to deceive men who were shrewd judges of an investment.

Merritt's expedition to New York was not solely for the purpose of raising capital. He was also concerned with labor supply. To this end he visited Utica, Rochester, and other places on the line of the Erie Canal, met the canal contractors who, with the Erie soon to be completed, were either already looking for future employment or would be shortly, and distributed notices advertising the contracts to be let on the Welland and the employment opportunities that would be available. This was an essential step, for canal construction called for skills which were not to be had in Upper Canada at this time. The contractors on the Erie had the necessary experience and equipment. They owned the ox teams, iron plows, and harrows; they knew how to build locks, dams, culverts, and towpaths, and how to follow an engineer's instructions; they could mobilize more easily than anyone else the unskilled labor previously employed on the Erie; they were accustomed to the informal credit arrangements involved in subcontracting and hiring. Beyond this, the largest contractors were men of capital who would invest in the Company if they were given contracts and would probably accept part of their pay in the form of stock. American labor, equipment, and experience were almost as essential as American capital.

Merritt entered into provisional agreements with two large contracting firms, Ward & Hovey of Montezuma and General Beach of Rochester.[71] These firms were later to obtain the important Deep Cut contracts. Skilled labor was not neglected. He obtained from Benjamin Wright, the Connecticut engineer who had supervised the central section of the Erie, the recommendation of Nathan Roberts, who had won his spurs as engineer of the western section, described by Wright as "a prudent, careful man, and free from any visionary plans of internal improvements."[72] Roberts was later to act as consulting engineer on the Welland. Merritt intended to lose no opportunity of profiting from Erie Canal experience.

From Bridgewater on October 18 Merritt wrote to his wife: "I have succeeded far beyond my most sanguine expectations. Have got the necessary Amt. of stock subscribed by the most respectable and influential men in the money market in New York."[73] This might seem to imply that he had sold in New York all the stock not taken up in Canada, but this was not the case. Before he left for New York, Canadian subscriptions amounted to $50,000. When he returned, $30,000 remained to be subscribed.[74] New York subscriptions must therefore have reached a total of $80,000, or precisely half the total capitalization. There can be little doubt that had these subscriptions not been obtained the Welland Canal Company would never have commenced operations.

In the closing months of 1824 preparations for beginning construction were rapidly pushed ahead. On November 15 the first contracts were signed, bids being submitted by no less than fifty contractors, most of whom were probably Americans attracted by Merritt's publicizing activities.[75] In view of the controversy over the Ontario terminus, the section on the top of the escarpment was the first to be undertaken. Contracts were let for the section from the Welland River to Lock No. 1, which on the plan then being followed was at the head of the west branch of Twelve Mile Creek. This section included what was already emerging as the major obstacle — the two to three miles of high ground between the Welland and the edge of the escarpment. There was no possibility of running a feeder to the top of this ridge; either a tunnel or a deep cutting was necessary. The former was chosen and a contract for a tunnel two miles in length was taken by Alfred Hovey. Its dimensions were to be sixteen feet eight inches wide by sixteen feet six inches high, and timber rather than masonry was to be used for the supporting structure.[76]

On November 20, 1824, excavation was begun, with a simple ceremony to mark the occasion. Merritt was later to remark with pride that construction was not halted for a single day until vessels passed from lake to lake five years later. The canal that opened for traffic in 1829, however, was very different from that begun in 1824. Already there were indications that plans, and with them estimates of cost, would have to be drastically revised. A depth of four feet was adequate on the Erie, which was a barge canal of considerable length. It was much less justifiable on the Welland, connecting two navigable lakes by a short artificial navigation. Restriction of the Welland to the dimensions of the Erie would entail transshipment of cargoes from sloops and schooners to barges at one end of the canal, and then back again to lake vessels at the other. If this was a disadvantage from the Canadian point of view, it was much more serious in the eyes of those Americans who looked upon the Welland as a means of avoiding the two hundred mile haul by barge on the Erie from Buffalo to Syracuse. Two transshipments, one at each end of the canal, would have destroyed any competitive advantage the Welland might otherwise have possessed.

It is hardly surprising, therefore, that pressure for enlargement of the proposed dimensions came first from the New York stockholders. On December 22, 1824, they wrote to Keefer, then president of the Company, urging him to apply for a new charter and to build the canal on a much more ambitious scale. "We ought to keep in view," they argued, "sloop, as well as boat navigation, in order to render the stock valuable."

> . . . We beg leave to recommend to the consideration of the directors, how far it is practicable (now) to make the Canal large enough for sloop navigation over the ridge from the Chippawa River to the descent towards Lake Ontario. . . Should this not be deemed prudent at present, but keeping it in view, we think it would be advisable to have an *open cut*

instead of a tunnel. We submit that if this part of the Canal should be cut for sloop navigation the other parts hereafter could be done without any material inconvenience and would greatly increase the supply for hydraulic purposes.

In case of the enlargement of the dimensions of the Canal, it might become necessary to apply to the Legislature for an extension of privileges and an increase of capital.[77]

Reinforcing these suggestions from New York were certain military considerations. A four-foot canal would be unable to accommodate gunboats and would not permit the movement of naval vessels from one lake to the other.[78] This was a consideration which the directors could not afford to neglect, for in its present form the canal was not regarded with favor by the colonial authorities. There were two reasons for this: the preponderance of American capital, and the proximity of the canal to the frontier. Either by itself might have been overlooked; together, they were serious. Merritt himself believed that an invading force could never hold the frontier districts long enough to interrupt seriously the flow of military supplies through the canal, but Lieutenant Governor Maitland took a different view. Apparently laboring under the delusion that the directors had decided on Niagara as the Ontario terminus, Maitland felt obliged to recommend to Lord Bathurst that the Company's application for a grant of land should not be approved:

> If the Canal were conducted into Lake Ontario as was originally intended, through any of the several streams that run into the Lake to the westward of the Niagara River, it would afford, in the event of hostilities with the United States, a secure line of communication for troops, stores, &c. — but as by the present plan it is to be brought into the Niagara River immediately under the guns of the American fort, this object, which must to the Government be of first importance, is entirely lost.[79]

Further, Merritt's success in mobilizing American capital blunted the obvious weapon which could have been used to bring about a change in the route. Had the land grant been really indispensable, it could have been made conditional upon the directors agreeing to run the canal through less exposed territory. But, thanks to the American subscriptions, it was no longer as necessary as it had been. "Your Lordship may perhaps be disposed to doubt," wrote Maitland discreetly, "whether it be advisable to subject a considerable landed property in this country to the control of a company so constituted. It is moreover believed that with the aid of these foreign subscriptions the undertaking will be attempted whether the assistance now prayed for from the Government be conceded or not." Bathurst, impressed by these arguments, refused the grant.[80]

But Maitland was mistaken in believing that the directors had decided on Niagara as the Ontario terminus. No such decision had been taken, although his informants may have led him to believe that it was a foregone conclusion. This was one matter on which Merritt would not compromise.

"They are making great efforts in Niagara," he wrote to his wife on November twenty-fourth, "to get the Canal to terminate there . . . but it will not do." [81] The fact that such a misapprehension on Maitland's part, with its serious consequences, was possible illustrates the lack of effective communication in this period between the directors and the executive government. This was a matter soon to be remedied.

There is little doubt that the pressure for enlargement could have been resisted at this time, and that if it had been resisted the Welland Canal would have been completed sooner and with far less strain on the financial resources of the province. But each interested group felt that it had something to gain, either from enlargement or from the legislative proceedings which application for amendment of the charter would occasion. If the canal were once more thrown into the political melting-pot, who could say what changes might not result? The interests of the New York and Albany group have already been mentioned. In the legislature the Niagara merchants could bring their heaviest artillery to bear, and they had some reason to believe that if Niagara could equal the claims of Twelve Mile Creek for a barge canal, it would far surpass them for a ship navigation. From the point of view of defence, too, it was clear that strategy would be far better served were the canal built on an enlarged scale.

What of Merritt and his St. Catharines friends who in these early months were fighting to retain possession of the canal route? In the first place, so long as they could retain control and block efforts to change the route, they had everything to gain from enlargement. A larger canal would mean more water power, larger mills, and a more extensive business. Secondly, although by applying for amendment of the charter they ran the risk of losing control, they as well as the Niagara people could hope that in the new charter some one definite route would be specified. If they played their cards well, that route would be Twelve Mile Creek, not Niagara. They had a good case. If military factors alone were considered, the best route was the Grand River – Burlington Bay line originally surveyed by the government. If the convenience of trade were paramount, no terminus could have better claims than Niagara. What was Twelve Mile Creek if not a happy compromise between these two extremes? It did not require much perspicacity to foresee that the lieutenant governor would never assent to a bill that ran the enlarged canal "under the guns of the American fort."

In addition, Merritt had strong personal reasons for favoring a larger canal. On January 13, 1825, he wrote to his wife, "Our canal is like money, it requires great exertions to get it and still greater to keep it. The Niagara people and the whole frontier have . . . combined to take it from us and I am *determined* they shall not have it." [82] In a letter to his father-in-law, Jedediah Prendergast, he stated bluntly, "My whole personal interest in this undertaking is the value it will attach to my property on the route," and complained, "I labor under every disadvantage for want of support, not having any person of consequence or capital on the line who has a correct view of its importance." [83] Some decisive action was clearly necessary to put an end to these uncertainties. Merritt continued:

> In case we compleat a small canal and the public once begins to realize the advantages they will never be satisfied until the Government make a larger one. . . This would lead to further exploring and I am satisfied from the experience already obtained there is a cheaper route than ours — which shall be nameless at present. These circumstances induce me to urge the immediate adoption of this, which when once completed sets the matter at rest for ever.

Whatever may have been this "cheaper route than ours" which Merritt declined to name even in private correspondence, only by getting legislative sanction for the construction of a full-scale canal through Twelve Mile Creek could he make sure that no other canal would be constructed to divert the trade of the Lakes and the finances of the province away from the Welland.

But no less impelling a motive for seeking amendment of the charter was provided by the small success which Merritt had so far achieved in winning for his project the positive approval and sanction of the provincial government. Lieutenant Governor Maitland, originally favorably disposed, had found himself unable to recommend the Company's petition for a land grant. John H. Dunn had deemed it best, on second thoughts, to decline the offer of the presidency. And stock subscriptions from the officials of Upper Canada's capital had not been generous. The principal reasons for this lack of enthusiasm for Merritt's project seem to have been two: the first was distrust of the ability of Merritt and his friends at St. Catharines to take more than a purely local view of their responsibilities; and the second, suspicion of the preponderance of American capital. Now, if construction of the canal was to go ahead smoothly, and especially if it was to be built on an enlarged scale, it was little short of essential that these sentiments of doubt and suspicion should be overcome, and that the lieutenant governor and his coterie of advisers should be induced to adopt a more positively coöperative attitude to the Company. The simplest and most certain way to do this would be to give them more of a say in its management. And if, in the process of effecting this, some way could be devised of minimizing the threat of American influence without sacrificing the assistance of American capital, so much the better. Application to the legislature for a new charter opened up the possibility, not only of increasing the capital stock and enlarging the dimensions, but also of making certain changes in the pattern of control, particularly through changes in the election of directors.

This stage in the Company's history concluded, therefore, with certain concrete tasks accomplished and certain difficult problems awaiting solution. The project for a Niagara canal had passed from the realm of ideas to that of action. Merritt, motivated in the first instance by the desire to improve his property on Twelve Mile Creek, had successfully mobilized local support and won legislative sanction for his undertaking. Important groups of investors had been interested, experienced engineers and contractors had been recruited, and appeals had been made for the active assistance of the British and provincial governments. A clearer though still inadequate conception of the physical dimensions of the project had been achieved. There remained, besides the massive but still largely unknown problems of construction, the difficult tasks of securing adequate financial support and neutralizing the potential or actual hostility of the various groups who felt their interests threatened. To these tasks Merritt and his associates now addressed themselves, utilizing the revision of the charter by the legislature as an opportunity to enlist new financial resources and new political allies.

CHAPTER THREE

CONSTRUCTION

THE PROBLEMS OF CONSTRUCTION FACED BY THE WELLAND CANAL Company were unlike any that had previously been encountered in North America. Specifically, they differed widely from those which had been successfully surmounted in the construction of the Erie Canal, the project on which most of the engineers and contractors employed on the Welland had received their training. A depth of only four feet on the Erie had simplified lock design and construction; the many rivers and lakes of northern New York State had minimized difficulties of water supply; no very great heights of land nor abrupt changes in level had complicated the planning and execution of the route. The Welland, in contrast, had to surmount, within the space of a few miles, a difference in level of over three hundred feet. Water supply was complicated by the presence of a ridge of high ground between the Welland River and the brow of the escarpment. Locks with an effective depth of eight feet posed problems of design and construction which differed not only in size but also in kind from those presented by locks with a depth of four feet. All these difficulties were aggravated by primitive technological equipment, acute financial stringency, and the total inexperience of those responsible for management. These general considerations must be borne in mind in analyzing the problems of construction encountered by the Welland Canal Company.

Despite the severity of the weather, work on the canal continued during the last months of 1824 and the beginning of 1825. The mouths of the tunnel at each end were excavated to bottom level and a shaft sunk in the middle to test the nature of the ground.[1] Here the first serious difficulty arose, for the middle shaft was flooded before the desired depth was reached and had to be abandoned. This meant not only that the tunnel scheme would have to be dropped, but also that a cutting through the same ground would be very hazardous. Abandonment of the tunnel project (at a loss to the Company of nearly £3000) provided yet another reason for a revision of estimates and a change of plans. Early in February 1825 it was finally decided to apply to the legislature for amendment of the charter and financial assistance.[2]

On February 25 the act granting the new charter was approved by the Assembly and on April 13 it received the lieutenant governor's assent. No financial assistance accompanied the statute, although the legislature did pass a resolution approving in principle a loan to the Company of £25,000. This amended act of incorporation represented, in one aspect at least, a clear victory for Merritt and the St. Catharines group. It permitted an increase of capital to £200,000, which was the major change, but it also laid down in detail the route to be followed. The canal was to terminate in Lake Ontario at the mouth of Twelve Mile Creek; that is to say, it would pass through St. Catharines and not Niagara. Further, by specifying enlargement to the dimensions of schooner navigation, the act made it certain that the line of the canal would pass down the eastern branch of the Creek, or directly through the property of Merritt and the Keefers, and not, as formerly, down the western branch through DeCew's property, since the Company's engineers reported that the latter ravine was too narrow to accommodate locks of the larger size.[3] DeCew thereupon withdrew from the Company entirely, while the Niagara group became bitterly hostile to the Company and remained so throughout its existence.[4]

The act departed from the charter of 1824 in a number of respects not directly connected with enlargement. Some of these changes were to prove important later. In the first place, seven directors, not five, were to be elected annually, and each director had to be both a resident of Upper Canada and a stockholder to the extent of at least twenty shares. These apparently innocent provisions were later to mean that, on a strict interpretation of the charter, only eight individuals were qualified to serve as directors of the Welland Canal Company, for only 232 shares were sold in Upper Canada and only eight residents of the province held over twenty.[5] With seven places to be filled on the board, palace revolutions were clearly impossible. Secondly, the stock voting scale was changed. The holder of five shares was now entitled to one vote; of twenty shares, two votes; of fifty shares, three votes; and of one hundred shares and upwards, four votes. This change, of course, was not in the interest of a large investor such as J. B. Yates who, with a total investment in the region of 720 shares, had no more voting power than if he had held only one hundred and who, as an American, could not become a director himself.[6] These two changes, taken together, effectively denied to American investors any influence, through formal channels of representation at least, in the management of the Company. The annual elections of directors were merely a matter of ringing the changes on the eight qualified candidates. When this convenient arrangement was broken up, it was through the appointment of directors by the provincial government.

One further change related to the provision made for eventual government purchase. In the act of 1824 government purchase could be consummated only after thirty years had elapsed, and on condition that the stockholders were repaid the amount of their investment plus twenty-five per cent. The new charter retained the twenty-five per cent clause, but extended the waiting period to fifty years and added the further proviso that the stockholders must have received on an average at least 12½ per cent per annum on their investment.

The canal as planned at this time may be briefly described. In reality there were two canals, with two summit levels and two entrances on Lake Erie. One section, however — that from Lake Ontario to the Welland River — was common to both and was to be constructed first. In this section the canal was to pass from Lake Ontario up the watercourse of Twelve Mile Creek, ascend the escarpment through a ravine, and enter the Welland River by means of a deep cut through the dividing ridge. This deep cutting, later to be the source of considerable difficulty and expense, was to be a mile and three quarters in length, with a maximum depth of fifty-four feet six inches. The ridge was believed to consist entirely of firm clay and no very great engineering problems were anticipated.[7] Between Lake Ontario and the Welland River there was a difference in level of about 310 feet, which would require thirty-five locks. The cost of this first section, sixteen miles long, was estimated at £113,000, including the harbor on Lake Ontario.[8] The Welland River was to be both feeder and summit level.

The second section consisted of the natural waterway of the Welland River. Here the only construction believed to be required was a towpath. The canal would join the Welland about eight miles upstream from the point where the Welland entered the Niagara River at the village of Chippawa, just above the falls. On the completion of these two sections vessels would be able to pass from one lake to the other, by ascending the canal to the Welland River, passing down the Welland to Chippawa, and making their way against the current up the Niagara River to Lake Erie.

The third section was supplementary to the other two and consisted of a cut about twelve miles in length from the Welland River by way of Forks Creek to the Grand River. This was the cut which was to drain the marsh in Wainfleet. Originally this section of the canal was to be on a level with the surface of the marsh and fed by a feeder from the Grand River above the rapids. In 1825, however, it was decided to make the cut sixteen feet deep and to have it enter the estuary of the Grand River directly, so that Lake Erie would become the feeder and summit level for this section. At the mouth of Grand River a harbor was to be constructed, so that the canal would then have two entrances on Lake Erie. The Grand River entrance, which was a considerable distance from the Canadian–American frontier, was intended to become the major British naval base on Lake Erie. From the commercial point of view, which presumably weighed more heavily with Merritt and his associates, it was believed to have the further advantage that it would be open for traffic earlier in the season than either the Niagara River entrance or the entrance to the Erie Canal at Buffalo, for winds and current blocked the Niagara River and Buffalo harbor with ice for two or three weeks after the more sheltered Grand River entrance was open. Nevertheless, it is hard to see why this supplementary and by no means indispensable extension of the canal bulked so large in the Company's plans at this time. Probably the desire to reap some advantage from the land grant in Wainfleet, together with the fact that H. J. Boulton, a director of the Company, was deeply involved in land speculation in the Grand River area, were significant factors.

The canal was to be built on a scale large enough to accommodate the schooners and sloops then navigating the lakes. This was construed to mean a depth throughout of not less than seven feet six inches, a width at bottom of thirty-four feet, and a width at surface level of fifty-four feet six inches, except in the Deep Cut where, for reasons of economy, the width at bottom was to be only fifteen feet and thirty-two feet at surface.[9] The lock chambers were to be built of timber, one hundred feet long by twenty-two feet wide, with seven and a half feet of water on the mitre sills. These were the minimum dimensions necessary if the canal were to serve naval purposes. Early in 1826 it was decided to increase the depth of the canal to nine feet six inches and to enlarge the dimensions of the locks to one hundred and twenty-five feet by thirty-two feet, in order to accommodate steamboats. Three locks on this larger scale were built between Merritt's property at St. Catharines and Lake Ontario before scarcity of resources compelled a return to the smaller dimensions. The use of timber for the lock chambers meant higher cost for maintenance than would have been required for stone locks, but the initial cost was lower and they would be easier to enlarge later. Locks of this type had to be entirely renewed at the end of ten years, for the timber above water level deteriorated rapidly.

In July 1825 construction was begun in earnest, agreements being signed with the contractors which called for completion of the Welland River–Lake Ontario section by April 1827. In September work was begun on the Deep Cut and by the end of 1825 excavation was in progress at a number of points along the line. The late start, however, meant that little more than preparatory work could be done before frost put a stop to digging. During 1826, however, considerable progress was made. By the end of October 1,330,704 cubic yards of earth had been excavated out of an estimated total of 1,457,238, and 202,707 yards of embankment had been completed, leaving 155,445 yards still to be constructed. Monthly expenditures averaged £7000 and by November 10 a total of just over £69,400 had been spent. The first three quarters of a mile north from the Welland River was practically completed, the towpath having been finished and the water let in. On the Deep Cut, where the greater part of the labor force was concentrated, just under half the excavation was completed and bottom level had been reached at one point. On the five-mile section descending the escarpment four locks were completed by the end of the year, except for their gates. The St. Catharines–Lake Ontario section with the larger locks would be navigable during the following season. The record for this first full year of operations, in short, was good.[10]

Early in the following year a Scots engineer named MacTaggart, employed by the British government on the Rideau Canal, was instructed by Colonel By, in charge of that work, to inspect and report on the progress of the Welland.[11] His report was, in general, not favorable.[12] He singled out for especial criticism the wooden lock chambers which, in his opinion, were badly constructed and inefficient. Certainly they must have made a poor showing when compared with the expensive masonry on the Rideau, and MacTaggart's vivid warning that, with the first freshet, they would float down the canal like so many bird cages was enough to frighten the timid. In this and other instances of less importance, however, it appears that MacTaggart took little account of the limited means at the disposal of the Company, a consideration which Barrett and Thomas, resident engineers on the Welland, were never permitted to forget.[13] From the point of view of capital cost and speed of construction, timber lock chambers and other improvisations were fully justified. A substantial part of MacTaggart's disapproval must be ascribed, it would seem, to the prejudices of a British-trained engineer confronted with American construction methods. His report does not appear to have had any serious repercussions and is mentioned only because it was the first report on the canal by an engineer not connected with its management.

By September 1827 work was so far advanced on the northern or Lake Ontario–Welland River section that tenders for the southern or Grand River section were called for. Contracts for this section were let to Messrs. Monson, Simpson & Company on October 4, and a beginning made with the slow task of draining the swamp. By December, when work on this section was halted through financial difficulties, 72,000 cubic yards of earth had been removed and drainage ditches carried into the swamp for three to four miles.[14]

On the Lake Ontario–Welland River section, Beach, Hovey & Ward, the American contractors who had undertaken the Deep Cut, were released from their contracts, as they were bankrupt and had failed to meet the specified date for completion. The board thereupon offered a prize of £125 for the best design for an excavating machine submitted to them, which was won by a certain Oliver Phelps, formerly a subcontractor for Hovey & Ward.[15] The whole of this section was then put under contract to Phelps. Heavy rains in the fall caused delay, and at the end of October all work was suspended. Only 371,643 cubic yards of earth remained to be removed from the Cut. The section from there to St. Catharines was finished and ready for water, with the exception of two locks and 12,000 cubic yards of earth to be removed the following year. The section from St. Catharines to Lake Ontario was already in use. Only the Deep Cut remained as an obstacle to the completion of the canal.[16]

The year 1828 was critical. The financial resources of the Company were under severe strain, in spite of assistance from the imperial and provincial governments. Energies were concentrated on the Deep Cut section. If this could be completed by the end of the year, the first two sections of the canal from Lake Ontario to the Niagara River could be opened for traffic during the following summer.

Under the supervision of Phelps, the contractor, and Barrett, the engineer, work on the Deep Cut was recommenced late in April. By October two sections of this cutting were completed. Progress was facilitated by the digging of a narrow ditch through the cutting, through which scows could be brought up to carry away the excavated material.

On November 9, however, when it was thought that only two more weeks' work remained to complete the cutting, a disaster occurred which resulted in a complete stoppage of work and threw the whole future of the canal into jeopardy. The banks of the Deep Cut collapsed. This was partly due to the steep angle at which they had been cut, and partly to the fact that the excavated material had not been deposited far enough back from the edge of the cutting. The real source of the trouble, however, was more fundamental. It lay in the fact that excavation of the bottom of the cutting had reached a bed of loose sand, the presence of which had previously been quite unsuspected. As soon as this level was reached and water allowed to enter, this sand was carried away in the form of silt, so that the banks were undermined.

According to the best engineering advice then available to the Company, this disaster made it impossible to continue the canal on the original plan.[17] Use of the Welland River as the feeder necessitated lowering the bottom level of the Deep Cut to the level of that river. Since this was now impossible because of the sand, either the work would have to be given up completely, or a new feeder found which would bring in a supply of water at a higher level, thus enabling the bottom level of the Deep Cut to be raised. New surveys were therefore ordered, and engineering skills supplemented by the enlistment of James Geddes, one of the most experienced canal engineers then available in North America.[18] Geddes and Barrett ran new surveys in November and December and submitted their reports early in 1829.

The solution they proposed was bold but practicable. The key lay in the Grand River section, which depended on Lake Erie, not the Welland River, for its water supply. The elevation of the waters of Lake Erie above the sand level in the Deep Cut was not in itself sufficient to give the desired eight-foot depth, even if a feeder were brought in directly from the lake, but there were two alternatives which promised a possible solution. One was to dam the mouth of Grand River so as to form a reservoir above the Lake Erie level; the other was to tap Grand River at a point several miles from its mouth and from this higher elevation to bring water down to the canal through a long cutting. The engineers recommended the first alternative.[19] They proposed to build a dam across the mouth of the Grand River sufficiently high to raise the water five feet above Lake Erie. A long cutting could then be made direct from this reservoir to the Deep Cut, passing over the Welland River, the original feeder, by an aqueduct. They estimated that by this plan they could bring in a supply of water which would provide a depth of eight feet in the Deep Cut, even though no further attempt was made to lower the bottom level.[20]

What Geddes and Barrett were proposing was something quite different from the Grand River section of the canal as originally planned. That had been a relatively short cutting, involving no dam across the mouth of the river and by no means essential to the effective functioning of the River Welland–Lake Ontario section. The new plan involved a very much longer cutting and meant that the whole canal, from the mouth of the Twelve Mile Creek to the Grand River estuary, would be from the hydraulic point of view one system, the effective operation of which depended primarily on the Grand River dam, the long feeder from Grand River to the Deep Cut, and the aqueduct over the Welland River.

Besides the longer feeder, the dam, and the aqueduct, the new plan necessitated additional locks at each end of the Deep Cut — two at the south end to enable vessels to pass from the canal to the Welland River, and two at the north end to connect the new higher level in the Deep Cut with the old level from that point to Lake Ontario. Further, it meant that the large sum of £86,000 expended for the Deep Cut excavation up to that date had been almost entirely wasted.[21] True, there was the partial compensation that, once the water level was raised, the width of the Deep Cut would be no less than one hundred feet, and the directors argued valiantly that the new plan would result in a much better canal than the old one, but the fact remained that this basic change in plans put the completion of the canal years, not weeks, distant and involved the Company in very heavy expenditures for which no provision had been made. This is quite apart from the very serious blow to public confidence which these disasters occasioned.

Changes in the route, as always, provoked objections. In this instance the most serious opposition came from the British naval commander, Commodore Barrie. Barrie protested strongly against the proposed Grand River dam, arguing that it would destroy any possibility of using the estuary as a naval base. He therefore insisted that the dam should be constructed not less than eighteen miles upstream. When the Company objected that this would involve lengthening an already lengthy feeder and adding greatly to its cost, Lieutenant Governor Colborne compromised by insisting that the dam should be built at least two miles upstream. In the outcome it was decided that the river should be dammed five miles from its mouth, at a place later known as Dunnville, and a cutting made from there to the feeder.[22] Barrie also objected to a short cutting which the Company proposed to make between the Welland and Niagara Rivers, pointing out that such a cutting would violate government land reserves and that permission had not been obtained. Although this was technically correct, Merritt had, it seems, obtained informal sanction from Lieutenant Colonel Phillpotts of the Royal Engineers who, until prodded into activity by Barrie, thought it too small a matter to be bothered with. In this case the lieutenant governor sided with the Company and the work was allowed to proceed. Here as elsewhere, the close personal connections between the board of directors and the provincial executive proved highly useful.[23]

The whole line of the new feeder from the Deep Cut to Grand River was put under contract on January 31, 1829. The line was not properly laid out, however, until April, and construction did not begin until early in May. Work on the Grand River dam, begun in January, was suspended in March because of Barrie's objections, and construction did not begin at the new location until early in June.[24] On the line of the feeder progress was delayed by illness among the laborers in the marsh section. These delays were a serious matter. The Company was near the end of its financial resources, and it was common knowledge that the provincial government would extend financial assistance only if the canal was open for traffic in the following season. In the meantime work was carried on by hand-to-mouth credit arrangements. Each contractor agreed to accept partial payment for work done in proportion to the means at the disposal of the Company. Normal contracting procedure was discarded to permit concentration of labor and equipment on sections where the work was lagging, particularly on the line of the Grand River feeder.[25]

The Grand River dam, built of trees, brush, and gravel, was completed by the middle of July and, with the completion of the feeder and aqueduct, closed at the end of September. This enabled the whole canal to be tested for the first time. Water was admitted to the feeder on October 7, and immediately turned off again, as the dam promptly sank several feet. Not until November 6 was the water raised to the necessary level, and a full supply was not available until the middle of that month.[26] These mishaps delayed the opening of the canal, planned originally for November 24. Severe frosts caused further delay and when, on November 30, two schooners finally passed through the canal from Lake Ontario to Buffalo harbor, their crews had to cut a passage through several inches of ice. Ceremonies planned to mark the official opening of the canal were cancelled as it was believed success was too uncertain to justify them. Nevertheless, the immediate task had been accomplished; ships had passed from one lake to the other by means of the canal.

But the event had, in reality, little more than symbolic importance. That two small ships had been forced through did not mean that the canal was ready for traffic, nor that the difficulties of the directors were over. The Company ended the year heavily in debt, and there was little immediate prospect of a volume of traffic sufficient to pay interest on their obligations, far less a dividend to the shareholders. In the construction of the canal durability had been sacrificed to economy and speed, and low initial costs meant continuing expenditures for repair and maintenance. The wooden lock chambers and the Grand River dam, to take only two examples, required constant attention if they were to continue to function. The Grand River feeder, which had been constructed in extreme haste, was too small to provide a reliable and adequate water supply and was navigable only by small boats. The Welland and Niagara Rivers provided the only usable entrance on Lake Erie, which meant that the navigation was circuitous and slow, the strong current on the Niagara being a serious drawback.

The task facing the directors in January 1830 was therefore twofold. In the first place they had to attract traffic through the canal. To this end tolls were set very low: 4d. per barrel for flour, 6d. per barrel for pork, 1s. per barrel for ashes, and 20s. per M. for pipe staves.[27] Plans were also laid for the formation of a subsidiary enterprise, the Erie and Ontario Transportation Company, which would build storehouses, purchase steamboats, and run a regular passenger and freight service between ports on both lakes and the canal harbors.[28] Secondly, the sections of the canal already built had to be kept in repair, the banks strengthened, the feeder enlarged, and the harbor on Lake Ontario — now known as Port Dalhousie — completed.

As if these two tasks, both essential to the survival of the Company, were not enough to occupy their attention and finances, the directors decided early in 1830 to undertake the construction of a new section of the canal which would provide a direct entrance on Lake Erie.[29] This new extension was strongly recommended by Geddes, the engineer, as a means of avoiding reliance on the dangerous and inconvenient navigation of the Welland and Niagara Rivers.[30] The cost of this new cutting was estimated at $100,000, a sum for which no provision whatsoever had been made.

No work beyond surveys was done on the proposed new route in 1830, the entire resources of the Company being devoted to widening and deepening the feeder, repairing the Grand River dam, and maintaining other sections of the canal.[31] Expectations of a large volume of traffic were disappointed by the renewed failure of the dam, and produce which had accumulated in anticipation of the opening of the canal on the date announced was sent instead over the Niagara portage, charges on which had recently been reduced to match the canal tolls. By the time the canal was opened this valuable and highly important early season traffic had disappeared. Several vessels drawing seven and a half feet of water did, however, pass through the canal late in the season, thus enabling the directors to claim that the work had been "fully tested."

Preparations were made to prevent a repetition of these misfortunes in the following year. Storehouses were put under construction at Dunnville, Port Robinson,[32] and Port Dalhousie. A line of boats was being organized to make daily trips between Grand River and Port Dalhousie, and the board announced that "effort will be made in the ensuing season to procure a sufficient number of vessels to leave Prescott every day, if not oftener, for Port Dalhousie; thence to Sandwich, touching at the intermediate ports on Lake Erie." These and other measures were designed to deflect the lake trade routes away from the Erie Canal and the Niagara portage. The increased volume of traffic anticipated for 1831, when the Ohio canals would be nearing completion,[33] gave them an added justification, but the Canal Company was in no position to support unprofitable subsidiaries.

Little work was done during 1831. The progress of construction and improvement was by this time geared directly to legislative grants — the only source of capital to which the Company still had access — and the necessary assistance was not obtained until the middle of March. Choice of a Lake Erie terminus for the new cutting was left by the legislature to the discretion of the board. On the recommendation of the engineer and after a personal inspection by John Warren [34] and J. B. Yates, a place known as Gravelly Bay, renamed Port Colborne, was selected.[35] Work on the new Lake Erie extension was put under contract late in June, but progress was slow, unusually wet weather being at least partly to blame. An expenditure of £3000 was authorized for the construction of a harbor at the mouth of Grand River — a work which the board had at one time expected (and, it must be admitted, with considerable justification) would be undertaken by the government, in view of its naval and commercial importance.

Hopes for a high volume of remunerative traffic were again disappointed. Lack of confidence in the canal on the part of lake shippers, which the mishaps of the previous year had done nothing to remove, was accentuated by the circulation in Buffalo, Cleveland, and other ports on Lake Erie of a rumor to the effect that slides in the Deep Cut had once again blocked the canal.[36] This fabrication was apparently not denied in time to prevent forwarders on both shores of Lake Erie from making other arrangements for the shipment of their produce, so that the bulk of the spring produce business was again lost. Such tactics at least demonstrated that the Erie Canal interests in Buffalo were aware of the potential competitive challenge of the Welland.

Probably of no less importance, however, in explaining the failure of Lake Erie forwarders to take advantage of the favorable freight rate differential represented by the Welland Canal route was the absence of adequate credit and transportation facilities on the line of the canal. St. Catharines could not compete with the commercial credit extended by Buffalo mercantile houses, backed as they were by the resources of the New York market, and Niagara, even if it had been disposed to help, was little better off. No regular lines of communication had yet been formed between the different ports on Lake Erie and those on Lake Ontario. No vessels had yet been designed for the double voyage on the lakes and the navigation of the canal. On the canal itself only four or five boats were available for freight. Three storehouses had been purchased by the Company and a steamboat acquired which was to serve the double purpose of towing vessels up the Niagara River and conveying produce from the American side. But even these forwarding operations, puny in comparison with the barge fleets and warehousing facilities available on the Erie, were discontinued at the end of the season, when the directors announced that their attention would thereafter "be confined exclusively to keeping the canal in a state of repair for transportation only, leaving forwarding, and all business connected therewith, open to individual competition." This meant that the Canal Company would in future play a passive role in the promotion of through traffic.

In spite of these difficulties, the Company had something to show for the two seasons in which the canal had been open. Tolls for the two seasons amounted to over £3607, and this in spite of the fact that the canal had so far been quite unsuccessful in breaking the Erie's monopoly of the Ohio trade. As the board hopefully pointed out, "the increase alluded to is entirely exclusive of the New York trade, scarcely a ton of which passed this route last season [1831]. The transit is wholly from Upper Canada, and to and from Oswego — principally wheat down and salt up. This trade is confined to Lake Ontario; and from the number of superior flouring mills recently erected at Oswego, cannot fail of increasing to an immense extent." [37] Failure to attract any part of the American Lake Erie trade was, however, hardly a matter for self-congratulation. As the directors themselves stated in another connection, "It was never anticipated by the most sanguine, that this work would remunerate the Stockholders without drawing a portion of the trade of Ohio to and from the New York market." Hopes for capturing this trade, now that the Company had withdrawn from direct participation in forwarding, centered on the completion of the direct cut to Lake Erie.

Work on this cutting was pushed forward vigorously during 1832, financed by a large loan granted by the legislature in the previous year. Serious delay was caused, however, by an outbreak of cholera among the laborers. When the epidemic passed, it was too late in the season for the contractors to finish the cutting that year as had been planned. Work on other sections of the canal was not seriously delayed. The canal and feeder

were overhauled; the Grand River dam was reinforced and "made permanent"; a new berm bank was erected along the entire line of the feeder;
and waste and stop gates were built at several points. A long and serious
interruption of the navigation resulted from the blocking of the feeder by
grass in the marsh section; to prevent a repetition, the feeder was deepened
during the winter from Grand River to the main line of the canal.[38]

Traffic during 1832 showed a slight increase, though by no means as
large as had been anticipated. A significant feature was the increase in
wheat from American ports, amounting to 100,000 bushels. Upward traffic
was still principally salt, 35,000 bushels of which passed the canal during
the season.[39] A great increase in American traffic was confidently expected
for the following year, when the direct Lake Erie line would be open.
Canadian freight, on the other hand, was expected to decrease "as the
continued emigration consumes the greater part of the surplus produce now
raised." Apparently the board did not believe that the westward movement
of population on the American side would have a similar effect.

By March 1833 the directors could announce the completion of the new
cutting and the opening of a direct line of navigation from Port Colborne
on Lake Erie to Port Dalhousie on Lake Ontario, a distance of only
twenty-eight miles. This improved canal, however, like the old one, was
completely dependent on the Grand River feeder, as the Deep Cut remained
above the level of Lake Erie.

The completion of this cutting ostensibly brought to an end the work of
constructing the canal. Nothing further should have been necessary except
routine administration and upkeep. In their annual report for 1832, however, the directors called attention to certain minor improvements which
they alleged to be necessary if the canal were to be put in a perfect state
of repair. To carry these out they petitioned the legislature for a loan of
£25,000. This was refused. The provincial government undertook, instead,
to purchase that part of the Company's stock which remained unsold,
amounting to some £7500. But the spending of this sum was taken out of
the hands of the directors and entrusted to three commissioners appointed
by the legislature.[40]

The duties assigned to these commissioners included deepening the
feeder, repairing and maintaining the locks and canal, and suggesting improvements. In their report at the end of the year, however, they remarked
with some acerbity that they had been engaged in finishing the canal,
rather than repairing it. The whole of the new Lake Erie cutting, for example, had had to be deepened, some parts being one foot above the proper
level. To obtain the judgment of an independent authority, the commissioners procured the services of Benjamin Wright, dean of American canal
engineers. Wright submitted a comprehensive report, in which he largely
exonerated the Company from charges of lack of economy.[41] He felt com-

pelled, however, to recommend substantial changes and improvements which, while certainly necessary to put the canal in perfect condition, were quite beyond the means at the disposal of the Company. Among these recommendations were the deepening of the feeder to six feet, the complete reconstruction of all the locks within four years, improvement of the harbor facilities at Grand River, Port Colborne, and Port Dalhousie, and extensive repairs on other sections of the line. His most damaging criticisms were aimed at the locks. He had no objection to wooden locks as such, if they were properly constructed, but he felt that the design of the Welland Canal locks was very faulty.[42]

Wright's report clarified the situation considerably. It was now clear that if the canal were to be kept in operation, far less enlarged, considerable further expenditures were required. Capital for such expenditures could come only from the provincial government, for the canal and its revenues were already mortgaged to the British government and could not be offered as security to private lenders. The commissioners therefore concluded their report by recommending that the canal should be made a government work, pointing out that

> . . . the cost of such solid and substantial repairs, alterations and improvements, as Mr. Wright has suggested, are assumed to be quite beyond the resources of a private Company; which fact, in addition to other considerations, leads to the conclusion, that the Canal ought to become entirely public property. The great navigable communications of the country, like its highways, should belong only to the Province, and be entirely and solely subject to the control of the Legislature. Under this impression, the Commissioners respectfully suggest, that the interest of the private stockholders should be purchased by the Province, and that the Canal should thus be rendered in name, as it always has been in fact, and must be in effect, a *national concern*.[43]

No immediate action was taken on this recommendation. In January 1834, however, a committee of the Assembly reported in favor of granting additional aid, perhaps convinced by Yates' argument that "it would not be proper with a due regard to public faith to suffer the Company to die, and then claim the forfeited property," [44] and in March an act was passed increasing the Company's capitalization by £50,000 and authorizing a subscription by the provincial government for the whole additional amount. Precisely half of this sum was used by the Company to pay off old debts to contractors, persons awarded land damages, and others.[45] Little could be done with the remainder before the navigation opened, but during the season the Grand River dam was again reinforced and the harbors at Grand River and Port Colborne extended. Contracts were also negotiated for urgent repairs required on the line of the canal.[46]

On November 15 the canal was closed to permit the contractors to proceed with the work. In spite of this minor curtailment of the season, statistics of freight traffic were encouraging. Tolls increased to £4300 as against £3618 in 1833,[47] and a total of 570 schooners, 334 boats and scows, and 66 rafts passed the canal. No less than 23,422½ barrels of pork paid toll, as against only 9611 in 1833, and 392,055 feet of square timber compared with only 30,942 in the previous year. The activities of the Grand River Navigation Company, another of Merritt's projects, in opening up the western peninsula of Upper Canada were responsible for a substantial proportion of the increased traffic, but equally significant were the encroachments of the Welland on the Ohio–New York trade. Of the 264,919 bushels of wheat which passed the canal during 1834, only 18,464 came from Canadian ports on Lake Erie; the remaining 246,455 bushels came from American ports, and of these 234,285 were consigned to the New York market by way of Oswego. Further, the directors were able to report that twenty new vessels were in process of construction on the American side of Lake Erie, designed specially for the Erie–Ontario trade, and similar activity was evident in Canadian shipyards.

At the end of 1835 the story was much less cheerful. Repairs and improvements were now urgently required, but the funds of the Company were exhausted. In addition, it was £3487 in debt, exclusive of estimates for work required.[48] Freight traffic was considerably less than had been expected. For this, three reasons were suggested. In the first place, a severe frost and snowstorm in May had destroyed a great part of the crops in Ohio and western Upper Canada.[49] Secondly, the lower lock pit on Grand River failed, completely shutting off all the produce which would otherwise have come down the river and through the canal. And thirdly, a fictitious report was circulated in certain of the New York papers to the effect that the canal was to be closed for repairs on November first, and that no produce should be shipped from Oswego later than October 25.[50] In spite of these difficulties, the board reported that the amount of produce passing the canal was nearly three times greater than in the previous year, and the tolls, if the figure of £5807 can be trusted, showed an increase of approximately 35 per cent.[51]

The question of buying out the private stockholders was debated in the legislature during this year, but no action was taken. A bill to provide a small loan to enable the Company to keep the canal open was reserved by the lieutenant governor. To carry it through the year, the board adopted a suggestion made by J. B. Yates and issued their own promissory notes, redeemable in one year. These notes were issued in payment to contractors and laborers and were accepted as currency in the towns along the line of the canal and by the storekeepers of the neighborhood.[52]

The same method of financing was used in 1836, and proved highly successful. The directors congratulated themselves in their annual report that by printing their own money they had been enabled to "relieve those individuals who had so long and so patiently waited for payment of damages long since due." This expedient, the legality of which was at least questionable, combined with short-term credit extended by the Bank of Upper Canada, enabled the Company to survive a trying year. On July 10 J. B. Yates died, depriving the Company of a source of emergency credit and the New York stockholders of their spokesman and watchdog. Between February and April the Company had to defend itself at length and in detail before a suspicious select committee appointed by the legislature to investigate serious charges of fraud and corruption laid against the officers of the Company by William Lyon Mackenzie, the Reform leader, who had been appointed by the Assembly to the board of the Company in the previous year. Though substantially cleared of these charges, largely owing to Merritt's able conduct of the defence, the directors were unable to secure further aid during this year. "No material was provided — every thing was postponed or delayed under the delusive assurance of public aid; and the Directors at the opening of the navigation were left £8,000 in debt, without any visible means of keeping the canal in operation." [53]

The effects of this interruption in the flow of government assistance were little short of disastrous. Up to October 1 the canal was closed for ninety-three out of the 184 days during which it should have been open for navigation. The locks, now nine or ten years old, were rapidly decaying and required immediate replacement. Further, the old threat of a competing canal on the American side of the Niagara River, checked by Merritt's energetic action in 1824, made a new appearance in a more dangerous form. Surveys had already been completed, the supporters of the project appeared undismayed by the estimated cost of between two and a half and five million dollars, and their engineer was only too accurate in his prediction that "if the Niagara Canal on our side should *merely be determined on*, the great efforts now making by the Canadians to give the Welland Canal a greater degree of efficiency would probably be rendered unavailing, and it would eventually sink into disuse." [54] Clearly the impasse could not be allowed to continue. Stopgap aid, humbly petitioned for by the board and grudgingly granted by small majorities in the Assembly, would no longer suffice. What was required was nothing less than a complete reconstruction of the canal on a permanent basis. Only in this way could it ever become self-supporting. Only in this way could the perpetual draining away of public funds be halted. Only heavy capital investment could put a stop to the unending process of "tinkering" with the canal, and the repairing or replacement of one part or another as the cheaply-constructed property deteriorated. Small wonder that the directors closed their annual report by expressing their desire that the canal should become public property.

On November 1, 1836, the directors submitted to the provincial government a petition for a loan of £100,000. This request, which outwardly differed little from its many predecessors, actually set in motion the process of government purchase. In March 1837 the legislature passed an act which went far beyond the Company's petition. All previous loans were converted into stock, and an additional subscription was authorized for the completion of the canal in a durable manner with stone locks.[55] At the same time the number of directors was reduced to five, three of whom were to be appointed by the government and two elected by the private stockholders. Effective control of policy was therefore by this statute removed from the hands of the private investors.

The act also provided for a complete survey of the canal by two competent engineers not previously connected with the work. The appointment was given to N. H. Baird and Hamilton H. Killaly, who submitted their report early in 1838.[56] Without recommending any drastic changes in the plan of the canal, they recommended enlargements the total cost of which was estimated at just over £300,000. Of this sum approximately £65,000 was to be expended on the improvement of the harbors at Ports Dalhousie and Colborne, and £13,000 on the construction of a junction and graving dock at Dunnville. The remainder was required for widening and deepening the feeder, which was still proving highly unsatisfactory, making a slight change in the route between Thorold and St. Catharines, deepening the canal to eight feet six inches, and enlarging the locks. Limited by their instructions to locks measuring twenty-four by one hundred and ten feet, Baird and Killaly nevertheless concluded their report by recommending that they should be constructed at least forty-five by one hundred and eighty feet, with eight feet of water on the mitre sill, in order to accommodate the steamboats then appearing on the lakes in increasing numbers. The additional cost, if this latter recommendation were adopted, they estimated at £250,000.

At this juncture the imperial government intervened. Political deadlock in Upper and Lower Canada, culminating in the abortive rebellions of the crisis year, 1837, had called attention to the urgent need for constitutional reform, and had led to the appointment of Lord Durham as governor general of all the British North American provinces, with almost dictatorial powers. Very shortly after his arrival, Durham recommended in the strongest terms to Lord Glenelg, the colonial secretary, that the canal system of the Canadas should be completed, with the aid of imperial credit if necessary. Glenelg in reply promised that the matter would receive serious attention, but emphasized that there might be difficulty in the House of Commons over renewed proposals for expenditures on Canadian canals, and that the imperial government could give no pledge of funds. Durham was authorized, however, to have a survey of the whole route from Lake Erie to tidewater made by a competent officer of the Royal Engineers.[57] Lieutenant Colonel Phillpotts was selected for the job, probably because he had been chief engineer on the Cornwall Canal.[58] His instructions were to report fully on the estimated cost of constructing a line of canals from Lake Erie

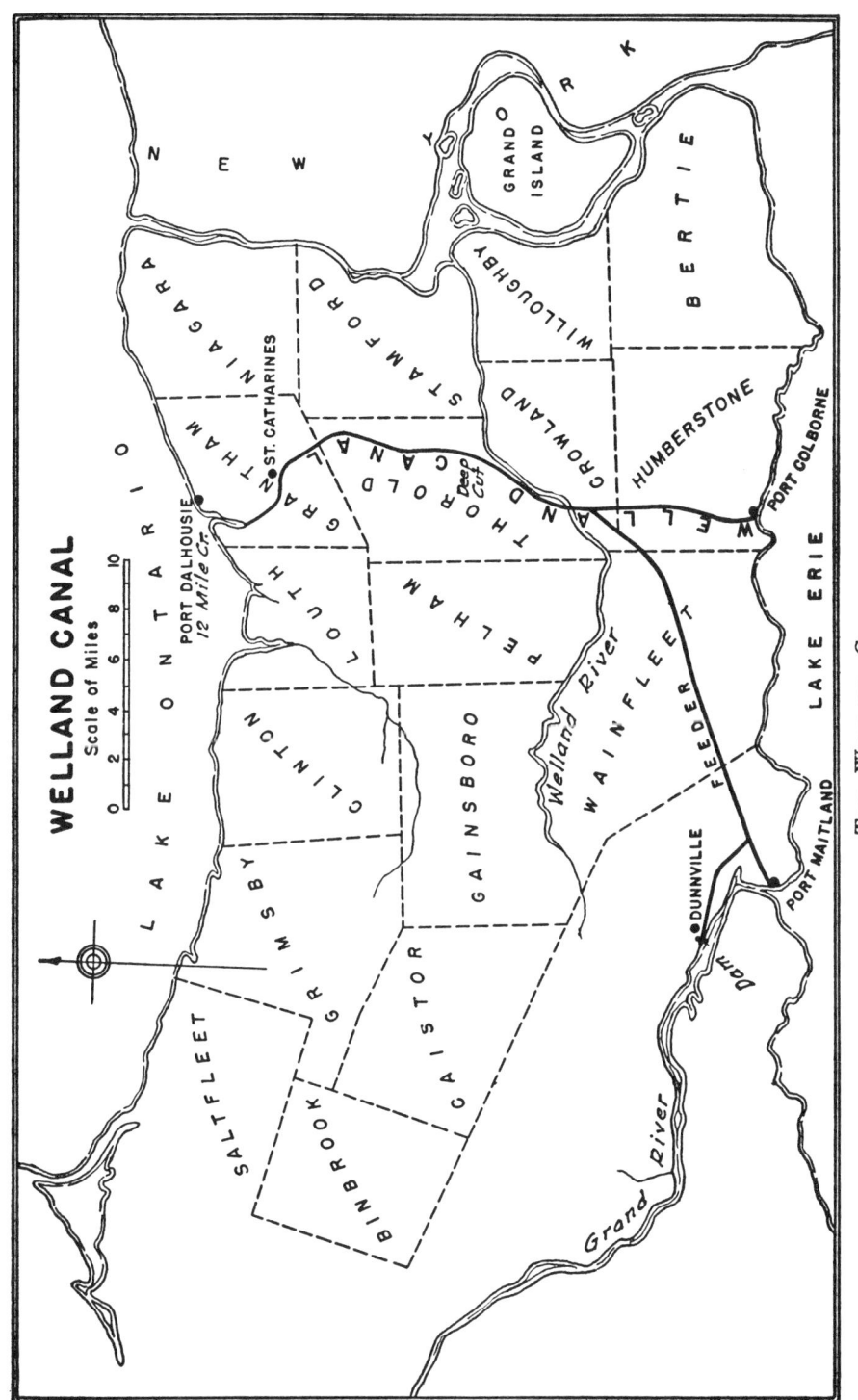

THE WELLAND CANAL
as completed in 1833

to Montreal on the same scale as the Cornwall Canal (that is, with locks two hundred by fifty-five feet, and nine feet of water on the mitre sills), the time required for completion, and the probable traffic from both American and Canadian sources that might be expected to arrive at Montreal and Quebec by this route.

At Phillpotts' request, the board of directors of the Welland Canal, who had been preparing to begin the reconstruction of the locks on the smaller of the two scales mentioned by Baird and Killaly, agreed to postpone their operations until he could complete his examination. His first report, dated December 31, 1839, contained a strong recommendation that the Welland should be reconstructed with stone locks on a much larger scale, and pointed out that "unless we open an uninterrupted navigation for *large freight steamers*, capable of conveying a cargo of at least 300 tons, *without transshipment* before they arrive at Montreal or Quebec, we have no chance whatever of securing any great portion of that vast and important trade which must ere long be carried on between the Western States and the Atlantic Ocean." He refrained from comment on the importance of the Welland from the military and naval point of view. That, he felt, was sufficiently obvious and had already been brought to the attention of the imperial government. What he wished to emphasize was its commercial value. From this point of view enlargement was essential and must be undertaken quickly.

> . . . it is quite impossible, in the present state of the work, to insure the navigation being kept open much longer unless the whole canal be immediately put into an efficient and permanent state of repair. . . if permanent and efficient measures be not adopted without delay, there is great danger that this highly important communication will soon become impassable.[59]

Phillpotts' emphasis on the dangers of delay was by no means exaggerated. While his report was in preparation the condition of the canal was going from bad to worse, and the need for capital becoming desperate. At the beginning of 1838 the directors reported to Lieutenant Governor Sir Francis Bond Head that the canal could be kept open only at an average annual loss of about £14,000.[60] Reconstruction and enlargement, they argued, would decrease the cost of maintenance and repair, but not enough to offset increased interest charges. They therefore concluded their report by recommending as a matter for serious consideration whether or not the canal should be abandoned as a navigable waterway and used as a source of water power only.

This report had its effect in an unexpected quarter. The New York stockholders now sent a memorial to the provincial government, praying that they be compensated for their investment in what they blandly termed " a public work which, for usefulness and profit, under proper management, is not equalled in America." [61] An act for this purpose passed the provincial legislature in 1839 but was reserved by the lieutenant governor. Reintroduced in the first session of the legislature of the now united provinces of Canada in 1841, this act finally became law on July 5 of that year.

The passing of this act marked, for all practical purposes, the final dissolution of the Welland Canal Company. Earlier in the year the maintenance and operation of the canal had been placed under the Board of Works, and in September the legislature voted £450,000 for its permanent reconstruction and enlargement. With this grant began the process of widening and deepening the canal which has continued to the present day.

CHAPTER FOUR

FINANCE

THE RELATIONSHIP WHICH EXISTED BETWEEN THE ENGINEERING difficulties of the Welland Canal Company and its financial problems does not require extended discussion. The scale on which the canal was constructed and the speed and efficiency with which its construction was carried through dictated the amount of capital required. Expectations as to future earnings, volume of traffic, strategic importance in the broadest sense, and, to a degree, speculative concern with land values, together with conditions on the money markets of New York, London, and Montreal, determined the ease with which this capital could be obtained and the security which was demanded. The pace of construction, in turn, depended very largely upon the volume of funds available. Errors and miscalculations in the one sphere had immediate repercussions in the other; and progress in both depended directly upon the effectiveness with which certain necessary entrepreneurial functions were performed.

The original charter of 1824 authorized the Company to issue 3200 shares of common stock of a par value of £12 10s. 0d. currency each, making a total capitalization of £40,000. Almost the whole of this amount was subscribed by the end of 1824. Over one half of these subscriptions came from persons resident in New York State; of the remainder, about £6000 were subscribed in Montreal and Quebec, and another £6000 in Upper Canada. No attempt had yet been made by the promoters to approach British investors, a fact which did not predispose the lieutenant governor and his advisors in their favor.

On February 25, 1825, the Upper Canada House of Assembly passed a resolution to lend the Company £25,000 and to permit an increase in capitalization. When on April 13 the amended act of incorporation became law, no financial assistance accompanied it, but a motion was passed that a loan be granted during the next session.[1] Hopes for obtaining a loan of the same amount from Lower Canada were dashed at the end of March when the legislature of that province dissolved before James Gordon, then the Company's treasurer, could present his petition.[2]

The new charter, although it increased the authorized capital to

£200,000,[3] meant in the short run a decrease rather than an increase in the Company's resources. The act provided that persons who had subscribed under the old charter could now withdraw and be repaid their subscriptions, if they so desired. Forty persons, representing a total of 170 shares, took advantage of this clause, most of them being residents of Niagara who were unwilling to support the Company now that the St. Catharines route had been definitely chosen.[4]

The withdrawal of these investors, though a serious blow, was offset to some extent by new subscriptions, a total of 232 shares being sold in Upper Canada. Most of these new subscriptions were small, and only eight individuals invested the £250 necessary to qualify them for a seat on the board of directors. These eight were: John Henry Dunn, John Beverley Robinson, William Allan, Henry John Boulton, D'Arcy Boulton, Colonel Joseph Wells, George Keefer, and W. H. Merritt.[5] With the exception of Keefer and Merritt, then, the passing of this new charter marked the exit of the original group of merchants and millers of the St. Catharines–Thorold district who had supported the canal project in its initial stages. In their place we find a new group, considerably higher in social rank, markedly political in their interests. Dunn, Allan, and Wells were members of the Legislative Council, Allan being in addition president of the government-sponsored Bank of Upper Canada.[6] Robinson, the attorney general of the province, and H. J. Boulton, the solicitor general, were leading members of the Assembly. D'Arcy Boulton, father of H. J. Boulton, was a judge of assize. As a group, they may be taken as representing the political and social elite of the colony.

Dunn, H. J. Boulton, Keefer, and Merritt were elected directors for the year 1825, the remaining seats on the board being occupied temporarily by three persons nominated by the legislature: James Irvin, Simon Mc-Gillivray, and J. C. Buchanan. The first official act of these directors was to draw up a new petition for a land grant. Presented to Lieutenant Governor Maitland, this petition was forwarded to Bathurst at the Colonial Office on May 19, accompanied by a strong recommendation that it should be granted, now that the entrance on Lake Ontario was to be at least ten miles from the frontier and the canal itself large enough for naval purposes.[7] Bathurst acquiesced in the recommendation, but instructed Maitland that the grant was not to be made final until the whole capital stock of the Company was subscribed.[8] Maitland, interpreting these instructions loosely, made the grant final in 1826, on the assumption that the completion of the canal was then no longer in doubt. By these means the Company acquired title to about 13,000 acres of land in the township of Wainfleet, an asset of which, as events turned out, they were unable to make effective use. Nevertheless, the success of this petition amply demonstrated the new solidarity of the relationships between the canal board and the provincial executive.

At the same board meeting a decision was taken which proved to be one of the most ill-advised in the history of the Company. At the instance primarily of Simon McGillivray and John Galt, commissioners of the Canada Company,[9] it was decided that precisely one half of the total capital stock, or 8000 shares, should be reserved for sale in Great Britain, to be disposed of through the agency of that Company. Of the remainder, 4000 shares were to be sold in the Canadas and 4000 in New York.[10] The reasons for this decision were explicitly stated in the *Annual Report* for 1825, and they had nothing to do with the ease or difficulty with which subscriptions could be obtained in the various places. New York subscriptions were limited to one quarter of the total solely because the board was "anxious to preserve the management of the Company under British influence." The support of the Family Compact, the lieutenant governor, and the Colonial Office was obtained only at a price.

To dispose of the £100,000 of stock reserved for England the board relied upon McGillivray. His plan was intrinsically a sound one: the directors were to communicate with "certain intelligent and leading individuals in the city of London [that is, the Canada Company], who, if they could be once induced to embark in this project, would at once ensure its success, and from the mere circumstance of their names being engaged in it, would at once fill your subscription, and bring your stock to a premium." [11] In addition, an agent was to be sent to London with maps, profiles, and statistics, to explain the project in detail. But no direct approach was to be made to the private investor. The Welland Canal Company was to be introduced to the London market, not as a speculation, but as a sound investment properly sponsored by respectable backers.

On the basis of this decision Dunn, the president of the Company, visited New York, Montreal, and Quebec during May and June. In New York he succeeded in selling not only the quota of stock reserved for that market but £25,000 in addition, which was deducted from the amount allocated to the Canadas. A total of 6000 shares ($300,000) were sold by private arrangement before the subscription books were opened to the public, the heaviest investors being, as before, John B. Yates and his associates. Dunn later reported, and the statement was confirmed by Yates, that he could have got the whole issue of £200,000 subscribed in New York at this time without difficulty, but that he did not feel free to cut down the amount reserved for England.[12] Another £25,000 of stock was sold in Montreal, Quebec, and Upper Canada. This left only the £100,000 reserved for the English market still unsold.

McGillivray was unwilling to go further with the Canada Company negotiations until he had personally inspected the line of the canal. He was unable to do this until September, being deeply involved in bankruptcy proceedings connected with his mercantile business in Montreal. Similar difficulties prevented him from undertaking the London mission himself when his tour of inspection was completed.[13] In his place he recommended one of the directors, Henry John Boulton, the solicitor general, and this choice was approved by the board.[14] Boulton's instructions were to offer the situation of permanent agent in England to Galt, secretary of the Canada Company, and to request Galt to form a committee to handle the Welland Canal issue. He was not to attempt to sell the stock himself.[15]

Once this decision was taken, events seem to have got completely out of control. Dunn, the president, left for New York. McGillivray took himself off to Montreal, pausing only to instruct Merritt to purchase for him certain choice parcels of land on the line of the canal.[16] Boulton thereupon took matters into his own hands. He drew up in his own name a very comprehensive power of attorney, authorizing him to receive subscriptions up to £100,000, and sent it to Merritt with a request that he should sign it as secretary under the Company's seal, promising that he would get Dunn or William Allan to sign it also.[17] Merritt complied with the request, although he had no right to use the seal, and Boulton left at once for Montreal, instructing Merritt to forward the plans and other papers to him in care of McGillivray.[18] He found time, however, to make out a draft on the Company for £300 sterling to cover his expenses, which Merritt also signed in the belief that the payment had been approved by McGillivray, which it had not.[19]

Boulton took ship for England on October 16, armed with his expense money, the power of attorney signed by Merritt alone, and a large package of blank receipts. The plans and profiles did not arrive in time and he did not wait for them. Meanwhile in Upper Canada the recriminations began. Dunn, informed on his return to York of Boulton's precipitate departure, wrote to him in consternation that he was not to make use of his power of attorney, but it is doubtful whether Boulton ever received the letter.[20] McGillivray gloomily predicted, "I think the very extensive nature of this [Boulton's] commission would startle cockney capitalists, who, be it remembered, are a very timid and suspicious race as to all things out of their reach or knowledge." [21] Merritt in self-defence remembered his too easily satisfied suspicions and protested that "when Mr. Keefer mentioned to me that Mr. Boulton had made out the draft, I stated that I had never been paid until the mission was fulfilled, and in justice to myself must state most distinctly that I never would have consented to that payment had I not conceived it had Mr. McGillivray's approbation." [22] But Allan bluntly told him that he had no right to use the Company's seal, that the power of attorney was invalid, and that "it appears to me that Mr. Boulton is not provided with any thing but your grant of £300 stg. and that he took care to get it without loss of time for fear of another Board objecting to it, which I should certainly have done." [23] Dunn was pessimistic and inclined to take the blame on himself: "Mr. Boulton may, and he may not, sell the stock. I am not without my fears and doubts — he, I think, was the most

improper person to be employed on such a mission, and when the speculators in London see one individual with such power and authority as
Mr. Boulton possessed himself of, is one strong reason, in my mind, that
there should be some apprehension . . . I am very sorry such a transaction
should have happened whilst I hold the office I do in the Welland Canal
and . . . trust I shall be exonerated by the Company." [24]

But fears that Boulton might misuse his questionable power of attorney
were groundless. He failed to make any use of it at all. Once in England,
he devoted little attention to the Company's business. He sold a few shares
to individuals he happened to meet, made no immediate effort to have the
stock sponsored by the Canada Company, and did not even write to his
associates in Upper Canada until the following March. [25] The only damage
he did to the Company was the loss of time he caused, but this was more than
enough. In December 1825 panic struck the London capital market. The
speculative boom which had carried stock flotations to a peak disappeared
overnight. A few Welland Canal shares had been sold before the bubble
burst, but even on these it was almost impossible to get the installments paid.

The opportunity had, in fact, been lost, and was never to return in quite
so favorable a guise. It was many years before the eight thousand shares
which had been reserved for England were fully taken up. Deprived in
effect of half its capital through laxity of organization and personal ir-
responsibility, the Company was crippled before ever its operations were
fully begun. The entire capital stock could have been disposed of in New
York, if the directors had not felt constrained to limit American participation. It could have been subscribed in London, if the right man had been
sent with proper introductions and authority. But these opportunities were
now gone. Meanwhile the Company limped on, casting hopeful eyes on the
public purse and financing itself by heavy and frequent calls on the New
York stock. [26]

The directors had agreed that they would make no financial commitments until the stock was fully subscribed. [27] On the basis of the American
and Canadian subscriptions, however, and in the belief that the London
mission would be successful and that the legislature would grant a loan,
contracts were let in July 1825, before Boulton left Montreal. Writing to
his father-in-law on Christmas Day of that year, Merritt reported cheerfully,
"The work on the Canal is getting on briskly . . . and should no unfore-
seen obstacle take place the whole Canal will be finished the ensuing year
[1827]." [28] Yet danger signals were not long in appearing. By December
1825, or five months after the contracts were signed, 20 per cent had been
called in on the stock subscribed in New York and the Canadas, and Yates
and his friends were complaining loudly. [29] Speaking before a select committee of the Assembly late in 1825, Dunn stated that the New York stockholders, most of whom had been hard hit by the financial crisis, would

probably refuse to pay further installments unless steps were taken to assist the Company until the subscriptions from England were available.[30] Impressed by these arguments, the committee recommended that the loan be granted, on the grounds that it would alleviate the pressure on the Canadian and American stockholders and enable the Company to push ahead with construction without waiting for the shares to be sold in London.[31] If we are to judge from the evidence submitted, no one seriously doubted that the London subscriptions would be available in the near future. Yet the loan of £25,000 finally granted on January 30, 1826, was far from being short-term credit: repayment was to be in three equal installments in two, four, and six years, with interest at 6 per cent payable semiannually.

This assistance enabled the Company to continue operations during 1826. During the summer of that year a belated attempt was made to withdraw the stock reserved for England and dispose of it in New York. In May the Company's New York agent, a man named Proctor, became insolvent and Yates and McIntyre were appointed in his place.[32] Yates immediately urged on the directors the necessity of placing the unsold stock,[33] and in the following month a letter was sent to Boulton instructing him to close the subscription list unless the stock was completely sold within fourteen days of the receipt of the letter.[34] Anticipating that Boulton would not succeed, Merritt approached the New York banking house of Prime, Ward & Sands, agents of the Barings, and offered them a commission of two and one-half per cent if they could get the remainder of the Welland Canal stock subscribed.[35] The offer was refused, on the grounds (as Merritt reported) that "the opening of this canal would be injurious to them inasmuch as it would divert the course of trade from New York to Montreal, and . . . no persons in New York would be found to embark in the undertaking on this account." Meanwhile Boulton seems to have bestirred himself, for a letter was received from John Galt, secretary of the Canada Company, informing the directors that a committee of five of the directors of that Company had been formed, headed by Charles Bosanquet, to act on behalf of the Welland Canal Company in London.[36] This offer was accepted by the board on September 2.[37]

The Canada Company's action brought no immediate relief. In September Yates was authorized by the board to raise in New York a loan of $50,000 or $100,000, whichever was more convenient, on the Company's bond and on the security of the grant of land in Wainfleet "on the supposition that the Company will have it in their power to offer that security by the time it can be ascertained by Mr. Yates whether he can succeed in effecting the loan." [38] He was also authorized to sell any stock he could, but in neither case was he successful. The stock by this time stood at a 50 per cent discount in New York.[39] A total of eight hundred shares had been forfeited for nonpayment of installments, in most cases after 25 per cent had been paid in.[40] Commercial distress in Montreal and throughout the

United States led to large quantities of stock being thrown on the New York market for what they would bring, most of them being bought up by Yates and his associates. At the end of 1826 Yates held 2150 shares in his own name, and in the name of himself and his partners no less than 4000 (nominal value $200,000).[41] Of this amount one thousand shares had been acquired by transfer, or in other words had been purchased by Yates in an attempt to support the market.

Thus, after barely one full season of operation, the Welland Canal Company found itself in serious financial difficulties. For this state of affairs the failure to sell the shares reserved for England, with the consequent necessity for heavy and frequent calls upon the New York and Canadian stockholders at a time of severe monetary stringency, was immediately responsible.

Before the end of 1826 a situation developed which appeared to make this failure slightly less serious. On September 30 of that year a dispatch was received from Lord Bathurst, the colonial secretary, stating that the British government was prepared to grant to the Welland Canal Company a sum equal to one-ninth the estimated cost of construction, on condition that government stores and vessels were permitted to use the canal without paying toll.[42]

The origin of this offer, which was apparently quite unexpected, is not without interest. During the summer of 1825 a commission of engineers had been appointed by the imperial government to inspect and report on the state of the province, with particular reference to its military security and communications. In their report to the Duke of Wellington, master general of ordnance, the commissioners devoted considerable attention to the Welland Canal which, they believed, would "materially assist in the defence of this [the Niagara] frontier" provided it was constructed on a large enough scale. They therefore recommended that "on this subject very clear instructions ought to be sent from England and . . . that the patronage and assistance of His Majesty's Government ought only to be afforded upon the positive understanding that the locks are not to be less than twenty feet wide so as to correspond with the Grenville and Lachine Canals." [43] As we have seen, the locks were already being constructed on these dimensions, but on this point the charter was only permissive; what the commissioners wanted was a positive guarantee.

The precedent for imperial aid to provincial canals was to be found in the Lachine Canal in Lower Canada, for which a grant of £12,000, or one-ninth of the estimated cost, had been made on the same conditions which were now being laid down for the Welland. The commission of engineers had given £147,240 as the estimated cost of the Welland;[44] taking this figure as correct, Bathurst now offered to grant to the Company the sum of £16,360 sterling, to be paid in four annual installments, on condition that an act be passed by the provincial legislature to authorize the Company to pass government stores and vessels free of charge and to make it a statutory requirement that the locks should be at least twenty-two feet wide.

This offer was immediately accepted by the Company, and the necessary enactment was hustled through the legislature by the middle of February 1827.[45] Authority to draw for the first installment, however, was not immediately forthcoming and, as we shall see, the Company never received the grant. In the meantime, new attempts were made to raise capital by the sale of stock.

The committee appointed by the Canada Company in London had so far been unsuccessful in disposing of the shares reserved for that market. New York also was unreceptive, as Merritt's fruitless offer to Prime, Ward & Sands had demonstrated. Excluded from these two sources of capital, the Company turned once again to the provincial legislatures of the Canadas and, early in 1827, presented petitions for aid, praying that the governments of the two provinces should purchase stock in the Company. Both of these applications were successful, though by narrow margins.

In Upper Canada the petition was referred in the usual manner to a select committee, which reported itself strongly in favor of granting the Company's request. After referring to the fact that the greatest pressure had up to then been borne by the New York stockholders, the report went on to state that no reliance could be placed on the prospect of receiving subscriptions in England. The committee therefore recommended that the legislature should provide "immediate and effectual support" to the Company.[46] On the basis of this recommendation a motion to purchase £50,000 of stock in the Welland Canal Company was carried in the Assembly by a vote of twenty to eighteen, a motion to reduce the amount to £25,000 having been defeated by a rather wider margin. The whole of this subscription was to be made available immediately, in order that the Company might be enabled to press ahead with the work without the necessity for frequent and heavy calls on the New York stockholders. The Company was required to deposit with the receiver general a bond for £20,000, to be forfeited if interest at 6 per cent were not paid semiannually until one year after the completion of the canal to Grand River.

In Lower Canada the Company's petition narrowly escaped being drawn into the constitutional conflict between the governor general, his nominated Councils, and the elected Assembly. At the start of the session Lord Dalhousie, in an effort to obtain legislation granting a permanent civil list, announced that all money bills for local purposes would be rejected unless the Assembly voted the money necessary for the service of government. When, however, a bill granting £25,000 for the purchase of Welland Canal stock was approved by the Assembly, Dalhousie felt impelled to make an exception. His reasons are perhaps best expressed in his own words:

When I received Sir Peregrine Maitland's dispatch on this subject by a gentleman [Merritt] especially sent with it, I lost no time in recommending it to the favourable consideration of both Houses. I had little hope that any greater consideration would be given to it in the Assembly, than to the recommendations on other matters, but it was immediately taken up warmly, and passed rapidly. I felt that I ought not to allow our Provincial disputes to be interposed in what so deeply interested our Sister Province, and I also rejoiced to see a first instance of that mutual support by which the Canadas will stand or fall hereafter. I therefore gave the Royal assent to the Bill . . .[47]

The ready support accorded the bill by the French-Canadian legislators was indeed surprising. Dalhousie surmised, probably with some accuracy, that the bill was passed in order to demonstrate "a spirit of liberality in the Assembly while the odium for rejecting such grants would fall upon the Council or upon His Majesty's Government."

As a result of these two successful petitions, the first few months of 1827 saw the finances of the Company in a much healthier condition than its directors had any right to expect. But they were still not out of danger. As financial resources increased, so did estimates. Writing on March 10, before news of the success in Lower Canada had arrived, Dunn gave to the lieutenant governor a lengthy account of the Company's finances.[48] Of its £200,000 authorized capital stock, £93,000 had been subscribed by private individuals, but of this a total of £10,000 had reverted to the Company through nonpayment of installments. On the remaining £83,000, 27 per cent was still to be paid in. In addition, the Company now had available the £50,000 subscribed by the government of Upper Canada, together with the grant promised by the British government — a total, Dunn estimated, of not less than £93,000.[49] Estimates of the total cost of the canal had now risen to £230,000, of which £90,000 had already been spent. This left £47,000 or, as Dunn put it, "not more than £50,000," still required to enable the Company to bring the work to a successful conclusion.

Having arrived at this convenient figure, Dunn reminded the lieutenant governor that the imperial government had expressed a readiness to advance money at low rates of interest for objects of public benefit, and went on to say:

. . . it has suggested itself to the Directors that if His Majesty's Government would consider the actual expenditure of £170,000 as sufficient security to render it prudent to afford the accommodation alluded to, and would raise by loan in England the funds still wanting, say £50,000 sterling, the Directors, relieved from the uncertainty of stock being subscribed by individuals, might safely proceed to put the Western Section of the Canal from the Welland to the Grand River at once under contract, and the certainty would be afforded of the navigation being completed with the least possible delay; it need scarcely be mentioned that if the remaining £57,000 stock should be subscribed in America it would of course enable the Company immediately to redeem the loan.

We may pause at this point to consider some of the implications which Dunn did not draw from the figures he presented. Work on the canal was at this time progressing in quite a satisfactory manner. The catastrophic slides in the Deep Cut had not yet occurred; no drastic recasting of plans and estimates had yet taken place. Nevertheless, it was already clear that the task was beyond the unaided power of the Company. Only public assistance had enabled it to survive as long as it had, and only by continuing and generous transfusions of public funds could it hope to complete the task it had set itself. The basic fact which no juggling with figures could hide was that out of a capitalization of £200,000 — itself less than adequate — private individuals had subscribed only £83,000. If the Company had adhered to its initial resolve not to commence operations until the capital was fully subscribed, the canal would not have been begun. The Welland Canal Company was already degenerating into a privately-controlled institution for the disbursement of public funds.

The strategy which the Company would follow in seeking future public assistance was also foreshadowed in Dunn's letter. It was based on the assumption that no legislative body concerned with the welfare and security of Upper Canada would suffer the Company to die. If this were conceded, the rest followed almost automatically. Unless further aid were forthcoming, the Company would have to cease operations. But if the Company ceased operations, the parts of the canal already built would fall into decay, and an unfinished canal was worthless. Unless further aid were granted, therefore, the investment already made by the public would be completely lost. The more capital the legislature invested in the canal, the more it had to invest if it wished to preserve its earlier investment.

Dunn's letter was forwarded by Lieutenant Governor Maitland to the Colonial Office on March 12, 1827, with the usual recommendation that it should be favorably considered. It was not well received. The Treasury, little impressed by Dunn's account of what had already been accomplished, informed the Colonial Office that they could not recommend Parliament to lend any money for the completion of the canal upon any security the Company could offer. They stated, however, that if the provincial government were to guarantee payment of interest on the loan and set up a sinking fund for redemption of the principal, an imperial loan might be arranged. A week later Huskisson forwarded the refusal to Maitland. Before the dispatch arrived Maitland wrote again to urge that the loan be made, offering this time the land grant as security. But nothing was done, either at this time or later, about the suggested provincial guarantee.[50]

Toward the end of the year another attempt was made, through the agency of J. B. Yates, to sell stock and obtain a loan in New York, but without result.[51] The funds available to the Company had by this time shrunk to a mere £39,000, including in this figure the promised "one-ninth" grant from the British government. Against this there was required to finish the canal from Lake Ontario to the Welland River £40,000, and from there to Grand River another £50,000, or £90,000 in all with no allowances for faulty estimates and unanticipated disasters.[52] It was clear that, unless some as yet untapped source of capital was found, the Company would be unable to complete even the first section of the canal, far less the proposed extension. The sum required was approximately £51,000. If the 3107 shares which still remained unsold could be disposed of, the deficiency would fall to about £12,260.

This was a desperate situation. The Company, it was estimated, could continue operations up to the end of July 1828; after that, if no further assistance were obtained, it would be bankrupt. But where was capital available? To appeal again to the Canadian legislatures after so short a respite would be to invite failure. England or the United States were the only possibilities.

On February 14, Merritt submitted to the board of the Canal Company five suggestions:[53] first, to enlarge the capital stock to £300,000; secondly, to attempt to sell stock or raise a loan in the United States; thirdly, to send an agent to England to obtain the promised "one-ninth" grant; fourthly, to sell stock in England; and fifthly, to obtain a loan, in addition to the grant, from the British government. Of these, the first suggestion was clearly pointless. When the present stock could not be sold, what was the use of issuing more? As for the others, it was all very well to talk of selling stock in England or the United States, but not even the Canada Company had been able to find buyers for the Company's shares in London, and New York was no more receptive. Yates had already tried to raise money in the United States without success, and the British government insisted on a provincial guarantee and a sinking fund before any imperial loan could be considered. The delay over the "one-ninth" grant, however, was in a different category; perhaps something could be done about that. Almost as a last resort, the board decided to send an agent to England, primarily to arrange for the payment of the imperial grant but with a roving commission to sell shares or arrange a loan wherever opportunity offered. Merritt was selected for the job.

Every possibility of raising money in the United States was exhausted before Merritt left for England. He set out from St. Catharines on February 26. The tenth of March saw him in Philadelphia, presenting his facts and figures to Stephen Girard. But Girard had no money for Canadian canals and his answer was a decided negative. Returning to New York, Merritt called a meeting of the stockholders which resulted in the sale of six hundred and forty shares. Yates and McIntyre agreed to pay up the remaining installments on their stock and to make a temporary loan of £10,000, but none of the other stockholders could or would do anything to help. Applications to John Jacob Astor, to Prime, Ward & Sands, and to "a Jew, agent of Rothschild" brought a succession of refusals. Clearly there was no point in spending more time in New York. On March 16 he sailed for England.[54]

Once in England Merritt began what one writer has well described as a siege of the imperial exchequer.[55] On May 13 he wrote to his father, "Of all places this is the most tedious to get through Business in a hurry." [56] Nevertheless, he got results and he got them quickly. On May 5 he made his first attempt to see the Chancellor of the Exchequer. On the thirteenth of the same month the government decided to make the loan, but was defeated in the House on another issue before the decision became effective. The new ministry, however, honored the promise of its predecessor, and on July 11 an appropriation for a loan of £50,000 sterling to the Welland Canal Company passed the House of Commons without a dissenting vote.[57]

But all of Merritt's time was not spent waiting in the antechambers of Whitehall. Besides giving evidence before the select committee on the civil government of Canada, he succeeded in selling all the remaining stock of the Company, or 2467 shares, to private individuals — some of them distinguished public figures like the Duke of Wellington and Alexander Baring, whose names headed the subscription list, some of them to more obscure individuals like the Reverend Richard Blacow of Liverpool, who by investing his life's savings became the largest English shareholder.[58] This was the first successful attempt to interest the English investor in the Welland Canal.

At first glance, Merritt appeared to have carried out his mission very competently. There were, however, certain offsetting considerations, though Merritt himself made light of them. In the first place, the imperial loan was granted instead of, not in addition to, the "one-ninth" grant promised by Bathurst. The Chancellor of the Exchequer had given Merritt two alternatives: either a grant of £27,000, this being one-ninth of the new estimated cost, or a loan of £50,000. Convinced that £50,000 would complete the canal by the end of that year and totally ignorant of the disasters then impending on the Deep Cut, Merritt chose the latter, though not without some faint hopes that the grant also might still be obtained at a later date.[59] Further, as security for the loan, Merritt had mortgaged the canal itself, with all its property, tolls, and profits, to the British government. Interest on the loan was to be paid at 4 per cent per annum and the principal was to be repaid within ten years. If principal and interest were not paid promptly the canal would become government property.

The stock subscriptions also were not above criticism. Yates in particular was inclined to regard them with a jaundiced eye, remarking that they had been made by "some persons high in office and a few others of such standing and wealth that the smallness of the sum rather impaired than added to the estimation of the stock." [60] Further, as we shall see, some of the subscriptions were not final commitments to purchase.

Merritt had, in fact, succeeded a little too completely. What he accomplished in London was this: he mobilized sufficient capital to insure the completion of the canal on its original plan. It should be kept in mind that his mission was completed before the increase in estimates which resulted from the slides in the Deep Cut. Had these slides not occurred, Merritt's work in London might have marked a turning-point in the Company's fortunes.

As was inevitable, the board confirmed the arrangements he had made. The money, urgently needed before he left, was indispensable after the Deep Cut catastrophe. But a resolution passed at a board meeting held on December 15, at which Merritt was not present, illustrates the mixed feelings with which the imperial loan was accepted. The directors expressed their regret that the loan had been obtained only at the price of the grant — "a condition amounting in fact to the requiring a bonus of £27,000 for the loan of £50,000" — and went on to say:

> This arrangement is so unreasonably disadvantageous that the Board cannot believe it possible after the Canal shall be actually completed, the Government will refuse to accept the payment of the balance between the grant first proffered and the loan of £50,000 as an extinguishment of the whole loan. . . On behalf of the stockholders generally and especially of those whose deep stake in the Company would make the arrangement with the Government, if literally carried out, almost ruinous to them, the Board has felt it necessary to record the sentiment with which they have confirmed the arrangement.[61]

Their feeling that a hard bargain had been driven was not entirely unjustified.

Up to this point the Company appears to have paid the interest on its debts to the provincial government punctually and in full.[62] Henceforth the story was to be very different. The slides in the Deep Cut in November 1828 were, in fact, a major disaster from the financial as well as from the engineering point of view. The Company had expended during 1828 a total of £60,000.[63] As a result of Merritt's work in England the directors now counted on having at their disposal the imperial loan of £50,000 sterling (£55,555 11s. 2d. currency) together with approximately £38,837 from the new stock subscriptions, or a total of about £94,400. It appears, however, that something in the region of £40,000 was required to pay off past indebtedness to private individuals, so that funds actually available for work on the canal amounted to only a little over £50,000.[64] Barrett's estimates at the end of the year, after the Deep Cut incident, showed that £54,662 was required to finish the canal for ship navigation throughout, and estimates up to that time had always been exceeded.

Taking an optimistic view of the situation, the directors reported at the end of the year:

> The funds of the Company now amount to nearly as much as would cover the estimate of expenditure for the whole work, on the above estimate

of £54,662; but from the large sums we have had to pay for interest on loans, contingencies, etc., the Directors do not feel that they would act prudently in undertaking to complete the whole line the present season for ship navigation, with their present means, although they are satisfied that it would be far more economical . . . than to delay it for another year.[65]

They decided instead to construct the Grand River cutting which, it will be remembered, was now to act as feeder for the entire canal, on the minimum dimensions which they believed to be consonant with its effective functioning. If Merritt had not succeeded in England, even this would have been impossible.

Throughout 1829 the Company's financial position continued to deteriorate. Costs were higher and resources smaller than had been anticipated. After Commodore Barrie's protests (see above, pp. 63–64), the Grand River dam had to be moved five miles upstream. This meant delay and the loss of the $1500 already expended on the work. Fever among the laborers on the line of the feeder meant further loss of time and money. Meanwhile certain of Merritt's hard-won English subscriptions were evaporating. On November 21, 1828, the firm of E. & R. Ellice & Company had been appointed by the Canal Company to act as agents in handling the transfer of the imperial loan. They were immediately drawn on for £30,000 and warned that the remaining £20,000 would be required in the near future.[66] Both Ellice & Company and the Canada Company had pledged themselves to Merritt for the purchase of stock, the former for £15,000 and the latter for £6000.[67] On July 2, 1829, when the news of the Deep Cut slides reached London, Ellice & Company, with the commission for the transfer of the imperial loan safely in their pockets, refused to comply with their agreement to buy stock, and shortly thereafter the Canada Company also repudiated its pledge.[68] The Canal Company had considered these pledges as binding, and the failure to secure the £21,000 involved was a serious blow.

Harassed by these difficulties, the directors tried every expedient they could devise to carry them over until the canal should be completed. The equipment and tools which had been used on the Deep Cut were sold. Application was made to the Bank of Upper Canada for a loan and, after William Allan, vice-president of the Canal Company and president of the bank, had exerted his influence, a small advance was obtained on the personal security of the directors.[69] Late in the year J. B. Yates, in response to appeals for help, advised the Company to issue post notes payable to bearer at St. Catharines, New York, and Montreal, with a par value of £12 10s. 0d. ($50.00) and with interest at 6 per cent, but this suggestion was not adopted until several years later.[70] Finally in desperation the board had recourse to the extraordinary expedient of applying to the lieutenant governor, Sir John Colborne, for a personal loan of £10,000 and apparently

were successful.[71] Nevertheless, when the canal was opened for traffic —
after a fashion — at the end of the year, the Company had a floating debt
of £15,467 in the form of arrears due to contractors and unsettled claims
for damages, while cash in hand amounted to a mere £152 19s. 11d.[72]

The completion of the canal not only opened up for the first time the
prospect of obtaining funds from revenue, as distinct from investments or
loans, but also provided the directors with the excuse they needed to apply
once again to the Upper Canada legislature for financial assistance. A loan
of £25,000 was requested — enough to pay the Company's debts and leave
a little over for maintenance and repair — together with authority to increase the capital stock to £300,000. The petition was referred to a select
committee which included the Radical leader, William Lyon Mackenzie;
and toward the end of January a report was submitted which recommended
that the loan be refused, but that authority should be given to the Company
to increase its capital stock. Ten reasons were given for refusing the loan,
of which the first and probably the weightiest was: "Because the Province
is already deeply in debt, which has been chiefly contracted on account of
this undertaking." [73] Of the other nine, one related to the fact that the
canal was now mortgaged to the British government, thus depriving the
provincial government of security for the loans already made, and one to
the withdrawal of the promised British grant. Both these arrangements
appear to have been bitterly resented by the Reform party. The other
objections were purely political in character, reflecting the grievances of
the Reformers.[74]

In spite of this hostile report a majority of the Assembly voted in favor
of making the loan, thus bringing the investment of the provincial government in the canal to a figure of £100,000 — "which," as the lieutenant
governor commented, "is a large sum for the limited revenues we pos-
sess." [75] The capitalization was not enlarged.[76] A similar petition to the
legislature of Lower Canada was a failure, the French-Canadian Assembly
being in no mood to repeat the gesture of five years before.

During these early months of 1830 strenuous efforts were made by
Yates to raise money in the United States. They were unavailing. On January 2 he reported to Merritt:

> I have made every effort in my power to induce some of the capitalists
> here [Albany] and in New York to receive the paper of the Company
> but have not yet been able to succeed. . . A loan might be made for a
> term of years if the faith of the Govt could be procured for the payment
> of the interest. . . My expressions of confidence were made on the suppo-
> sition that as the security was undoubted and money was abundant here,
> there would be no doubt of success. But I was mistaken. The Banks do
> not wish to give a currency to the paper, and Individuals will not even
> examine it.[77]

On the eighteenth of the same month he used what was for him unusually strong language to protest against drafts drawn on him by the Company. "I am without power," he asserted, "if I do accept I cannot pay . . ."

> . . . The canal, together with the contracted littleness of the Gentlemen who ought to have aided it, have destroyed not only my power to aid any further, but if I can escape ruin I shall be fortunate. The wretched policy of passing all the drafts, too, through the hands of persons who are decidedly hostile to the canal & in the hope of realizing its resources & arresting its progress, have repeatedly attempted to destroy us & that by the most insidious and cowardly means.
>
> If the draft is presented to me here I dare not accept it, until I know what reliance I can place of the means to take it up. You will pardon me, but I can do no more. We can borrow what we please if your Government will lend its credit & guarantee the debt but without [that] we can do nothing.[78]

Again the familiar pattern repeated itself. First the Canadian legislatures were approached, then the New York bankers, and finally England. This time, however, it was decided that Yates should go to England himself. There was still stock to be sold, thanks to the defection of Ellice and the Canada Company, and there was still hope, though precious little, that the British government might soften the terms of its loan and perhaps even make the grant originally promised. In any event the attempt had to be made, for the Company needed money and there was apparently none to be had in North America.

Yates' objectives in going to London were very much the same as Merritt's had been in 1828: to obtain the "one-ninth" grant from the British government; to raise a loan, either from the government or from private sources; and to sell the remaining stock.[79] The question of the imperial grant was now, however, very much more difficult, for Merritt had explicitly refused it, accepting instead the £50,000 loan. There was no good reason for hoping that the clock could be turned back, although Yates carried with him petitions from the Company and the Upper Canada Assembly to that effect. The most that could be hoped for was some modification of the terms of the loan, and this was in fact all that Yates obtained. The Company was released from the obligation to pass government stores and vessels free of toll. This relaxation, the Treasury considered, was "not . . . unreasonable" in view of the fact that the Company had given security for the loan and for the payment of interest. And with that very minor concession Yates had to be content.[80]

When it became clear that the grant was not to be obtained, either in addition to the loan or as a partial offset to the interest payable on it by the Company, Yates looked elsewhere. Attempts to raise a loan from private sources encountered the objection that the Company had already mortgaged its property and profits to the British government, and had to be abandoned. But some success was achieved in placing the unsold shares.

With the aid of letters of introduction from New York acquaintances, Yates managed to sell 470 shares to individual members of the mercantile house of Fletcher Alexander & Company, with authority to draw for the money immediately, but (and here Yates' words had better be quoted directly) "two separate negotiations at different times for the whole balance of stock [which] I verbally closed were broken off in consequence of the unfavorable opinion decidedly expressed by the partners in a highly respectable commercial house in the Canada trade who for some cause had taken a stand against the Canal Company." [81] In consequence Yates was constrained to do what he could in the way of placing small blocks of stock with individual investors, and in this manner sold several hundred shares. But it was slow and painful work, and not what Yates regarded as proper for a man in his position:

> After being there so long a time without hearing any direct information
> of the state and progress of the canal, and the unfavorable account that
> reached us through the Montreal papers, my situation became exceedingly
> embarrassing in the disposition of stock. A species of personal respon
> sibility was obliged to be assumed in the representation that no object
> of this sort ought ever to require, and which never fails to impair con
> fidence in, if it does not injure the character of the person making it.

Although this peddling of shares was not to Yates' taste, he had been very successful. In all he sold a total of 1158 shares, leaving only 459 still to be disposed of. Equally significant for the future history of the Company, however, were two by-products of his London visit. The first was his meeting with a certain Captain Ogden Creighton. Creighton seems to have ingratiated himself with Yates immediately; he wrote a pamphlet for Yates to distribute, and helped him to find purchasers for the stock. He was later to act as Yates' Canadian agent, for Yates, being an alien, could neither be a director nor hold real estate in Canada. The second development was foreshadowed in a significant phrase in the report from which we have quoted above. The reason given by Yates to explain his failure to obtain a loan from private sources was his "not having any power to enter into a negotiation for a loan sufficient to remove the lien of the Government." The implication was obvious: had Yates been given the authority, he believed he could have freed the Company from the encumbrance which was excluding it from the money markets of New York and London.

Yates returned from England convinced that the only hope for the private shareholders lay in raising from private sources a loan large enough to pay off all the Company's obligations to the Canadian and British governments. This view was not entirely consonant with the wishes of the Canadian directors, who looked forward with equanimity to the prospect of continued government assistance and — possibly — eventual government purchase. None of these directors, we must remember, was a large stockholder, and most of them were prominent members of the provincial executive. As far as they were concerned, government purchase would constitute a natural and proper conclusion to their efforts. To Yates this view was anathema.

The next application for aid to the Upper Canada legislature almost precipitated conflict between these two policies. A request for a loan of £25,000 was referred by the Assembly to a select committee under the chairmanship of H. J. Boulton, the man who had bungled the Company's first mission to England. Boulton took the bit between his teeth and hustled through the committee a report recommending that the government should lend the Company, not the £25,000 asked for, but £200,000 — enough to pay off the loan made by the British government as well as all previous provincial loans.[82] This proposal was clearly intended to give a final quietus to the policy Yates was advocating; as the report stated, "The Province will, in the event of the recommendation being adopted, be the sole creditor of the Company, and hold a lien on the Canal, which shall prevent the Company ever looking to any other quarter." In other words, Boulton and Yates both were concerned to consolidate the Company's debt; but whereas Yates was insistent that the capital required should come from private sources, Boulton looked in the first instance to the legislature.

The Assembly at first adopted the report but later, finding on reflection that £200,000 was rather a large pill to swallow, changed it to a loan of £50,000, and this only on condition that the directors should furnish individual security that this sum would be used to complete the whole canal, harbors, and so on, and that the government would be indemnified against the payment of the interest and one half the principal. J. B. Yates, Alexander Yates Macdonell (Yates' nephew, a Canadian), and Merritt became personally liable for the amount required and the act received the lieutenant governor's assent on March 19, 1831.[83]

To finance this loan the province issued debentures for a corresponding amount, but in this instance the issue was not handled as it had been previously — that is, by direct sale of the debentures. Indeed the province itself, its credit weakened by successive grants and loans to the Company, was in no very secure financial position by this time. An attempt during 1830 to float a £100,000 bond issue for the financing of internal improvements had proved a failure.[84] To circumvent this difficulty, the debentures were on this occasion issued directly to the Canal Company, to be disposed of as best the directors could arrange it. This procedure had been suggested in Boulton's report, and preparations had already been made to put it into effect. On October 26, 1830, Yates had received a blanket commission to negotiate a loan "to the amount which he may deem necessary to pay off those incumbrances, and for the purposes of the Canal, with any individuals, bodies corporate or politic, in any way or manner he may conceive best adapted for the interests of the Company." [85] On March 10 he was empowered to offer the provincial debentures as security, and on May 11, 1831, arrangements for a loan at 5 per cent interest were concluded with the Bank of the United States. The provincial securities were to be deposited with the bank as collateral on a dollar-for-dollar basis as and when the money was required, an arrangement which (so the directors congratulated themselves) "allows the Company their own time to sell them, as well as the opportunity of selecting the best market aided by the influence of the Bank." [86]

This was not the only piece of financial legerdemain going on at the time. The mortgage given to the British government covered, as we have seen, the whole canal and its revenues. This included the land owned by the Company, in particular the large grant in Wainfleet, and the water power privileges. These were potentially valuable assets, but no attempt had yet been made by the Company to realize on them.

On October 26, 1830, Yates offered to purchase all the landed property of the Company, together with the rights to sell or lease the surplus water, for the sum of $100,000 payable in installments over ten years.[87] The board, while agreeing that such a sale was desirable inasmuch as the efficient utilization of the water power demanded an investment of capital beyond the means of the Company, felt some hesitation about accepting his offer. At the next board meeting, on November 3, hesitation was more marked. The directors "conceived they would assume too great a responsibility to close with his proposal without having more information respecting the value of the property to be disposed of." [88] They therefore instructed Merritt to advertise the sale in the newspapers of New York, Boston, Montreal, and elsewhere, offers to be received before March 1, 1831. The matter was also brought to the attention of the stockholders in the *Annual Report* for 1830, in a manner not calculated to arouse their suspicions:

> It has been deemed advisable to offer for sale on or before the first of March next, all the lands and hydraulic situations belonging to the Company on the line of the Canal, as they can be managed to better advantage by individuals; and the increased toll from the erections that must be immediately placed on the line in order to render them profitable to the purchasers . . . will be an equivalent for the increased value of those situations which the Company propose to surrender.

When the first of March arrived, however, the highest outside offer received was only $30,000. Yates immediately renewed his original bid of $100,000, and the property (which was, of course, still burdened by the mortgage to the British government) was sold to him at this figure.[89]

Since Yates, being an alien, could not legally hold landed property in his own name in Upper Canada, he formed a partnership with his nephew, A. Y. Macdonell, and with Ogden Creighton, and had the title to the land

and hydraulic rights made out to Macdonell as his trustee. This partner-ship came to be known as the Hydraulic Company. Its formation was highly important, not only because it marked the sale of the Company's land and water privileges and introduced a small but powerful inner clique into the canal management, but also because, although the sale itself does not appear to have been "rigged" in any way, it aroused considerable hostility, particularly among the Upper Canada Radicals, whose political power in this period was rapidly growing. Land speculation was a familiar rallying cry among reformers and agitators in Upper Canada, and the Hydraulic Company seemed tarred with the same brush as the Canada Company and the highly controversial Clergy Reserves. In a sense they were right: the hydraulic purchase was a speculation. Yates now owned land and water-power rights which were potentially of very great value indeed,[90] and the Canal Company got very little in return. True, they re-ceived a bond for £25,000 and an undertaking that £1500 would be paid as interest on that bond every year. But as a matter of fact very little of this annual payment ever reached the hands of the Canal Company. Year after year the interest payable was cancelled in consideration for damages due the Hydraulic Company for failure of the water supply, draining of the canal to facilitate repairs, and similar reasons.[91] The effect on canal tolls was negligible.

Shortage of cash and short-term credit was no less a problem at this time than shortage of capital. The £50,000 grant from the provincial government could be expended, under the terms of the act, only for the completion of the canal. It was not available for the liquidation of the Company's floating debt, amounting to approximately £11,000.[92] Most of this debt consisted of sums due the contractors for work performed and unsettled claims for land damages. If the latter could safely be left pending from year to year, the former could not. Delay in paying the contractors had immediate repercussions on the rate of construction.[93] Further, finan-cial stringency occasionally led to acute distress among the laborers and, if allowed to continue, could lead to the breaking up of the labor force.[94]

Normally, short-term credit was obtained by drafts on Yates — a prac-tice against which he protested vigorously on several occasions — or by advances from the Bank of Upper Canada against security provided by the directors as private individuals. These sources were now drying up. Yates was in difficulties with his lottery business and would probably refuse to honor the Company's drafts. The Bank of Upper Canada was growing obdurate. In October 1831 Ridout, the cashier, informed Merritt that the bank would discount no more notes bearing his name, as he had failed to meet on maturity two drafts for a total of £2150.[95] Allan, president of the bank, stated bluntly, "For my own part I have seen no inducement for any Person to come forward and assume the responsibility of a large sum for

the use of the Public . . . I dare say a little money is of the utmost consequence now in [the] progress of the Canal — but it is not a little that does
for your wants — it is large sums — that will only do for you." [96] Provincial loans or grants-in-aid earmarked for specific purposes did nothing
to help these problems, while the mortgage to the British government stood
in the way of any consolidation of debts through the agency of private
lenders.

In an attempt to find a way around this difficulty a memorial was drawn
up by the directors early in 1832 and forwarded to the Colonial Office,
praying that the imperial government should give up the mortgage in so far
as it related to the lands and hydraulic privileges, or in other words that
the mortgage should be interpreted so as to cover the canal itself and the
revenue from tolls only.[97] There is little doubt that the initiative for this
proposal came from J. B. Yates and his associates in the Hydraulic Company. In the spring the answer arrived: Lieutenant Governor Colborne was
to use his own discretion in the matter, but the Treasury insisted that,
before releasing the Company from the mortgage on the hydraulic property,
he was to assure himself that ample security remained for the loan and
that there was a "reasonable probability" that the tolls would be increased.[98] Suspecting, perhaps, that cancellation of the mortgage would
benefit the Canal Company less than it would Yates personally, Colborne
for the moment did nothing.

In the meantime the Company again petitioned the legislature for a
loan of £25,000, offering as security the bond given by the Hydraulic Company. A committee of the Assembly reported favorably, but the legislature
refused to sanction the loan. Instead, they left the mortgage in the Company's hands and subscribed for £7500 of stock, the money to be expended
on the maintenance and repair of the canal by three commissioners appointed by the legislature.

The refusal to make the loan and the appointment of commissioners
amounted in effect to a vote of censure on the directors. All the Reform
members and many of the Tories objected strongly to the way in which
Merritt had negotiated the imperial loan and were uneasy about the sale
to the Hydraulic Company. Acceptance of the Hydraulic Company's bond
as security for a provincial loan would have been tantamount to giving
legislative approval to both these arrangements. But the fact remained that
this new government subscription did nothing to relieve the Company from
the pressure of its debts. At the end of 1832 the Company owed £11,814
to contractors and had unsettled land damage and other claims to the
amount of £8000. Work indispensable to the opening of navigation was
estimated at £6319.[99] The legislative subscription would cover this last
item, but not the other two.

Efforts were renewed to raise money on the security of the Hydraulic
Company's bond.[100] On February 16, Merritt appealed once again to the

lieutenant governor to release the Company from the mortgage on the hydraulic property, pointing out that the existence of this prior lien had frustrated all attempts to raise money:

> After ascertaining the House would neither lend us £25,000 on the security of the hydraulic works, nor relinquish any part of the stock held by Government, I made an arrangement with certain individuals to take this security from the Welland Canal Company and become personally responsible to the Bank for the amount required to pay off the debts £12,000, which the Bank assented to. . . It appears however since the Act has passed, I misunderstood the extent of the security some of these gentlemen intended to go, in consequence of which the negotiation has failed.

This, he continued, had placed the directors, and himself in particular, in a most embarrassing situation, since commitments had already been made in expectation of receiving the loan:

> . . . the contractors and laborers prosecuted the work with the greatest diligence, expecting payment as a matter of course when done. The Directors as well as myself knew we could not pay them unless we obtained a further loan. Still we urged them on at all hazard to get the canal open the present season, to effect which we have incurred debts to the amount of £11,000. . . I have offered to mortgage my own personal property to the Bank, in addition to the personal security of three or four individuals for the loan of £4,000. If obtained we may still sustain the character and credit of the Company. If not, I deem it due to my own character His Excellency should know the cause.[101]

Colborne responded by consenting to release the Company from the mortgage on condition that the debt of £11,000 to the contractors was paid and that the remaining £14,000 was expended on completing the feeder and the canal. Wishing, however, to have a clear opinion on the validity of the bond executed by the Hydraulic Company in payment for its property, he consulted his attorney general, H. J. Boulton. Boulton, not for the first time, found his personal interests slightly at variance with the plans of the board. Owning as he did extensive stretches of land in the Grand River area, he had no wish to see the traffic of the canal diverted away from Grand River by the completion of the direct cut to Lake Erie. Accordingly he argued persuasively that Colborne should refuse to release the Company from its mortgage until the full £25,000 offered by the Hydraulic Company was paid, stating that, unless Yates and his associates could raise the whole sum due, he did not think it prudent to allow "persons in the United States" to acquire such a valuable property, especially since the property would readily fetch £25,000 and probably much more if it were freed from the mortgage.[102]

Influenced by this patriotic counsel, Colborne informed the board that he would consent to the release only if the whole £25,000 which the Company proposed to borrow on the security of the Hydraulic Company's bond were expended on perfecting the feeder and completing the new cutting to Lake Erie.[103] This, of course, did not suit the Company at all; what was required was security for a loan sufficient to pay off their floating debt, now at the end of 1832 amounting to about £17,000. Merritt therefore wrote to Colborne's secretary in an effort to settle the dust which Boulton had so successfully raised:

> His Excellency is willing to grant the relinquishment if £25,000 is raised and expended on the canal, or if the Directors will guarantee it shall be done. The property is now sold for that sum, £25,000 — they only require £11,000 to pay the debts, and find a relinquishment first necessary to raise that sum or even a small part of it. They will then have the residue coming from the sale now made, which they will guarantee shall be laid out on the Canal if required, thereby giving all the security ever contemplated.[104]

At the same time he appealed to Dunn for coöperation:

> I have seen His Excellency who appears to feel a responsibility in making the relinquishment after the Attorney Gen. having given so vague and doubtful an opinion on the subject. . . if you could see His Excellency on the subject he would, I am sensible, grant the relinquishment — without it the security is not valid, and we will get the work in needless confusion; with it I can borrow the money and pay off all demands.[105]

Finally Colborne granted the release, and Creighton and Macdonell were dispatched to New York to obtain a loan on the security of the Hydraulic Company's bond. They did not succeed. Later in the year, however, Yates managed to obtain a loan of £25,000 which was used, not to pay off the floating debt, but to complete the new harbor on Lake Erie, now named (with a nice sense of appreciation for services rendered) Port Colborne.[106] If we ignore the small amounts paid by the Hydraulic Company as interest, this loan was the only benefit derived by the Canal Company from its land grant and water-power privileges. On the debit side of the ledger must be put the political hostility aroused by the sale, the split with Boulton, and the resignation of Dunn from the presidency as a result of his refusal to become personally liable for further advances from the Bank of Upper Canada.[107] Merritt was elected president in his place, at a salary of £400 a year. Dunn had apparently served without remuneration.

For the time being this marked the close of the Hydraulic Company incident. The appearance of Benjamin Wright's report at the end of 1833 resulted in a noticeable change of sentiment toward the canal, particularly in the Assembly. He exonerated the Company from charges of waste and mismanagement and gave it as his considered opinion that, the total expenditure up to March 1833 having been £356,955, "there must have been good economy to accomplish so much as has been done for the sum above stated." [108] This was a verdict not lightly to be set aside, for Wright was without doubt the most experienced canal engineer on the North American continent. Nevertheless, on grounds of principle and because of the size of Wright's estimates, the commissioners appointed by the legislature recommended that the canal should be made a national work. They also took it upon themselves to suggest

> . . . that the Welland Canal Company owe a large floating debt to many individuals in the country for contracts performed by them — the nonpayment of which has caused great distress; and they submit for consideration the propriety of making immediate provision, for further payment of the debts of the Company, in which the credit of the Province, as well as the Canal Company, may perhaps be thought to be in some measure involved.[109]

This favorable report was submitted to a legislature which in the same session had voted no less than £350,000 for the construction of the Cornwall Canal, the only part of the improvement of the St. Lawrence which could be undertaken without the coöperation of Lower Canada. A petition from the Welland Canal Company for assistance produced results in strong contrast with the meagre subscription of the previous year.

The first result of the petition was a debate in the Assembly on the question of government purchase of the canal. It seems probable that the purchase would actually have been made at this time, had not two serious obstacles presented themselves. The first was the alienation by the Canal Company of its lands and hydraulic privileges, and the second the attitude of the New York stockholders. Regarding the former, the commissioners had expressed themselves in strong terms:

> It is . . . just cause for regret, that the hydraulic privileges created by the Canal should ever have been alienated by the Company, as it has established a separate interest, which already has produced, and will continue to produce great trouble and inconvenience; and they cannot avoid remarking on the manifest inexpediency of suffering a great public work, upon which so much money has been expended, to be in the slightest degree injured or incommoded, for the sake of any minor advantages.

Provincial purchase was politically, if not theoretically, impossible until these lands and water privileges were repurchased. The attitude of Yates and his associates in New York interposed a further difficulty. The commissioners had written to the private stockholders to inquire on what terms they would surrender their title to the canal. The New York stockholders held out for full payment of principal and interest and made it clear that they would much prefer not to sell, if only adequate financial assistance was obtained from the government. Yates, for example, wrote to the committee of the Assembly, "None of the accidents which have occurred have lessened my ideas of the intrinsic value of the property. I know the country by which it will be supported, and the result is inevitable." [110] He therefore proposed as an alternative to government purchase that the legislature should advance a sum sufficient not only to place the canal in such a state of repair as would insure its success, but also to restore its credit and enable it to discharge its debts. Debts to private individuals owed by the Company amounted at this time to nearly £25,000; the sum necessary to place the canal in a fit state for traffic was estimated by Wright at £8500.

The demand for full principal and interest removed government purchase from the realm of practical politics, for the time being at any rate. The provincial finances would not permit it. Even the £7500 subscribed in 1833 had been raised only by makeshift expedients; the commissioners appointed in that year had closed their report by calling the attention of the Assembly to the fact that

> . . . upon applying to the Receiver General for money, they were informed that the debentures for the loan authorized by the Legislature had not been taken up and that consequently he had no funds. The difficulty which thus threatened the Commissioners in the execution of their duty, was only surmounted by Mr. Dunn's becoming personally responsible at the Bank of Upper Canada for the whole of the sum authorized by the Act, as it was required.[111]

And on June 21, 1833, Baring Brothers had informed Dunn:

> We are fearful . . . that the rates of interest to which you are restricted by the Legislature, will not hold out sufficient inducement to investors to become subscribers to the loan you offer us; at the same time that they are too low to be a profitable investment of its capital by a House carrying on an active business. We are not able, therefore, to comply with your wish, by stating any terms at which we would be willing to contract for the loan in question, which would not be at variance with the stipulations alluded to in your letter.[112]

For the time being, therefore, provincial purchase was left in abeyance. Instead, on March 6, 1834, the legislature passed by the narrowest of margins an act authorizing the purchase of £50,000 of stock, the capitalization of the Company being increased to £250,000 to accommodate the subscription. Government representation on the board of directors was increased to three members out of seven.[113] To raise the necessary funds the receiver general was authorized

> . . . to raise by loan on debenture from any persons or bodies corporate or politic who may be willing to advance the same upon the credit of the Government bills or debentures authorised by this act a sum not exceeding £50,000, debentures payable not less than 20, not more than 40 years after date, with interest at six per cent if payable in Canada, five per cent if payable in England.

The Assembly being equally divided, the act was passed by the casting vote of the Speaker.

The drift toward government ownership and control did not go unopposed. Ever since his return from England in 1830 Yates had been pressing for a consolidation of the Company's obligations, and in particular for some method of freeing the Company from the mortgage held by the British government. In this endeavor he could count on the coöperation of many of the members of the Upper Canada Assembly. Indeed, on April 1, 1834, that body drew up an Address to the King, praying that the imperial loan of £50,000 be relinquished. The address pointed out that the province had now given assistance, by subscriptions and loans, to a total of £207,500; that three directors were appointed by the legislature; that the Company had a right to expect, by the terms of the dispatch of 1826, a grant of one-ninth the estimated cost of construction; and that

> . . . from the amount of debt due to, and the security held by His Majesty's Government on the said Canal, the Company have been and still are unable to obtain further loans, otherwise than from the Revenues of this Province — that the increased value of Crown Lands, which will be produced by the completion of this work, besides the advantages which the Mother Country will derive from the extention of commerce in consequence thereof, will in the opinion of this House more than compensate for the expenditure of the fifty thousand pounds, which will not exceed the one-ninth part of the cost of the said canal.[114]

But the appeal was in vain. The colonial secretary, Spring Rice, refused to reverse the decision of his predecessor, on the ground that it would set a bad precedent for future assistance to important colonial projects.[115]

Once this possibility was ruled out, the range of alternatives open to the board narrowed considerably. The payment of a dividend was a far-distant possibility; meanwhile, the canal still needed capital. It was futile to look to private investors so long as the Company remained encumbered by the mortgage to the British government and by the various loans made by the legislature of Upper Canada. Two possibilities only presented themselves: either to continue to rely on the provincial government for financial aid, in which case increasing government control and final government purchase were certain; or to attempt to mobilize sufficient private capital to pay off all government loans and subscriptions and to carry on under private ownership.

As events turned out, both these lines of policy were pursued simultaneously, the former mainly by Merritt and his friends in the Upper Canada legislature, the latter by Yates, acting in direct contact with financial houses in New York, and in Upper Canada through his associates, Macdonell and Creighton. A certain breach in the former solidarity of the management resulted, but in the beginning this was not serious. Merritt, although he seems to have regarded eventual government purchase as both inevitable and desirable, was prepared to coöperate with Yates as long as the line of policy pursued by the latter showed any prospects of success;

and Yates for his part, though anxious to free the Company from all dependence on government, took pains not to obstruct Merritt's negotiations with the legislature.

The first development was a partial victory for Merritt's policy. In June 1834 the Canal Company bought back its real estate and hydraulic rights. The alienation of this property, as we have seen, was one of the main reasons why government purchase had not already been consummated, and furthermore the use of water for mills and machinery had interfered with the working of the canal. The negotiations for repurchase were handled by a committee of the board composed, significantly, of the three government directors. Yates was extremely reluctant to sell, but agreed to do so in order to simplify his own affairs and the relations between the Canal Company and the government.[116] The terms finally arranged were not unfavorable to him. The Canal Company returned to the Hydraulic Company the bond for £25,000 originally given in consideration for the transfer, and also gave its own bond for £17,500, payable in fifty years with interest at 6 per cent payable semiannually. This second bond was, of course, intended to represent the capital which Yates had invested in his property. The Hydraulic Company was, however, permitted to hold about two hundred acres of land at Allanburgh and Port Colborne, together with certain mill sites at Humberstone.[117] The rental on these lands, together with rents on lands already sold, would equal the interest payable on the £17,500. This agreement, therefore, followed the pattern of the original purchase agreement by minimizing the actual transfer of cash between the two companies.[118]

Meanwhile Yates had not been idle. On November 3, 1834, he wrote to Merritt:

> I think I can negotiate a loan for one million of dollars or any less sum we may need to pay off all our debts to the Govt. I have commenced a negotiation with the Agent of a strong European House in case the Govt are not willing to purchase this winter to loan us that sum, so that we may be independant, & if I am not mistaken it will be accompanied with the inquiry what the Govt will charge for its stock interest in the canal. . . I would by no means make the move for the Govt to purchase but keep quiet and merely make a general report of prospects.[119]

On January 7, 1835, he laid down the minimum terms on which he was willing to accede to Merritt's policy:

> If the Government would be willing to convert their stock into a loan & consolidate it with their own debt & withdraw the Govt representative in the Board & give a credit of 30 years including the £50,000 to the British Govt, I would have no objection to hazard my property in such [a] new engagement. If we could not pay the debt, let the Canal & all with it go.[120]

By April he was certain that a loan could be raised from private sources, and by September he was ready to urge immediate action. "It has become important," he wrote to Merritt, "that the Welland Canal Company should make a proper effort to stand by itself & pay off the Government."

> . . . Its increased estimation in public opinion, in consequence of the steady increase of its business & evident prospective importance, is now such that I am encouraged from the interviews I have had with men in correspondence with the most prominent money lending houses in Europe, to think we can now make a loan to enable us to consolidate our whole debt & permanently renew the locks. A proper & energetic effort for this purpose may accomplish it.[121]

Finally in November he wrote to Merritt urging him and Creighton to come to New York at once. "We must have a full & free conversation. I cannot write what I wish to propose. You will approve of it & so will every friend to the Province and the W.C.C. We have no time to lose — let us now act with promptness & vigor & the victory is ours." [122]

Yates' confidence was not unfounded. With a caution praiseworthy in a businessman, though annoying to the historian, he never divulged in correspondence the identity of the European financiers with whom he was in communication. Merritt himself was informed only on his arrival in New York with Creighton, then the Company's treasurer, in November 1835. The negotiations must, however, have gone smoothly, for late in December Creighton forwarded to the lieutenant governor a letter from "certain mercantile Houses & Individuals in the City of New York" inquiring whether he felt himself authorized to dispose of the government interest in the canal, and if so on what terms.[123] And here an unexpected difficulty arose, for the only statute which referred to the possibility of selling government-owned stock was that passed in 1827 (8 Geo. IV, cap. 17) which authorized the lieutenant governor to sell at not less than par.

Presumably this technicality could have been circumvented, given time. But events in the political sphere were now moving too fast, and late in 1835 the long-germinating hostility to the Canal Company, closely linked as it was to the inner clique of the Tory party, developed into open attack. Leader in the assault was William Lyon Mackenzie, radical demagogue and journalist. Appointed to the board of the Company by the legislature early in 1835, Mackenzie had spent five months ingratiating himself with his fellow directors and burrowing through the Company's chaotic account books. He emerged on October 21 with a series of startling charges of fraud and defalcation on the part of the Company's officers, which he proceeded to publicize in a broadside entitled "The Welland Canal."

If Mackenzie had wished to do the greatest possible amount of damage to the Company, he could hardly have chosen a better moment. Merritt, who by this time had managed to get himself elected to the Assembly, succeeded in having the whole matter referred to a select committee which, after prolonged inquiry (which might well have been abbreviated had not

Mackenzie held the government printing contract) finally emerged with a verdict of "not proven" on all serious counts. But the damage had been done. It was all very well for Creighton to urge Merritt, "Your policy is to put everything off *to the last* — *bother* them until the end of the Session and all will go well — eventually they *must* purchase the work," [124] but the fact remained that Yates' negotiations had been effectively halted at their most delicate stage, the flow of public assistance interrupted, and confidence in the canal badly shaken. Yates did his best to turn the crisis to advantage: if the government were dissatisfied with the management of the canal, then let them sell their interest in it and divest themselves of all responsibility. He had his offer ready and the government had only to accept.[125] But this was to ignore the political aspects of the situation. Mackenzie and his followers were determined to make political capital out of the Welland Canal, and it would have taken more than a fair offer from a New York financier to deflect them from their purpose.

The bitterness of the attack did what no other crisis in the history of the Company had succeeded in doing: it broke Yates' confidence. On February 27, 1836, he wrote to Merritt:

> The scoundrel has by his publications done injury that it will require time to repair. But I cannot see why the proposition I make in my letter is not acted upon if they want to sell out & let us take the canal. . . We can raise what we want if our debt is consolidated & no more danger of legislative interference, and if so much noise had not been made I might have negotiated for a sufficient sum within the year by loan. I cannot say more than I have said. I am tired out and wish I had never seen the canal, or anything connected. It has embittered my life here as well as there. They must do as they please . . .[126]

There were not to be many more letters from Yates, and those that did follow echoed the same note of despondency and disgust. On July 10, 1836, he died, and by his death put an end to all serious efforts to free the Company from its dependence on the legislature. Nothing more was heard of the million-dollar loan. From this point on, eventual government purchase became inevitable.

At the end of 1836 the Company had a floating debt of £1208, to which had to be added about £2500 for land claims and £6346 for necessary repairs. Cash in hand amounted to only £295, leaving £9853 to be provided.[127] To keep the canal open, stopgap aid to the amount of £2000 was voted by the legislature, but the bill was reserved by the lieutenant governor so that for the whole of the season the Company was left to fend for itself. The results were disastrous. During 1836, indeed, the Welland Canal Company touched the nadir of its fortunes. Complete bankruptcy was avoided only by the desperate expedient of issuing the Company's bills as currency and by Merritt's efforts in prevailing upon private individuals to endorse the Company's notes.[128] But it was clear that an impasse had been reached. Another such year and it would be impossible to keep the canal open, far less undertake the extensive repairs which were by now urgently necessary.

On August 6, 1836, the board decided to ask the private stockholders for authority to open negotiations for the sale of their interest in the canal to the provincial government. The necessary permission having been given at a general meeting held on November 2, a memorial was presented to the lieutenant governor praying that the province would buy out the private shareholders.[129] As if to emphasize the request there appeared on November 29 the report of a select committee on the Welland Canal which recommended "making the Welland Canal strictly a public work" and suggested as suitable terms for purchase the issue of provincial debentures to the private stockholders on a dollar-for-dollar basis, with further debentures to be issued for back interest when the revenue from tolls should reach a figure of £50,000 per annum.

But the end was not yet. The legislators of Upper Canada were not so eager to purchase the canal that they could not afford to procrastinate, and there were some who, like John Macaulay, still toyed with the idea of dual control, believing that "it would be well if the New York capitalists still retained their interest in the Canal." [130] On March 4, 1837, there was passed an act which, although it finally effected the long overdue reorganization of the Company's finances, made no mention of government purchase. The capitalization of the Company was increased to £597,300, of which the government of Upper Canada was to hold £454,500 — £209,500 to represent a consolidation of previous loans and subscriptions, and a new subscription of £245,000 for the permanent reconstruction of the canal with stone locks. The remaining lands held by the Hydraulic Company were to be repurchased, and the board was prohibited from expending any of the new subscription until it could show a valid conveyance of the property. The number of directors on the board was reduced to five, so that the three government-appointed directors held a majority. This act therefore marked the end of private control.

It is clear that this statute was intended as a substitute for outright purchase. On the one hand it deprived the private stockholders of effective control over their investment; on the other, it protected their financial interest by laying down (though not unambiguously) the priority in which future revenues were to be distributed. The act provided that

> . . . the tolls received upon the canal, after deducting the amount required for the charges now made thereon by law or so much thereof as shall be necessary, shall be first annually applied to discharge the interest which will accrue upon the said sum of £245,000 to be advanced for the purposes aforesaid, and the remainder of the income received by the said Company shall be divided among the private stockholders until it shall equal six per cent on the amount of their investment.

Only after these charges had been deducted was a dividend to be paid on the stock held by the government.

If the full amount thus voted by the legislature had been raised and expended on the reconstruction of the canal, this compromise between governmental and private control might have proved workable. On grounds of principle the stockholders could complain, as in fact they subsequently did, that they were deprived of the control over their property without their consent, but it can hardly be said that the arrangement was inequitable to them. Indeed, the private stockholders themselves later claimed that, had the statute been permitted to continue in effect, the amount actually derived as revenue from the canal between 1839 and 1842 would have been sufficient to pay 6 per cent on the government subscription of £245,000 and 6 per cent on the private stock, and still leave an annual surplus of £7816.[131] But as a matter of fact, the act was inoperative almost from the start. Just as the stock market crash of 1825 had frustrated the first attempt by the Company to sell its stock in England, so the panic of 1837 broke before this last and largest provincial subscription could be raised. Only £68,144 of the promised £245,000 was actually realized. After April 1837 the province could not sell its bonds,[132] and the Canadian rebellions of the same year completed the debacle.

In this atmosphere of bankruptcy and rebellion, the three government-appointed directors drew up a report to the lieutenant governor in which they demonstrated to their own satisfaction that the canal could be kept open for navigation only by incurring an annual net loss of about £14,000.[133] Taking a very pessimistic view of possible future increases in traffic, they raised the question — and left no doubt which way their own judgment was inclined — whether it might be wiser to "let the Canal go to decay," using it is a reservoir for water power only, rather than aggravate the province's already serious financial difficulties by continuing to pour money into the work. Such a report, backed as it was by the authority of a majority of the board of directors, represented a direct threat to the interests of the private stockholders. The act of 1837 had excited no protest when it was accompanied by the promise of reconstruction and a guarantee of participation in revenues; it took on a very different aspect with threats of abandonment in the air. If the canal was to be abandoned, what hope could the private stockholders entertain of ever receiving any return on their investment? Clearly, under the act of 1837, none. Their only hope lay in the passing of an act which would enable them to withdraw their capital entirely, by exchanging their shares for the rather less dubious security of provincial debentures. Accordingly in March 1839 the New York stockholders memorialized the provincial legislature as follows:

> . . . in 1837, they learned with dismay, that without their knowledge or assent, the management of their property was taken from them by the

Legislature and vested under the control of the Government, a measure
which, without remuneration, they believe to be unprecedented in any
country. That if the true spirit and meaning of the Act had been adhered to, it would have insured the Government interest on their loan,
and the Shareholders a dividend, inasmuch as the expenditure would
have been gradual from year to year, and the income, as on all other
Canals, would have increased in progressive proportion. They conclude
in praying that, as the control of their property has been wrested from
them, they may be repaid for their outlay in constructing a public work
which, for usefulness and profit, under proper management, is not
equalled in America.[134]

This energetic protest proved effective. Two months later a bill passed
the legislature providing for the purchase of the private stock in the canal
by the provincial government. Debentures were to be issued, payable in
twenty years, in exchange for the private stock, the exchange being at the
option of the shareholder. These debentures were to bear interest at 2 per
cent for the first two years, 3 per cent for the third year, and so on up to a
maximum of 6 per cent. This plan, which seems to have been originally
suggested by John Beverley Robinson, the chief justice, was designed to
minimize the immediate burden on the provincial finances. Further, as
soon as the tolls on the canal reached a figure of £30,000 per annum, each
former stockholder was to receive debentures for the back interest due to
him since his stock was first subscribed.

The issue of provincial debentures, however, was not the easy matter
it had once been. The state of the provincial credit was now a matter of
keen concern to the British government, and the lieutenant governor, Sir
George Arthur, although he admitted that the Welland was "absolutely
indispensable" to the safety of the western part of the province, yet did
not think it proper to add to the public debt for the purpose of compen-
sating the private stockholders until the funds required to complete the
canal had been raised.[135] He therefore reserved the bill for the Queen's
approval.

A committee of the Assembly to which was referred the petition of the
private stockholders and the message of the lieutenant governor stating
that he had reserved the bill recommended that the matter should be decided one way or the other: either the private stockholders should be
bought out, or the government should divest itself of majority control on
the board of directors. They advised that an address be submitted to the
Queen, praying that the bill should receive the royal assent.[136] In accordance with this recommendation, a motion to address the Crown was carried
in the legislature on January 25, 1840. When, in accordance with the constitutional reforms of 1840–41, the first parliament of the now united provinces met in Kingston on June 14, 1841, the Welland Canal compensation
bill was one of the first measures introduced. It became law on July 5,

when Lord Sydenham announced that the royal assent had been granted on September 11 of the previous year.

But not even then were the difficulties over. This act also proved to be inoperative. Not only were certain of its provisions objectionable to the private stockholders, but also, and more important, the debentures issued proved to be unsalable at anything like their nominal value. Merritt went to England in 1841 in an attempt to market the issue, found that the bonds sold at a heavy discount, and returned bearing recommendations from the Treasury and Lord Stanley that the act be amended. In consequence, the act of 1843 (7 Vic. cap. 34) was passed. This measure provided for the issue of debentures payable in twenty years, bearing interest at 5 per cent if payable in England and 6 per cent if payable in Canada, with debentures for back interest to be issued when the canal tolls reached an annual figure of £45,000. This compromise proved acceptable to all parties, and the Welland Canal Company passed finally out of existence.

CHAPTER FIVE

ENTREPRENEURSHIP

ENTREPRENEURSHIP IS A WORD WITH MANY MEANINGS, AND CAN be defined in different ways depending on the matters in which we are interested and the problems we wish to examine. In this chapter we shall follow one simple and widely-accepted definition, according to which entrepreneurship refers to the functions performed by those who are responsible for the inauguration, maintenance, and direction of a profit-oriented enterprise. Entrepreneurship in this sense has two aspects: internal and external. Internally, it refers to the way in which the various people involved in the enterprise allocate among themselves the tasks which have to be performed if the enterprise is to survive. Externally, it refers to the way in which the relations between the enterprise and various "outside" groups, such as banks, competitors, customers, and governments, whose activities are important to the fortunes of the enterprise, are organized. For our present purposes the usefulness of the concept lies in the fact that it focuses our attention sharply on the activities of the handful of men, partly co-operating and partly competing with each other, who made up the entrepreneurial group. The most conspicuous figure in this group, although he by no means dominated it, was William Hamilton Merritt.

Merritt's official position in the Company was that of agent. The nearest modern equivalent would probably be general manager. His functions in this capacity were formally laid down at a board meeting on September 7, 1825:

> Mr. Merritt, residing at St. Catharines, shall have the general superintendence of the Engineers, Surveyors, Contractors, and all other persons in any way employed by the Company, and . . . he shall keep a private account with all the Contractors of the monthly performance of their work according to the Engineer's estimate, which he shall certify and transmit to the President, in order that the same may be laid before the Board; upon which he shall receive a draft for the amount to be paid to the parties on taking their receipt for the same.[1]

In his private memorandum book he described the functions he was expected to perform as follows:

> I have to attend to the whole line, keep a detail of the proceedings on each job, a copy of all accounts, decide on all plans and specifications

of Engineers, encourage and alternately censure each Contractor, urge them on as well as the Engineer, particularly that part which requires more labor, look out for contractors, find out what different jobs cost, to compare the value of excavation, and have my whole mind and attention placed on the work. To answer and attend to various applications, settle disputes, spend as much time in talking as working; paying money to various Contractors on the line.[2]

In terms of formal organization, then, Merritt was responsible to the directors for carrying out their decisions and paying to the employees of the Company the sums to which they were entitled. In informal terms, however, as preceding chapters will have made clear, his functions were considerably more diffuse. His job in the Welland Canal Company was more than a definite office with a certain prescribed range of functions and authority; it was, in his own eyes at least, a generalized warrant to act in whatever manner seemed to him best calculated to serve the interests of the organization. What it included and what it excluded were matters which Merritt decided largely for himself. There was, in fact, little that went on in the Company which Merritt regarded as outside his sphere of responsibility or beyond his competence to perform. When the most urgent problems were those of construction, it was Merritt who set up his bed in the corner of the Welland Canal office and inspected the line every day, listening to the complaints and excuses of the contractors, consulting with the engineers, and noting down in the "red Yankee pocket-book" at which political journalists were later to poke fun, the progress of the work and the estimates of money required.[3] When capital supply became the most urgent issue, it was Merritt who went to London and talked the Treasury into lending the Company £50,000. When the canal was open and ready for traffic, it was Merritt who communicated with the Cleveland and Oswego forwarders and arranged that special facilities should be provided for cargoes between the two ports. And when the scene of the Company's struggle for survival shifted to the floor of the Assembly, it was Merritt who, first as a witness and later as a member, justified the Company's insatiable demands for money and in 1835 conducted a spirited and almost singlehanded defence against Mackenzie and his accusations.[4]

This is a situation which requires explanation. How did the other directors come to permit Merritt this free-ranging and ill-defined authority? Why was he not prevented from arrogating to himself functions and duties so highly disparate in their nature? Was this arrangement useful to the Company, or did it contribute to its difficulties?

We may begin by pointing out that, although Merritt was by no means a large stockholder, he was more deeply involved in the success of the Company, in an emotional sense, than any of the other directors or stockholders. The costs to him of failure, in terms of reputation and social status, would have been immeasurably greater than to John H. Dunn or J. B. Yates, for example. He was, in consequence, strongly motivated to exert himself on the Company's behalf in whatever way he felt to be necessary. He felt himself to be responsible, not for the performance of certain specific functions, but for the Company as a whole. He thought of it as his project; he identified himself with the Company and his integrity with its good name. Consequently he welcomed, if indeed he did not seek, additional responsibilities. With these responsibilities, assumed rather than imposed, there appears to have come an almost unquestioned ascription of authority. Not only did Merritt himself feel responsible for the Company as a whole; he was, to some extent, recognized as being so responsible, and held accountable for its actions.

In addition, it should be emphasized that the Canal Company was from the beginning starved of trained and experienced personnel at every level in the organization above that of the engineers. Many of Merritt's duties came to him by default. The directors, apart from Merritt and Keefer, were government officeholders, not businessmen. They could at most attend a board meeting for a few hours once a month, but they had neither the time nor the ability nor probably the inclination to take any of the load of day-to-day management off Merritt's shoulders. Nor could he delegate much of his work to subordinates, even had he wished to do so. The Company could not afford more than the minimum in the way of office staff; there was a bookkeeper and a secretary, and that was all.

So far as we can tell, Merritt never complained of being overworked, nor was he ever inclined to take a strict view of what came within his jurisdiction and what did not, except in one particular respect which we shall note later. The question may well be asked, indeed, whether he was not too ready to assume the responsibility for functions which might well have been delegated or performed by others. One gets the impression that he liked to feel himself at the center of things, that he wrung positive satisfaction out of the belief that his actions and his decisions were the ones that counted. Certainly his appetite for responsibility was not quickly satiated. Was he abashed or flattered, one wonders, when in 1827 the president of the Company begged almost apologetically that he should let his colleagues know how the work was progressing? ". . . it cannot be asking too much. If it was to the extent of *good*, or *bad*, or indifferent it would be satisfactory to us." [5]

Combined with this tendency to accumulate responsibilities, one finds in Merritt a related characteristic, the relevance of which is so obvious that it almost escapes attention. Merritt was an immensely hard worker. The impression he gave is well illustrated by some of his wife's complaints. Returning from York early in March 1828, Merritt broke a rib when his coach overturned. He rested in St. Catharines for a few days only, and then set out for England, causing Mrs. Merritt to write in exasperation to her mother:

> . . . he was not well when he left home but you know how it is, if business calls if he is able to crawl he will go. . . . I told him after he got hurt he'd wear himself out, that he was nothing but flesh and blood as well as others and couldn't stand everything. I get so vexed sometimes, here's a Mr. Robertson [J. B. Robinson?] just back from England — but has done nothing, and there [sic] President and their Directors and Engineers, they don't any of them do any thing without H[amilton] is at their heels.[6]

Mrs. Merritt's opinion on this matter is probably not to be taken as entirely impartial, and certainly mere expenditure of energy is no index of efficiency. But there is no reason to doubt that, at least in the early years, it was the fruits of Merritt's almost compulsive activity which, more than any other single factor, kept the Company alive.

A man of this type — energetic, aggressive, and persistent — is likely to make a highly effective promoter, but to be less competent when it comes to the routine business of running an established organization. The very characteristics which are valuable in the one role may well prove inconvenient and a source of conflict in the other. There is, indeed, a certain amount of evidence to suggest that Merritt's tendency to monopolize authority and his overriding sense of urgency were not uniformly and without exception assets to the Company in its later years. For example, it is possible that some of the Company's construction difficulties arose partly because Merritt would not leave the engineers alone. Geddes, Barrett, and Roberts were, after all, reliable and experienced men — more experienced indeed, in canal matters, than Merritt himself. They did not need and may well have resented Merritt's perpetual supervision and his constant reminders that time cost money. Again, there is little mystery about the numerous corrections and erasures in the books of the Company which excited Mackenzie's suspicions and disturbed a trained accountant like Francis Hincks. They arose because the Company's books did not agree with the "private account" which Merritt kept by order of the board.[7] If there were discrepancies, it was the Company's bookkeeper who altered his figures, not Merritt. And lastly, in rejecting the British government's offer of a grant of one-ninth the cost and in mortgaging the Company's property and earnings in return for the £50,000 loan, Merritt was seizing a short-term benefit without giving sufficient weight to the long-term commitments involved. On more than one occasion, in fact, Merritt acted in a manner which suggests impulsiveness and the absence of proper checks on his judgment.

The people who stood to lose most, in a financial sense, from any errors of judgment which Merritt and his colleagues might make were, of course, the stockholders. We must realize clearly that there were no large stockholders among the directors. None of them except Merritt owned more than the minimum number of shares (twenty) necessary to qualify him for a seat on the board. Merritt himself owned only thirty-eight. Further, the total number of shares owned by private individuals in Upper Canada amounted to no more than 1½ per cent of the capital stock. In December 1836 the distribution of stock holdings was as follows: [8]

	Number	Percentage
Government of Upper Canada	8,600	43.0
Government of Lower Canada	2,000	10.0
Individuals in Upper Canada	297	1.5
Individuals in Lower Canada	1,106	5.5
Individuals in New Brunswick	40	.2
Individuals in New York	5,570	27.8
Individuals in England	2,411	12.0
	20,024	100.0

This table makes clear the importance of the provisions of the charter of 1825 which restricted membership of the board to residents of Upper Canada who owned twenty shares or more. In effect these provisions disfranchised stockholders who lived outside the province. If the charter was interpreted literally, there were only eight candidates for whom they could vote to fill seven seats on the board. Clearly the relationship between ownership and control in the Welland Canal Company was a very peculiar one.

So far as influence on the policy of the Company is concerned, there are only two groups of stockholders, apart from the directors themselves, with whom we need to concern ourselves. These are the government of Upper Canada and the New York State group under the leadership of John B. Yates. Yates himself owned the largest single block of stock held by a private individual, owning in his own name and that of his firm no less than 1500 shares at the time of his death in 1836. In addition he could when necessary command the proxy votes of the entire New York group. Voting, as we have seen, was little more than a formality; nevertheless, Yates had certain ways of making his influence felt and these we shall consider shortly. The government of Upper Canada, for its part, had the appointment of two and later three directors by virtue of its stock holdings; it could also affect the policy of the Company in other ways, however, such as by the granting or refusing of financial aid, by the appointment of commissioners (as in 1832) to disburse the funds allotted, by the investigations of select committees, by the views expressed in debate, and by the exercise of the considerable discretionary powers enjoyed by its executive officers. Since the directors of the Company, or at least those representing the private stockholders, were closely identified with what we may call the Government House clique, the Company could until the period after 1836 count with some assurance upon a friendly attitude in the Legislative and Executive Councils and on the part of the successive lieutenant governors. The Assembly was a different matter; here a more critical atmosphere was usual, particularly on the part of the Reform members.

For Merritt the overriding concern, to which all other considerations were secondary, was to get the canal built and open for traffic as quickly as possible. His primary interest was in the state and progress of the physical property. This attitude — very understandable in a man whose initial involvement in the project was due to concern over property values — contrasted in some respects with that of John B. Yates. For Yates the canal was first and foremost an investment. The progress of the work was for him not so much an end in itself, but rather a means whereby his property rights in the canal might attain a market value. He pressed continually for measures which would "give a value to the stock."

The explanation for this contrast in attitudes is to be sought, not so much in any difference in character or intellect, but rather in the very different economic circumstances in which the two men found themselves. Yates' principal business was not the canal but lotteries. For Merritt, whose financial stake in the Company was small, it was of little importance whether or not the shares fell below par, except in so far as it might threaten the survival of the Company and the completion of the work. For Yates, on the other hand, it meant the difference between bankruptcy and solvency. He had ventured into a project which carried all the surface indications of a profitable speculation and he had been badly caught. His initial investment in the Company had been made with borrowed money, and the shares purchased had been pledged as collateral for further loans. Ready and certain access to credit was essential for the successful operation of his lotteries. Anything which affected the value of Welland Canal shares, therefore, affected the solvency of his whole financial position, not to mention his prestige and reputation among the businessmen of New York and Albany.

But this is hardly a completely adequate account of what the canal meant to John B. Yates. His interest was more than financial. Hopes of monetary gain may have been responsible for his initial involvement in the project, but before his death in 1836 this sentiment had become overlaid with a faith in the value and prospects of the canal which was no less positive than that of Merritt himself. Certainly if what was required was someone to restrain Merritt from his optimistic excesses and cast the cold water of financial prudence on his inflammable imagination, Yates was not that man. Concerned with the value of his shares he may have been; but it is not recorded that on any occasion he advocated retrenchment or suggested that the Company should cut its coat to fit its cloth. It was primarily on his insistence that the dimensions of the canal were altered from four to eight feet depth. The decision may have been sound; but it does not appear that the difficulties which it would occasion, both technical and financial, were adequately considered at the time. He made no effort to dissuade the directors from undertaking the Lake Erie extension in 1831; indeed, he actively supported them. Yet this new work could well have been postponed until the Company's finances were on a sounder footing. Nor did the hazards of his lottery business deter him from forming the Hydraulic Company, a serious and quite unnecessary addition to his net liabilities.

In their chronic speculative optimism and their tendency to overreach themselves Merritt and Yates were two of a kind, and in general they worked together with considerable harmony. After all, there was no dispute between them as to the primary objective of their efforts: the completion of the canal. The sooner the canal began to produce revenue, the sooner would Merritt's ambitions be satisfied and the sooner would Yates' holdings of stock become marketable. It was in regard to the proper means of achieving this goal that the difference in their attitudes which we have mentioned showed itself, and in particular in regard to financial policy. Merritt regarded with equanimity, and indeed welcomed, each successive government grant and subscription. He saw no threat either to his own interests or to those of the Company in dependence on the legislature as a source of capital. The prospect of eventual government purchase he found by no means unattractive. After all, what did "the government" mean to him, if not the Executive Council, composed largely of his friends and fellow directors, the Legislative Council, dominated by the same group, and the Assembly, which might indeed prove bothersome on occasion but which could generally be counted on to grant what was requested? "The government" to Merritt was not an institution existing over and against the Company, but rather an instrument which the Company might use for its own purposes. Just as in his speeches and public papers he portrayed himself and his colleagues as acting *for* the province, so he expected the political leaders of the province to act *for* the Company. And until Mackenzie demonstrated that "the government" could be used as an instrument to destroy the Company as effectively as it formerly had given support, his expectations were not disappointed.

John B. Yates seems to have found this attitude hard to understand and harder still to accept. As a major stockholder, he was by no means content to let the government have the canal, even with repayment of principal and interest, unless complete and final bankruptcy were the only alternative. It was in the expectation of profits — large profits — that he had bought the stock, and that these profits, given time, would be realized he never doubted. To be sure, in the early years he had been as anxious as Merritt that the government should take an interest in the canal and demonstrate that interest by financial aid. But the successive encroachments of the legislature upon the Company's freedom of action he resented and feared. Earlier than any of the directors he recognized the danger implicit in Mackenzie's appointment to the board, suspecting (correctly, as it turned out) the imminence of the kind of organized political attack which he had learned to dread and respect in the lottery business. "The government" for him was not *his* government; with the officeholders and Councillors whom Merritt admired and attempted to emulate he coöperated because there was no alternative. But he had little confidence in their ability and less in their willingness to put the interests of the stockholders first and their own careers and reputations second.

Deprived during the Company's formative years of the power to influence directly by his votes the composition of the board of directors, Yates perforce had to devise other ways of safeguarding his interests. In the beginning he seems to have relied chiefly on his personal influence over Merritt, for whom he had a certain respect and with whom he was at some pains to remain friends. Regular correspondence, supplemented by frequent visits to Upper Canada, enabled Yates to exercise through Merritt a general supervision over policy, highly personal in its nature and dependent for its effectiveness more on Yates' greater business experience and wider financial contacts than on any formal authority. After 1830 Merritt showed signs of resenting these leading reins and of wishing to follow an independent line. It is significant that he declined to participate in the Hydraulic Company, though invited to do so. Yates thereupon strengthened his position by transferring or perhaps selling shares to Creighton and Macdonell, who thenceforth acted more or less as his deputies and who, being resident in the province, could serve as directors. Thus, either through Merritt or through Macdonell and Creighton, Yates was never without access to and influence over the decisions of the board. But this influence was always indirect and limited. In particular, Yates was largely powerless in the political field, where he felt himself to be and was regarded as an "outsider."

Yates had one other means of making his wishes effective, but he had to be sparing in its use. If provocation seemed sufficiently severe, he could retaliate against the board by threatening to deny them his services as a source of credit. To understand this it is necessary to bear in mind that relations between the Company and the Bank of Upper Canada, which was the only major source of credit available in the province, were never harmonious and on occasion could degenerate into something approaching open hostility. Credit could be obtained in limited amounts on the directors' signatures, or on the security of government debentures, but never on the basis of the Company's property or shares. Believing their proper business to be the issuing of notes by the discounting of commercial bills and accommodation paper, the bank's directors declined to extend credit to a canal company on the basis of real estate or unmarketable stock. The consequence was that the Welland Canal Company was chronically starved of short- and medium-term credit. Loans on personal security helped to tide the Company over more than one emergency, but involved a degree of risk unwelcome to most of the directors. Confronted with this highly conservative lending policy, the directors perforce had to adopt whatever makeshift expedients were open to them. On two occasions the Company issued its own "post notes" — interest-bearing securities which circulated as currency in the Niagara district. More frequently, however, credit was obtained by drafts at three or six months' date drawn on the firm of Yates & McIntyre or on Yates personally. Although Yates frequently found these drafts a source of acute financial embarrassment, he never failed to honor them.

Reliance upon Yates as a source of credit necessarily entailed the cession to Yates of a certain degree of authority. A threat by Yates to refuse drafts was a threat which had at least to be listened to. When, for example, Yates stated in January 1830 that he could "do no more," that he would honor no more drafts on his credit, but that the Company could borrow what it pleased if the government would only guarantee interest on the debt, we may be sure that Merritt and his friends in Upper Canada, even though they made no effort to do as Yates recommended, did not dismiss the matter offhand. But it is doubtful whether they took his threats as seriously as he intended them to. They knew quite well that Yates was rather in the situation of the man who has the bear by the tail and cannot let go. Too much of his fortune was tied up in Welland Canal stock to permit him to cut his losses and let the Company fend for itself. If the Company had ever become completely insolvent, all of Yates' friends in the Albany banks could not have saved him from bankruptcy, and his lottery business, founded as it was on a reputation for honest dealing and prompt payment, would have shared in the general ruin.

Although Merritt often spoke as if profits and revenue were important to him, his behavior suggests that they were, in his eyes, more symbols of achievement — evidences of the fundamental correctness of his so-called visionary designs — than ends in themselves. Although he liked to present himself as the guardian of the rights of the private stockholders, particularly in the negotiations with the government over provincial purchase, their interests and his aspirations did not always coincide. He was easily able to convince himself that what seemed to him the right thing to do would in the end redound to their benefit, and, as we have seen, there was really no way by which the private stockholders could bring him to heel. Far more real and important for Merritt were the opinions and beliefs which he encountered nearer home, in the newspapers, in legislative debates, and in the conversations and letters of his friends in Upper Canada. Here it was not the value of the stock so much as the canal itself as a physical entity and a political symbol which counted — the progress of construction, the number of ships which had passed through, whether the canal was just another piece of political jobbery or (as its protagonists claimed) truly a work of great national benefit. This was the scale of values which faced Merritt continuously and urgently, and which, in addition, was capable of being realized in terms of friendly or hostile action. Every petition for funds which the directors presented to the legislature was a standing invitation for criticism, praise, or blame. It was in the legislature that the fate of the Company was decided, and not decided once and for all but decided anew every year, for every year the Company needed capital and every year the legislators of Upper Canada had to make up their minds whether to cast the Company adrift or to continue subsidizing it out of the public purse. These were the sanctions which impressed themselves on Merritt as critical, and to their imperatives, expressed and implied, he struggled conscientiously to conform.

Particularly important for Merritt were the values and expectations of Upper Canada's social elite — that small group of lawyers, politicians, and officeholders which historians call the Family Compact. These were the people whom Merritt could not afford to alienate. Not only did they hold the balance of political power, which was in itself enough to make their coöperation and good will essential; they were also the people whom Merritt, as the son of a Loyalist, had been taught from childhood to regard as the leaders of society — men who should be respected, admired, emulated, and, if necessary, obeyed. To seek their friendship and approval was expedient, certainly; but it was also, for a man in Merritt's position, right and proper and natural. His Loyalist background, his army service, and his whole family tradition inclined him to accept without fundamental criticism their claims to social preëminence and their competence to define what should be for him correct and seemly conduct and what should not.

From the beginning he took pains to secure the participation of the leading members of the Compact and to phrase his conduct in conformity with their system of values. Writing in reminiscent mood in 1850, this is what Chief Justice John Beverley Robinson remembered most vividly.[9] Robinson had first heard of Merritt's scheme on his return from England in 1824. The general opinion then was, Robinson recalls, that Merritt was a "wild, visionary projector whose judgment it would be unwise to trust to"; many people regarded him as a person "wholly governed by views of private interest." But, says Robinson,

> . . . a very little communication with you convinced *me* that your motives were pure and disinterested and highly patriotic. . . What confirmed my confidence was the observing that you had the good judgment and right feeling to desire from the first that all money-transactions and accounts connected with the work should be in the hands of gentlemen with whom you had no connection and whose integrity was free from all question, and in the next place that it seemed your earnest wish to have the direction of the Company committed to gentlemen whom you could not hope to bend to any thing unworthy. . .

Robinson's adjectives are worthy of note: Merritt's motives had to be pure, disinterested, and patriotic. His views on the question of the profits to be derived from the canal are also of interest and must have been anathema to Yates. Writing in 1833, Robinson stated:

> As to the work yielding a revenue — that, however desirable for the publick, and most important to the few private stockholders whose stake is large, is in reality quite a secondary consideration. The grand object was to overcome a great natural impediment to the prosperity of the better half of our country. . . As to its being a work that will pay, I never laid stress on that branch of the question.[10]

Robinson's attitude toward the Canal Company in this respect may safely be taken as typical of that of the Compact. In such a climate of opinion it is readily understandable how Merritt, who in 1824 had stated bluntly: "my whole personal interest . . . is the value it will attach to my property," could say ten years later and apparently without conscious insincerity, "Canals ought never to be made, in any country, as objects of gain." [11] The prejudices and beliefs of the Compact were not to be infringed with impunity, while the terms of high moral principle in which they were typically expressed had, for a man like Merritt, a certain insidious attraction.

There is irony in the fact that it was this alliance with the Family Compact which in the end nearly ruined the Company. In seeking the support of the Tory bureaucracy in 1824 Merritt was doing the obvious and rational thing. The canal could never have been built if the Company had lacked sympathizers within the Tory party and advocates who had the ear of the lieutenant governor. Yet it was precisely this close identification of the Company's management with the personnel of the Family Compact which precipitated Mackenzie's attacks, the blocking of financial aid in 1836, and the appointment of a committee of inquiry determined to hold the Company guilty of every conceivable form of corruption and extravagance unless it could be proved otherwise. The political development of Upper Canada did not stand still between 1824 and 1836. The alliance which had been indispensable in the earlier year was almost fatal in the later.

The attitude of the Reformers to the Welland Canal Company was ambivalent. Drawing as they did much of their strength from the back-country settlers, they were at first inclined to look with favor on a project which promised to lower transportation costs, reduce the price of imports, and raise the amount which the farmer received for his produce. Thus the editor of the *British Colonial Argus*, who in one breath could say, "The full development of our internal resources . . . need hardly be looked for so long as we remain a dependent colony of manufacturing England," could assert in the next that the legislative grants to the Welland and St. Lawrence canals were "two green spots in the midst of desolation." [12] Mackenzie, too, was in the beginning quite prepared to write editorials in praise of the Welland Canal. Doubts grew in direct proportion to the amount of financial aid granted. The appointment of government directors to the board, at first without statutory provision but at the invitation of the Company, failed to palliate the growing suspicions of the Reformers. Hostility to "monopolies," echoing the sentiments of Jacksonian democracy, was accentuated by resentment of the Compact and fears that increased taxes might be imposed to meet the costs of government aid. Where was the money to come from? How was the interest on the ever-growing provincial debt to be paid? Not by import duties, surely, for the merchants would never permit it, and the French in Lower Canada were not likely to tax themselves in order to pay for extravagance in the upper province. By taxes on land, then? It seemed inevitable. The humble settlers of Upper Canada were to pay, while the aristocrats of the Compact lined their pockets by speculation and embezzlement.[13]

In addition, many of the Reformers were sceptical about the wisdom of concentrating such a large portion of the provincial finances upon this one project. Should not the benefits of government aid be scattered more widely? Thus in the debate on the Welland Canal loan in 1834 a Mr. Werden remarked that

> . . . it was a very popular thing . . . to see this mighty work progressing; but in the meantime, all the improvements in the interior of our country [were] to be neglected; there would be no pittance to be applied to our roads; our means would all be swallowed up in this immense canal.[14]

A fellow-Reformer, a Mr. Morris, thought it fallacious to argue that the Welland would benefit Upper Canada as much as the Erie had benefited New York,

> . . . inasmuch as the latter work was carried through the interior of that country, and promoted the prosperity and wealth of every section which it passed through; whereas the Welland Canal only connects two great Lakes, the navigation of which is already as good as it can be made.[15]

Further, even supposing the expectations of the supporters of the canal were amply fulfilled, would it be wise to leave it in the hands of a private company? Thus Dr. Duncombe, a leading Reformer, asked rhetorically:

> . . . shall this key stone in the arch of all our prosperity and greatness, as a commercial nation, be left in the hands of a private company, with privileges secured to them by acts of parliament, which their interest may induce them to use in a way that may prejudice the best interests of the Province? . . . Would this be prudent or wise legislation, to allow a company to control one of our principal sources of advancement, to use at their convenience the large funds of the public money which they have in their hands at present, and the additional sums that must be granted to save what has already been expended in the work? I think it would not.[16]

In so far as one can generalize in the matter — and generalization is dangerous, for the Reformers were a very heterogeneous group — it is safe to say that their hostility was directed not so much against the canal as a commercial project, but rather against the canal as a symbol of Tory exclusiveness and in particular against the alleged incompetence of its management. And it is very difficult to estimate what proportion of the accusations of inefficiency, extravagance, and general malpractice which they hurled at Merritt and his associates really took their origin in hostility to the Company and what proportion represented merely charges cooked up for political purposes to embarrass the government. Imputations of fraud and dishonesty are difficult to prove or disprove at this late date; suffice it to say that the committee of inquiry which investigated Mackenzie's charges in 1835 found no indications of criminal negligence or serious malappropriation of funds, and that examination of the evidence surviving at the present day does not suggest that the verdict was incorrect.[17] In any event, until Mackenzie unmasked his guns, the attitude of the Reformers could largely be ignored. They could talk and make a nuisance of themselves, but unless and until they could command a majority in the Assembly they could not make their views effective. The leaders of the Tory party, on the other hand, through their dominance of the Legislative and Executive Councils, could exercise a veto power at any time. They controlled the legislative grants which from 1826 onward literally kept the Company in existence, as well as a host of minor favors which were less obviously vital to the Company but which nevertheless made all the difference between active support and mere toleration. By comparison, the sanctions exercised by the Reformers must have seemed trifling and ineffective. Small wonder that Merritt conformed with such precision to the role marked out for him by the Compact.

While this is so, Merritt was well aware that his every action was watched by a cloud of hostile witnesses, eager to exploit for their own purposes every slip from grace. And his desire to satisfy both parties — to live up to what was expected of him by the Compact while at the same time giving to the Reformers no just excuse for attack — showed itself in a number of ways. Consider, for example, the matter of land speculation. Merritt, who knew in advance the route which the main canal and its branches would take, had ample opportunity to pick up at bargain prices parcels of land which later would rise appreciably in value. Yet it is not until 1832, when the canal was already completed, that we find him purchasing any land at all. In 1831 Yates offered him a sixth share in the hydraulic purchase, but this Merritt refused, stating in a letter to the board:

> I have refrained from purchasing any situation on the line of the Canal from its commencement, to avoid any ground for suspicion of having specu-

lated for private advantage, instead of selecting them for the benefit of the Welland Canal Company.[18]

Nevertheless, in the following year he did purchase several mill sites at Dunnville and others at Port Colborne in 1834. Justifying these purchases in the face of criticism, he pointed out that in no case had he bought or leased land directly from the Company, but always from private individuals who were presumably as well aware of the value of real estate as he was. And when this argument did not silence the critics, he offered in 1835 to relinquish all the land he had previously purchased, provided only that he was repaid the amount of his original outlay with interest.[19] His conduct in this respect, indeed, appears to have been prudently circumspect. David Thorburn, a Reformer and government director who had no reason to be biased in Merritt's favor, testified when questioned about the Dunnville purchase:

> Mr. Merritt along with Mr. Street [a local capitalist] is owner of the lands in which Dunnville is situated. The Directors conceived they ought to have more room at Dunnville. Mr. Merritt wanted the Company to have it without charge, but Mr. Street thought they ought to pay the full value of it as town lots. At the end of the bridge over the Grand River dam, where there is an immense quantity of water power, Mr. Merritt wanted the arbitrators on damages to consider the damages by the company of those lands favorably towards them (the Company). Mr. Street and Mr. Merritt's view of this was that they would get a profit from it, as a village would rise there, being at the end of a toll bridge and possessed of great water privileges.[20]

There is, in fact, no evidence to suggest that Merritt ever abused his position in the Company by speculation in land. The construction of the large "steamboat" locks between his property at St. Catharines and Lake Ontario (and nowhere else on the canal) is another matter; here perhaps Merritt permitted his private interests to take priority.

A similar attempt to steer a prudent middle course between the lofty but conveniently imprecise moral precepts of the Compact and the inflammable suspicions of the Reformers characterized Merritt's relationship to the handling of the Company's financial affairs. And here a difficulty of interpretation arises. We have already noticed that Merritt tended to regard himself as responsible for the Company as a whole and to take upon himself functions which were not necessarily implied by his formal position. When it came to the Company's money affairs, however, Merritt's attitude was very different. He steadfastly asserted that they were outside his jurisdiction and that he had no responsibility whatsoever for them. For example, in an attempt to refute Mackenzie's charge that "Mr. Merritt is sometimes paymaster, treasurer, and secretary all in one," he stated:

> The system always pursued since the commencement of the undertaking is as follows: the Engineer makes out the return monthly, or the Overseer

latterly, not having had occasion for an Engineer when keeping the canal in repair. These calculations are examined by the Secretary, then presented to the Board of Directors, who approve of [them] and order them paid. The Engineers or Overseers are the only persons responsible for the quantity or correctness of these returns; the Secretary, for the calculation. . . Not one pound of the funds of the corporation, since Mr. Black was first appointed Secretary, has ever come through my hands.[21]

And this description of the state of affairs was confirmed by John Beverley Robinson who, when Mackenzie's charges were first made public, wrote to Merritt as follows:

I have always rejoiced on your account that you had, from the first, nothing to do with the money, for the disposition to deny you justice has prevailed so strongly with many persons, that you could not have escaped imputations.[22]

What are we to make of these statements — the one admittedly a public assertion of innocence and therefore not the most reliable evidence, but the other a casual remark, a reference to something taken for granted, in a private letter? How are we to reconcile them with the obvious fact that Merritt was very deeply involved indeed in the Company's financial affairs, not only in the raising of money, the selling of shares, and the soliciting of loans, but also in the spending of it? How reconcile them, for example, with the testimony of a certain contractor rejoicing in the delightful name of Love Newlove, who stated in 1835 that Merritt

. . . has paid me a great deal of money at different times. . . He always paid me whenever and wherever I met with him and wanted it. If he had not the money of the Company he paid me with his own.[23]

What Merritt intended to convey by his statement was, of course, that he had no opportunity to defraud the Company, the best defence against charges that he had been guilty of financial peccadilloes being a demonstration that he could not have done so, even if he had wanted to. And in terms of formal organization his statement was correct. In terms of informal organization, however — which is to say, in terms of the patterns of behavior which characterized the Company as an actual functioning organization — they were very wide of the mark. Merritt had ample opportunity to indulge in petty cheating, if he had been so inclined. But there seems in fact to have been very little of this. As Mr. Newlove pointed out, Merritt was more likely to pay the contractors out of his own pocket than defraud them of their due. This was irregular, of course; but analysis of this and other instances on which Mackenzie fastened suggests that it was these irregularities which made it possible for the Company to function. Certainly Alfred Hovey was given unusually favorable terms for his Deep Cut contract; but two other contractors had already failed and no one else would touch the job. Was the work to stop for that reason? Certainly

$10,000 was lent to J. B. Yates while other creditors of the Company remained unpaid. But what was this in comparison with the sums which Yates had lent to the Company, often to his own extreme inconvenience? To Mackenzie's suspicious eyes these discrepancies between formal and informal organization represented so many opportunities for deceit and fraud. To Merritt and his associates they were necessary expedients, justified by the urgency of the task which faced them and by their mutual confidence in each other's personal integrity.

Merritt's attempts to avoid the slur of "private interest" in his real-estate transactions had no ill effects upon the management of the Company. The same can not be said of his refusal to concern himself formally with the Company's internal finances. If Merritt did not accept the responsibility for supervising the Company's receipts and expenditures, who did?

This is not an easy question to answer. It appears that on December 7, 1825, the board appointed a bookkeeper named Wenham and a secretary named Black. These individuals remained with the Company for about two years and established the system (if it may be dignified with that name) on which the accounts and records were kept. Some time after 1827 they were replaced by Beaton as bookkeeper and Clark as secretary. The names are of no importance, except as indicating that identifiable individuals performing these functions did exist; for it must be admitted that, if Mackenzie had not made the state of the Company's accounts the target of nine out of his thirty-odd accusations and thus elicited a certain amount of information on the subject, it would be quite possible to relate the whole history of the Company without mentioning that a bookkeeper or secretary was ever employed. In point of fact, they contributed little to the management of the Company. Their role was merely that of clerks; they were responsible for keeping a record of payments and receipts, but they had no executive authority and performed their tasks in a very unsystematic manner indeed.

Two years after the Company was formed, Dunn was surprised to discover that Black was ignorant of even the fundamentals of his job. He had asked Black to prepare a statement of the Company's transactions with a certain firm of contractors for submission to the board. The crudity of the resulting document can be guessed from Dunn's comments:

> I thought it needless to point out the form of such a statement to Mr. Black because I conceived he was perfectly acquainted with the nature of such an account, which should be a simple Debtor & Creditor, shewing the work done, and the money received of all the transactions between the Company and those Gentlemen from the commencement of the Welland Canal, and it should be such a Document as to shew, and to be kept in the office as a record, for the information of the Company and the public, instead of a parcel of detached and unconnected scraps of paper as was sent. Of all transactions there should be a regular state-

ment, and in future it must be done — it is time we should be on a regular system.[24]

Dunn did the Company's office staff a slight injustice; they did have a "regular system" of a sort, though whether it was any better than no system at all is open to doubt. It was described by the select committee of 1830 as follows:

> The accounts of the Company are kept according to a system laid down by Mr. Wenham . . . by which, instead of being balanced annually or semi-annually, they are left open until the several sections of the canal shall be completed; a mode of book-keeping which, however convenient it may be to the Directors, does not render the task of inspection more easy.[25]

Mackenzie, who knew something about accountancy, was less mild in his criticism. Evidence on the Company's bookkeeping methods is so scanty that his words are worth quoting at length:

> It does not appear that the Company have kept a regular book or cash account, shewing the whole of the receipts from time to time, and the payments as they were made to each person. . . As to the Italian method of book-keeping, so admirable in its results, it has not been followed so as to enable any accountant to balance the books. The estimates of work done, materials furnished, and labor performed, have been entered on the ledger by a single entry direct from an estimate, the copy of an estimate, or an estimate book, and not by a double-entry of debtor and creditor made on the journal from the original transaction. Day Book there is none, and as to concentrating the accounts in the ledger under general heads of receipt and expenditure, it has not been adhered to. A casual inspection of the petty books will shew that they differ materially in their results from the regular books of account.[26]

It is difficult to overestimate the serious consequences of this casual, unsystematic, and wholly inadequate financial housekeeping. It seems to have been literally impossible for anyone, even with the best intentions in the world, to get an accurate picture of the financial operations of the Company as a whole, or to decide with any confidence where money was being economically expended and where it was not. The system of "open accounts" described by the committee of 1830 meant that the directors were quite unable to say how much each particular section of the canal would cost until the work was finally finished, and by then it was too late to do anything about it. Small wonder that the estimates were exceeded. Every time the engineer submitted a statement of work to be done and an estimate of funds required, a good case could be made for authorizing it. Every time the estimate was exceeded, good reasons could be found why the original figure had been too small. After all, the engineers were honorable men. The directors, whenever they made one of their periodic applications to the legislature for financial aid, were rather in the position of the impecunious schoolboy who, having spent his pocket-money, asks for more, without being able to explain what he has done with the amount he had. There was no system by which a careful and detailed control could be exercised over the way in which the Company spent its money. The healthful discipline of methodical bookkeeping was entirely absent.

Now, since this is the case, it is really irrelevant to discuss at length such questions as whether or not Clark was a habitual drunkard, as Mackenzie alleged, or whether any of the Company's funds were misdirected to serve private ends. It is sufficient to point out that the committee which investigated the Company's affairs in 1835 described Clark, drunk or sober, as "quite incompetent for the discharge of [his] duties" and that Francis Hincks, who certainly examined the Company's books with no very sympathetic eye, stated on oath that he really did not think that any fraudulent intent could attach itself to any individual connected with the accounts of the Company. These matters, however interesting, are not of any great significance. What is significant is the fact of the existence of this amazing lacuna in the Company's structure — the fact that neither formally nor informally was there any provision in the Company's organization whereby the expenditure of funds could be systematically supervised and recorded. Rational bookkeeping and accounting, those hallmarks of capitalistic business organization, were nowhere to be found in the Welland Canal Company.

Part of the explanation for this state of affairs is to be found in the fact that, during the vital years when the pattern of organization was being developed, the Company was essentially an institution for the spending of money, not for its receipt. Its task was to invest, not to sell a service for a price. Money costs of construction could, in theory at least, be estimated with a fair degree of accuracy, but the other side of the comparison was missing. The canal produced no revenue at all until 1830, and even when in the following years revenue figures began climbing, they could not be used to set standards of performance for work then in hand. The Company's revenue was the result of expenditures incurred long before; it originated in one indivisible unit of fixed capital — the canal itself. So long as the canal was kept open and in repair, the revenue would be forthcoming.

The fact that costs had to be incurred several years before revenue appeared, combined with highly optimistic expectations of what the revenue would be, goes a long way toward explaining the laxity of the Company's bookkeeping and accounting methods. There was no yardstick against which proposed expenditures could be measured; or rather, the yardstick was that of the engineer, not the accountant. When everything was expenditure and nothing receipt, who could say that one item of expenditure would prove justified in terms of the final earning power of the canal and another would not? To what criteria could the directors appeal? Merely the chronically inflated expectations of future earning power which characterized this and indeed every other canal project of the period. What was the point of penny-pinching economy and frugality when the revenues of the future would amply repay a few pounds more or less spent on construction now? Time costs, not money costs, were the important consideration, and when it came to economizing time Merritt was as miserly as the most demanding critic could desire.

But it must be admitted that this is hardly a complete explanation. We might expect to find careless financial housekeeping in an enterprise where money was plentiful, but the Welland Canal Company was struggling against the inadequacy of its financial resources almost from the day it came into existence. Would it not be reasonable to expect to find the Company's directors obsessed with economy, husbanding every penny, subjecting every proposal for expenditure to careful scrutiny before authorizing it? Instead of which we find just the opposite: a seemingly irresponsible prodigality; a willingness to spend freely even when there was no money to be had; a desire to adopt any expedient, even to the extent of printing the Company's own money, rather than delay the progress of the work. How are we to explain this apparent paradox?

Several lines of explanation seem to make sense. In the first place, quite apart from their inflated expectations and obsession with time rather than money costs, the directors' policy of spending up to the limit and then appealing to the legislature for aid was, up to a point, sound political strategy. To approach the legislature while the Company still had funds available but not used would have been to invite a rebuff. "Spend what you have and then we shall see," would have been the inevitable response. But to appeal for aid with an empty treasury and an impressive array of debts was another matter, for no Upper Canada legislature, at least before 1836, was prepared to allow the Company to expire entirely. Perhaps we should not take too seriously Merritt's frequently-expressed concern over the large volume of long-unpaid land damage claims against the Company. In one sense at least these debts were assets to the Company, for they made its survival and solvency a matter of acute personal concern to a not unimportant sector of the electorate.

In the second place, bad though the accounting methods of the Company certainly were, they were probably not very different from ordinary commercial practice in Upper Canada at the time. Observe, for instance, the similarity between the "open account" system of the Company, whereby debits and credits were not balanced until each section of the canal was completed, and the typical system of the Canadian country storekeeper, who balanced his books — if he had any — only on the occasion of his annual purchasing trip to Montreal, when the results of the past year had to be assessed in order that arrangements for credit might be made for the season which was to follow. When Mackenzie was flaying the Company for its bad bookkeeping, it is noteworthy that he contrasted its methods, not with any contemporary Canadian enterprise, but rather with the precepts of a certain

manual recently published in Albany which had been recommended by —
of all people — John B. Yates' partner, Archibald McIntyre.[27] Supposing the
Welland Canal Company had looked around for an example on which to
model itself, where could an analogous case have been found? The Canada
Company and the Bank of Upper Canada were, in volume of money handled,
the only two institutions in the province which were at all comparable; and,
in respect of accounting practices, one being a land settlement company and
the other a bank of issue, methods would differ radically from those suitable
for a canal company. That their methods were one whit better than those of
the Company is, in any event, an open question.[28]

The normal safeguard against misuse of executive power in a private
corporation is the removal of the responsible officers by vote of the stockholders. In the Welland Canal Company, as we have had occasion to note,
this safeguard was ineffective, since the charter of 1825 laid down qualifications for election to the board which only a small handful of individuals
could meet. Responsible government was as uncharacteristic of the Welland
Canal Company as it was, in this period, of Upper Canada as a whole.
There was no means, except perhaps by complicated juggling with share-
ownership such as introduced Creighton and Macdonell to the board, whereby incompetent or irresponsible directors could be replaced, as Boulton's
misbehavior on his abortive mission to England in 1825 had eloquently
demonstrated.

It may well be that we need look no further than this for an explanation
of the inadequate internal organization of the Company. Only the development of an unusual degree of personal identification with the Company on
the part of the directors could well have compensated for the absence of
effective externally-imposed sanctions. But, except in the case of Merritt,
there is no evidence to suggest that the directors conceived of their role in
these terms. They were busy men; they had other work to do which had
prior claims on their attention and greater penalties attached to ineffective
performance. None of them had a large financial stake in the Company;
none of them had much to gain by a more careful attention to the details of
management. Their attitude is well illustrated by the following letter, written
to the lieutenant governor in 1829, in which they politely intimate that,
having done everything they can think of at the moment in the way of
raising money, they feel themselves to be divested of any further responsibility:

> The Directors cannot forbear remarking that their individual interest in
> this great public undertaking is very inconsiderable and merely taken
> in order to qualify themselves for the discharge of a very important and
> arduous trust; and having made earnest and repeated representations
> of the present state of the work, and the difficulty they have now de-
> scribed, they feel that they have relieved themselves from responsibility
> and done all that it is in their power to do as the mere representatives
> of the public and private stockholders.[29]

The directors, in a word, regarded their responsibilities as strictly limited. They saw their role as that of trustees, in some vague sense, of the public interest, rather than that of proprietors or representatives of the private shareholders. However honorable their intentions and however scrupulous their moral code, they were not prepared to devote wholehearted attention to the affairs of the Company. Nor, indeed, did they feel under any pressure to do so. Sanctions exerted by the private stockholders were rendered nugatory at an early stage; sanctions exerted by the legislature, though a matter of more continuous concern, did not become fully effective in this respect until 1836.

Consideration of the role which such men as Dunn, Boulton, Allan, and Robinson played in the Welland Canal Company leads one to look with suspicion upon the conventional generalization that it should have been built by the government, not by a private company. The most extreme statement of this point of view is to be found in William Kingsford's essay, *The Canadian Canals*, published in 1865. Kingsford, who was an engineer by profession and claimed to speak with some authority on canal matters, holds that the country was "taken by surprise" when Merritt and his associates petitioned for a charter. He does not doubt that, had the charter been refused, the Welland Canal would have been constructed by the government, as was the Cornwall Canal ten years later. But, he asserts, the government was "forestalled by the few, who laid their grip upon the work only to delay it by incompetency and mismanagement. . . We find a small clique of irresponsible men, with no special aptitude, taking possession of and to no little extent enjoying all the fruits, of the management of a project, which was national in its character." [30] He is quite certain that, had the government undertaken the work, it would have been completed more quickly and at less expense.

Such an argument, being hypothetical, is very difficult to refute. We may recall, however, that the original petition of October 14, 1818, was not a request for the incorporation of a private company, but a prayer that the government should appoint surveyors and take what other steps it deemed desirable for the construction of a Niagara canal; that it was not the petition but the report of the legislative committee on the petition which first mentioned the possibility of chartering a company; and that not until five years had passed after the appearance of this report did Merritt and his friends again approach the legislature, this time with a petition for a charter. There is no evidence to suggest that in 1818 Merritt and his fellow millers of Twelve Mile Creek would not have been quite content to see the project taken up by the government. On the contrary, had the financial resources of Upper Canada not been unexpectedly curtailed by the failure of Lower Canada to provide for the usual division of the customs duties, it is very probable that this is precisely what would have happened.

The five years which elapsed between 1819 and 1824 were of no small importance. These were the crucial five years which saw the Erie Canal transformed from a mere project into an all-but-completed reality. If we look at the matter in this light, the proper charge to make is that the Welland was constructed too late, rather than too soon. Be that as it may, by 1824 the Upper Canada government had had ample opportunity to preëmpt the Niagara project for itself, if it had wanted to. Official surveys had already been made. Merritt, with Niagara already hostile because of his insistence on the Twelve Mile Creek route, had at this time no influence in the legislature sufficient to override a settled determination to entrust the project to the government, had such a determination been present. The point is that it was not present. On the contrary, it seems to have been with something like a feeling of relief that the Upper Canada legislature delegated to a private organization the responsibility for a project which many still believed entirely visionary and which certainly involved considerable financial risk.

Kingsford's position is, in fact, untenable. Seven years elapsed between Merritt's first attempt to interest the government in the project and the final amended act of incorporation. The legislative process was expressly designed to check impetuous commitments made by an elected Assembly. The chartering of the Welland Canal Company was no piece of hasty legislation, but a deliberate and calculated act of government policy in which all branches of the legislature and all levels of colonial government participated. It could have been blocked at any time if powerful interests or responsible authorities had seen fit to oppose it.

Would the canal have been completed more quickly or at less expense if it had been built by the government? It is significant that contemporary critics of the Company made no such assertion. So far as Mackenzie was concerned, the government was in fact building the canal. Public money was being used to pay for construction, and the directors were either themselves members of the Compact or its dupes. Mackenzie would have laughed to scorn the idea that expenses would have been any less or "defalcations" any smaller, had the Welland Canal been formally entrusted to an executive department of the government. As he stated to the Lower Canada legislature, "The Officers of Government are the very people by whose mismanagement the Welland Canal has been brought into difficulty." [31] Government to him meant the government of his day — that is, the Family Compact — whereas to Kingsford it meant some ideally efficient Board of Works, such as could not have existed in Upper Canada in the 1830's. There is no reason to suppose that Kingsford, writing more than thirty years after the event, had a more correct idea of what the government of Upper Canada could and could not have done than did William Lyon Mackenzie who, whatever the defects of his vision in other respects, had a keen eye for the limitations of a colonial bureaucracy.

References to the successful construction by the government (after 1840) of the Cornwall Canal and the other St. Lawrence canals are beside the point, in the first place because of the important constitutional changes which took place at the end of the 1830's, and in the second place because the experience gained from and the precedent set by the Welland were very significant factors in these later undertakings. For instance, the Cornwall Canal was financed by provincial loans raised by John H. Dunn in London in 1834 and 1835. This was the first entrance of the provincial government into the London capital market; it was made possible in large part because the way had been charted by Merritt and Yates for the Welland. Significantly, it was Merritt who introduced into the Upper Canada Assembly the bill which empowered Dunn to float these loans. Further, a great deal of the effective propaganda which made the Cornwall Canal possible originated with the very men who had been associated with the Welland, and this for the excellent reason that the full potentialities of the Welland could not be realized without the complete canalization of the St. Lawrence. In this later development Merritt in particular played a strategic role; it is a historical commonplace that the completion of the St. Lawrence canal system was largely his achievement. Merritt could never have played this role had he lacked the experience and prestige gained from the Welland. To assert that the Welland Canal should have been constructed by the government is to read history backwards. It was in no small part because Merritt, his associates, and indeed Canada as a whole had learned their lesson on the Welland that these later transportation improvements took the form they did.

But one cannot, without a distinct feeling of unreality, discuss construction by the government and construction by the Welland Canal Company as if they were mutually exclusive alternatives. In its origin a creature of the state, the Company throughout its existence was in a very real sense an instrument of state policy. It was a mixed corporation, a classic example of the common institutional device by means of which, in the first half of the nineteenth century, legislatures throughout North America attempted to promote and regulate the course of economic development. Both legislative appointees and private individuals sat on the board of the Company; both public and private funds were used to pay for construction. Similar corporations, particularly in the fields of banking, canals, and turnpikes, existed in almost every state of the American union in this period; the state of Pennsylvania alone had invested over six million dollars in mixed corporations by 1843.[32]

The mixed corporation represented, in essence, an attempt to ally the capital-raising powers of the state with the entrepreneurial energies of private individuals. As a device for promoting economic development it had certain obvious attractive features, and also certain characteristic failings. It enabled the legislature to encourage and assist projects which seemed to be in the general interest but which were too risky, as business propositions, for private investors to carry through unaided. It made feasible the exercise of a certain degree of public control over enterprises which enjoyed monopolistic powers. And it held out the possibility, though usually it turned out to be no more than that, of supplementing public revenues by dividends from profitable operation. Each of these motives seems to have been present in the case of the financial assistance extended to the Welland Canal Company by the legislature of Upper Canada. The characteristic defects of the device, unfortunately, were also present: the inevitable pressure of political considerations upon Company policy; the difficulty of securing agreement among directors who were responsible to different groups with partly conflicting interests; the lack of procedures for insuring effective surveillance over the expenditure of public moneys; and the tendency for corporate survival to become dependent more upon effective lobbying than upon efficient management.

In the Canadian provinces the mixed corporation never achieved the popularity which it attained in the American states before 1850. For this the example of the Welland Canal Company may have been partly responsible. Certainly the fact that the Company had been chartered as a private corporation, and yet was charged with public responsibilities, introduced serious complications for its management. In the first place, it meant that the standards of performance which Merritt and his associates were expected to meet were ambivalent and imprecise. If the Company was a private organization, why should its directors be expected to concern themselves with military and naval strategy? Was that their responsibility? Why should private stockholders have to shoulder the expense of placating Commodore Barrie's whims and prejudices? Why should the Company pay for the construction of harbors and other ancillary works which would certainly be of far greater benefit to the province generally than they could ever be to the private stockholders? On the other hand, if the Company was an agency and creature of the government, if it was expected to bear in mind its responsibilities not only to the stockholders but also and indeed primarily to the general public, why did the Bank of Upper Canada steadfastly refuse to extend credit to the Company as such, insisting always that the directors as private individuals should provide security? Why should Merritt have to mortgage the Company's profits and property before aid could be obtained from the imperial government? Why should the Company's shares have to be hawked about the London money market like those of any bubble project instead of appearing with all the prestige and security of a provincial guarantee?

In the second place, the fact that the Company was legally and formally a private corporation, and yet actually looked and acted far more like an informal extension of the executive government, had important implications for the modes of conduct which were expected of its officers and the ethical standards to which they were expected to adhere. For example, to anyone who regarded the Company as nothing more than a private organization, many of Mackenzie's virulent denunciations must have seemed totally irrelevant. If "valuable mill sites [were] given away without recompense," was not this the Company's affair and no concern of the legislature? If "the President, Agent, and some of the Directors [were] engaged in forwarding goods on the Canal," what provincial or imperial statute was thereby infringed? If Merritt's expense account sometimes included brandy and cigars, should the legislature of Upper Canada take action in the matter?

From considerations such as these one may perhaps infer that, no matter what the legal form in which it was clothed, the Welland Canal Company was regarded by a significant body of contemporary opinion as in effect much more than a private profit-oriented business organization. The standards of performance to which its officers were expected to adhere and the ethical norms which they were expected to respect were such as we would normally regard as being typical of a governmental, rather than a business institution. And the reasons for this are, of course, sufficiently obvious. The job which the Company was chartered to perform was essentially of a public developmental nature. The individuals conspicuous in the management, with the exception of Merritt, were better known as politicians than as businessmen. Shortage of capital threw the Company into a state of dependence on the legislature which was continuous and obvious. The Company was not judged by the standards applicable to a private business because it did not act like one.

Three factors combined to bring the Welland Canal Company into intimate and continuous contact with the political authorities. The first and probably the most important was capital scarcity. Private capital, though supplemented generously by New York and Albany and hesitatingly by Montreal and London, was quite inadequate for the task. Dependence on the greater borrowing powers of the legislature was inescapable. The second was the requirements of provincial defence; all groups in Upper Canada and in Britain, whether favorably inclined toward the Company or hostile to it, recognized the importance of the canal in this respect. The third was what we may call an "accidental" factor: the qualifications laid down in the charter for membership of the board which, whether of design or not, resulted in a close identification of the Company with the inner circle of the Tory party.

The history of the Company, if it illustrates anything, illustrates the failure of its management and of the political authorities of the province to evolve a system of mutual aid which would at one and the same time insure the survival of the Company and avoid the alienation of politically influential sectors of the population. Financial aid from the legislature was neither generous nor predictable enough to enable the Company to complete the canal in a permanent manner. The significance of the canal for colonial defence was allowed to become a handicap, in respect of the terms on which aid was received from the imperial government, instead of an asset. The close alliance established between the Company and the Tory party, though probably indispensable in the initial stages, embroiled the Company in all the bitterness and petty factions of colonial politics and rendered its survival dependent upon the uncertain flux of popular elections. Capital shortage seems to have been of prime importance; if the Company had been able to free itself from financial dependence on the legislature, greater freedom of action in other respects would certainly have followed. But capital scarcity was, at the same time, the difficulty which the directors could do least to remedy.

The Welland Canal Company is sometimes referred to as a failure, but this is clearly too absolute a term. It is true that the stockholders received no return on their investment up to the time when reconstruction and enlargement was undertaken by the provincial government, although revenues were then showing a healthy upward trend. From this financial point of view the enterprise was certainly not a success. But to realize a profit for the shareholders was not the only or even the major purpose which the Company was organized to serve. There were other purposes, equally real, which were in fact achieved, although they could not be calculated in cash by the Company or indeed by anyone. The Welland Canal did break the monopoly which the Erie would otherwise have held over the commerce of western Upper Canada. It did accelerate the development of the western part of the province and of the Niagara peninsula. It did provide a strategically vital link between Lake Erie and Lake Ontario. These benefits are not easy to measure, but to appreciate their importance one need only consider what might have been the consequences if the Welland had not been built.

In these circumstances, to call the work a success or a failure adds little to our understanding of its historical significance. The real importance of the first Welland Canal becomes evident only when we consider its place in the full course of Canadian development. The Welland Canal was the first major step in the program of canal construction which set the pace for the development of the St. Lawrence economy during the next quarter-century. Once the first step had been taken, there could be no turning back until the entire program was completed. No single link in the St. Lawrence canal system could realize its full potentialities until the whole chain had been forged. The combination of heavy fixed costs and unused capacity presented problems which only expansion could solve. Further, the very limitations and defects of the Welland Canal Company made it certain that, when canals were built in future, the government and not private or mixed corporations would build them. Waterways were too vital to the Canadian economy, and the demands they made on overseas sources of capital too insatiable, for any but governmental organizations to undertake the task. The precedent set by the Welland Canal Company served not only as a stimulus but also as a warning to future generations.

The history of the Welland Canal Company is a history of muddling and of improvisation, of high hopes and cruel disappointments. In these respects it is typical of most of the human works which tradition labels great achievements. The men who built the canal were not overwise nor gifted with unusual foresight. Time and again they made serious mistakes, and even more often they deceived themselves as to the probable consequences of what they decided to do. They were men who saw a task which needed to be done and who, with all their inexperience, carried it through to completion as well and as expeditiously as they could in the circumstances which surrounded them. To exaggerate their success or minimize their errors would increase neither our understanding of the past nor our ability to take rational action in the present.

APPENDIX

REVENUE, TRAFFIC, COSTS, AND SOURCES OF CAPITAL

I. RATES OF TOLL

INFORMATION ON THE RATES OF TOLL CHARGED ON THE WELLAND CANAL during the period of private ownership is not as complete as could be wished. Shortly after the first opening of the canal in 1829, only four categories of freight were distinguished:

Flour	4*d*. per bbl
Pork	6*d*. per bbl
Ashes	1*s*. 1*d*. per bbl.
Pipe staves	20*s*. 0*d*. per M. (1200 units)

These were relatively low rates. In anticipation of objections on this score, the board pointed out that the rates were experimental and could be raised if necessary, and also that the cost of operating the canal was almost entirely overhead, which should be distributed over as large a volume of traffic as possible. Both these points were sound. Traffic through the canal had to be developed in competition with the Erie Canal and also with the Niagara portage, and for this low rates were essential. They were equally necessary if the Welland were to facilitate the speedy opening up of the western peninsula of Upper Canada.

The first change in these rates of which we have knowledge came in 1832. At the beginning of that year the rates were as follows:

	s.	*d.*	
Flour		4	per bbl.
Pork		6	per bbl.
Whisky		6	per bbl.
Ashes	1	0	per bbl.
Wheat		1½	per bushel
Pig iron, grindstones, and plaster	2	6	per ton
Castings (down)	3	9	per ton
Castings (up)	5	0	per ton
Merchandise	5	0	per ton
Square timber	15	0	per M.
Pipe staves	15	0	per M.
Saw logs		4	each
Salt		1½	per bbl.
Passengers		3½	each

It should be noted that the rate for pipe staves was reduced between 1829 and 1832 from 20*s*. to 15*s*. per M. This may perhaps be taken as an indication of the severity of competition with the Erie. Further, the 1832 rate favored the movement of flour rather than wheat. If we take the conventional ratio of five bushels of wheat to one barrel of flour, there was a differential of 3½*d.* per barrel in favor of having the wheat milled before passing through the canal.

Apparently no further changes in tolls were made until the close of the season of 1835, when there appeared the more elaborate schedule reproduced in Table I. It will be noticed that increases were made on several items: flour rose from 4*d.* to 5*d.*; pork from 6*d.* to 7½*d.*; salt from 1½*d.* to 2*d.*; pipe staves returned to their original rate of 20*s.*; and several other rates were increased. These changes suggest that the

TABLE I

Welland Canal Toll Sheet, 1835

RATES OF TOLL ON THE WELLAND CANAL—AS AMENDED.

DESCRIPTION OF PROPERTY.	THROUGH The whole Route.	FROM MOUTH OF Grand River to Dunnville, & *vice versa*.	FROM Dunnville to Port Robinson, & *vice versa*.	FROM Port Robinson to Thorold, & *vice versa*.	FROM Thorold to St. Catharines, & *vice versa*.	FROM St. Catharines to Port Dalhousie, & *vice versa*.	FROM Port Robinson to Port Colborne, & *vice versa*.	Chippawa Cut. Vessels not intending to pass through the Canal.	Chippawa Cut. Vessels intending to pass through.
	26 miles.	4 m. 60 ch.	20¼ miles.	6¼ miles.	4 m. 50 ch.	5 m. 18 ch.	12 miles.	16 chains.	
Flour, : : per barrel,	0 5	0 2	0 2½	0 1	0 1	0 1	0 1½	0 1	Same as if entering the Canal at Port Colborne, or Port Dalhousie.
Pork, : : "	0 7½	0 3	0 3¾	0 2	0 2	0 1½	0 2½	0 1½	
Ashes, : : "	1 0	0 4	0 6	0 3	0 2½	0 1½	0 4	0 2	
Whisky, : : "	1 0	0 4	0 6	0 3	0 2½	0 1½	0 4	0 1½	
Lard and Butter, : "	0 7½	0 3	0 3½	0 2	0 2	0 1½	0 2½	0 3	
Salt, : : "	0 2	0 0½	0 1	0 0½	0 0½	0 0½	0 0¾	0 0½	
Beer and Cider, : "	0 9	0 3	0 4	0 2	0 2	0 2	0 3	0 3	
Dried Fruit and Nuts, "	1 0	0 3	0 6	0 3	0 2½	0 1½	0 4	0 3	
Pitch, : : "	0 6	0 2	0 3	0 1½	0 1½	0 1	0 2	0 2	
Hams and Bacon, : per cwt.	0 4	0 1¼	0 2	0 1	0 1	0 1	0 1½	0 1¼	
Oil, : : per barrel,	0 7½	0 2	0 3½	0 2	0 2	0 1½	0 2½	0 2	
Bees' Wax, : "	0 6	0 1½	0 3	0 1½	0 1½	0 1	0 2	0 1½	
Fish, : : "	0 9	0 3	0 4	0 2	0 2	0 2	0 3	0 3	
Dried Fish, : per cwt.	0 4	0 1¼	0 2	0 1	0 1	0 1	0 1½	0 1¼	
Crackers, : per barrel,	0 7½	0 2	0 3½	0 2	0 2	0 2	0 2½	0 2	
Wheat, : : per bushel,	0 1¼	0 0½	0 1	0 0½	0 0½	0 0½	0 0¾	0 0½	
Oats, : : "	0 1	0 0¼	0 0½	0 0¼	0 0¼	0 0¼	0 0½	0 0¼	
Corn, Barley and Rye, "	0 1¼	0 0½	0 1	0 0½	0 0½	0 0½	0 0¾	0 0½	
Potatoes, : : "	0 1	0 0¼	0 0½	0 0¼	0 0¼	0 0¼	0 0¾	0 0¼	
Coals, : : per ton,	2 6	1 0	1 3	0 10	0 10	0 10	1 0	1 0	
Castings, : *up*, "	5 0	1 3	2 6	1 8	1 8	1 8	2 0	1 0	
do. : *down*, "	3 9	1 0	1 10½	1 0	1 0	1 0	1 3	1 0	
Pig Iron, : : "	2 6	1 0	1 3	0 10	0 10	0 10	1 0	1 0	
Grindstones, : "	2 6	1 0	1 3	0 10	0 10	0 10	1 0	1 0	
Plaster, : : "	2 6	1 0	1 3	0 10	0 10	0 10	1 0	1 0	
do. ground. : "	3 9	1 3	1 10½	1 0	1 0	1 0	1 3	1 0	
Furniture and Baggage, "	5 0	1 3	2 6	1 8	1 8	1 8	2 0	1 3	
Lard and Butter, : per keg,	0 4	0 1	0 2	0 1	0 1	0 1	0 1½	0 1	
Tobacco, leaf, : per cwt.	0 4	0 1	0 2	0 1	0 1	0 1	0 1½	0 1	
do. manufactured, "	0 6	0 2	0 3	0 1½	0 1½	0 1½	0 2	0 2	
Pipe Staves, : per M.	20 0	3 9	10 0	5 0	5 0	5 0	7 6	3 9	
W. I. do. : : "	7 6	1 3	3 9	1 10½	1 10½	1 10½	2 6	1 3	
Saw Logs, : : each,	0 4	0 1	0 2	0 2	0 2	0 2	0 3	0 1	
Square Timber, 12 in. diameter, and upwards, per 1,000 cubic feet,	25 0	5 0	12 6	7 6	7 6	7 6	8 9	5 0	
Flatted Timber, do. do.	20 0	3 9	10 0	5 0	5 0	5 0	7 6	3 9	
Small round building Timber, do.	12 6	2 6	6 3	3 9	3 9	3 9	5 0	2 6	
Shingles, : per M.	0 6	0 2	0 3	0 1½	0 1½	0 1½	0 2	0 2	
Barrels, : each,	0 2	0 0¼	0 1	0 ½	0 0½	0 0½	0 0¾	0 0¼	
Boards, 4-4 inch, per 1,000 feet,	3 9	1 0	1 10½	1 0	1 0	1 0	1 3	1 0	
Merchandise, *up* and *down*, per ton,	5 0	1 3	2 6	1 8	1 8	1 8	3 9	1 3	
Firkins, sm. casks, packages, &c. each,	0 2	0 0¼	0 1	0 1	0 1	0 1	0 1½	0 0¼	
Passengers, : "	0 6	0 2	0 3½	0 2	0 2	0 2	0 2½	0 2	
Onions, : : per bushel,	0 2	0 0¼	0 1	0 1	0 1	0 1	0 1½	0 0¼	
Oysters, : : per barrel,	1 0	0 4	0 6	0 3	0 3	0 3	0 4	0 4	
Vinegar, : : "	1 0	0 4	0 6	0 3	0 3	0 3	0 4	0 4	
Cheese, : : per cwt.	0 3	0 1	0 1½	0 1	0 1	0 1	0 1½	0 1	
Ploughs, : : each,	0 6	0 2	0 3	0 2	0 2	0 2	0 2½	0 2	
Hides, : : per cwt.	0 3	0 1	0 1½	0 1	0 1	0 1	0 1½	0 1	
Skins—Sheep, Deer, &c. "	0 3	0 1	0 1½	0 1	0 1	0 1	0 1½	0 1	
Horns, : : "	0 3	0 1	0 1½	0 1	0 1	0 1	0 1½	0 1	
Hay, : : per ton,	2 6	1 0	1 3	0 10	0 10	0 10	1 0	1 0	
Bran, : : "	2 6	1 0	1 3	0 10	0 10	0 10	1 0	1 0	
Bricks, : : "	2 6	1 0	1 3	0 10	0 10	0 10	1 0	1 0	
Fire Wood, : : per cord,	0 7½	0 2	0 3½	0 2	0 2	0 2	0 2½	0 2	
Cedar Posts, : : "	2 6	1 0	1 3	0 10	0 10	0 10	1 0	1 0	
Tan Bark, : : "	1 6	0 6	0 9	0 6	0 6	0 6	0 7½	0 6	
Stone, : : "	1 3	0 5	0 7½	0 4	0 4	0 4	0 6	0 5	
Wool, : : per ton,	5 0	1 3	2 6	1 8	1 8	1 8	3 9	1 3	
Stone Ware, : : "	5 0	1 3	2 6	1 8	1 8	1 8	3 9	1 3	
Flax Seed, : : per barrel,	0 6	0 2	0 3	0 2	0 2	0 2	0 2½	0 2	
Vessels, under 40 tons burthen,	5 0	5 0						5 0	
do. 40 to 50 do.	10 0	10 0						10 0	
do. 50 and upwards,	15 0	15 0						15 0	
Boats for Passengers, 3½d. per mile, or,	5 0	5 0						5 0	
do. for freight, : :	2 6	2 6	1 3	1 3	1 3	1 3	1 3	1 3	

Source: *Annual Report of the Welland Canal Company*, 1835.

new schedule was intended to mark the end of the initial period of development and that the board believed charges could be increased without risk of a serious fall in revenue.

In summary, the policy of the board in regard to toll charges appears to reflect a definite and well-considered line of action. Tolls were initially set low and raised slowly after increases in volume of traffic appeared to justify increases. Flexibility of charges to meet competition was not entirely absent.

II. TRAFFIC

Quantity series for several classes of freight moving through the canal are available for the decade 1831–41. Five of these series, three (square timber, pork, and wheat) representing mainly "down" freight and two (salt and merchandise) "up" freight, are presented graphically in Chart I, and statistics for these and other cate-

CHART I
Volume of Traffic on Welland Canal, 1831–1841
(uniform logarithmic vertical scale)

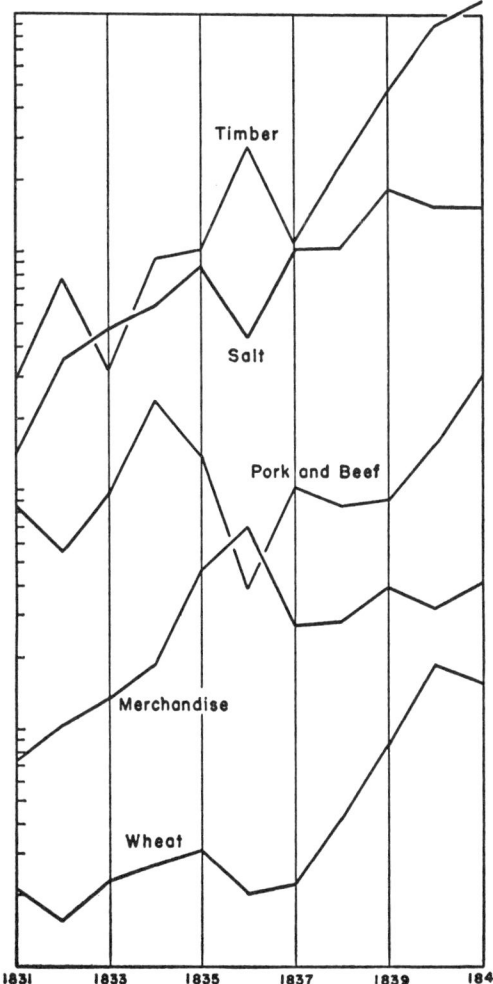

TABLE II

Freight Traffic, 1831–1841

(selected commodities)

	1831	1832	1833	1834	1835	1836	1837	1838	1839	1840	1841
Merchandise (tons & cwts.)	736/14	1032/00	1323/05	1880/05	4791/00	6996/10	2697/14	2779/04	3914/07½	3119/09	4051/00
Wheat (bushels)	210,105	155,170	229,675	264,919	301,635½	201,400	218,242½	414,919	864,846	1,833,765	1,579,966
Flour (barrels)	30,081	—	39,994½	27,702½	13,049	21,799	6,829½	49,082	66,855½	209,016½	213,483½
Pork & beef (barrels)	8,600	5,422	9,611	23,422½	13,907½	3,887½	10,395½	8,760½	9,053	15,624½	30,416
Saw logs (number)	4,189	—	17,914	5,939	18,047	24,968	11,237	5,174	10,294	5,942	11,300
Whisky (barrels)	1,795	—	601	332	552	699½	260	274	834½	1,515¾	1,950½
Salt (barrels)	14,182	34,546	46,552	59,641	87,297	43,891½	101,260	101,807½	184,562	156,597	156,138
Square timber (cubic feet)	28,500	75,992	30,942	94,380*	102,960	279,944	106,335	232,147	470,554	899,507	1,155,086
Pipe staves (number)	307,718	146,136	161,792	392,055	454,701	601,729	665,825	—	757,911	862,704	—
Boards (feet)	865,888	—	1,521,467	1,297,892	1,341,330	2,722,908	3,343,510	1,228,780	2,575,627	2,004,721	3,580,911
Coal (tons)	—	—	—	399¾	610½	305½	755¾	844	1,325½	938	1,422

Sources: *Annual Reports of the Welland Canal Company,* 1831–1841; Lt. Col. Phillpotts, *Report on the Canal Navigation of the Canadas;* J. L. McDougall, *The Welland Canal to 1841.*

* The *Annual Report* for 1835 gives 64,380 for this item; the figure in the Table is taken from the *Annual Report* for 1834.

gories are given in Table II. It should be noted that Chart I, together with the later Charts II and III, is drawn with a logarithmic vertical scale and is designed to show relative rates of growth and relative fluctuations only. Absolute figures should be read from the tables.

Study of Chart I and the quantity series reveals the wide fluctuations in volume of business experienced by the Welland Canal in this decade. The statistics, however, must be interpreted with caution. In no case are they to be taken as necessarily indicative in the first instance of business or crop conditions; what they show primarily is the condition of the canal itself. Thus in Chart I the trough in three of the five series in the year 1836 is probably to be attributed to two factors: the increase in toll rates at the end of 1835 and the fact that the canal was closed to traffic for over half the season. It is interesting to note that merchandise, the toll charge for which was not raised in 1835, showed no decline in 1836 but on the contrary reached the highest volume of the decade.

The trends of the five series charted may be adequately represented by straight lines, indicating on a semilogarithmic scale constant relative rates of growth per year. The approximate rates of growth appear to be 35 per cent for square timber,

CHART II

Vessels passing Welland and Erie Canals, 1831–1841
(*uniform logarithmic vertical scale*)

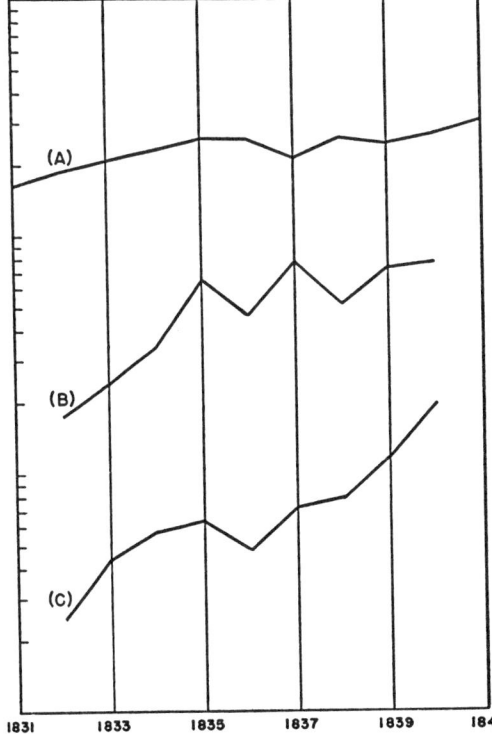

(A) Erie Canal: total lockages at Lock No. 26.
(B) Boats and Scows passing Welland Canal.
(C) Schooners passing Welland Canal.

23 per cent for salt, 8 per cent for merchandise, 15 per cent for wheat, and 8 per cent for pork and beef. Clearly, if the figures are reliable, the Welland Canal in this decade was enjoying a rapidly increasing volume of business.

It cannot be assumed, however, that the volume of wheat paying toll in this period moved uniformly in the direction, Lake Erie to Lake Ontario. In the years 1835, 1836, 1837, and 1838 the wheat crop failed in parts of the United States and wheat was imported from Upper Canada in spite of the American duty of 25 cents a bushel imposed in 1824. Crop conditions in Upper Canada were little better than in the United States, but such wheat surplus as did exist found its way to the states of New York, Michigan, and even Illinois, rather than to Montreal, although prices in the latter port were sufficiently high to attract wheat from Europe for milling. Part of the wheat traffic composing the series charted may well have passed from Lake Ontario to Lake Erie, rather than in the reverse direction.

Probably the steeply rising trend noticeable in the wheat series may be ascribed in part to the Colonial Trade Act passed by the British Parliament in 1831. This act removed all duties on agricultural produce entering the British North American colonies. American wheat could therefore profitably be exported to Upper Canada, milled there, and sent to England as colonial flour, taking advantage of the colonial preference accorded by the Corn Laws. American flour, on the other hand, was a manufactured product and was liable to a special duty even if exported by way of the St. Lawrence. The act of 1831, which created a highly profitable business for Upper Canada millers, must have contributed in no small measure to traffic on the Welland.

Chart II presents two further series which may be taken as indicative of the volume of freight passing through the Welland Canal — those for schooners, and for boats and scows. The steadily rising trend, representing an exponential rate of growth, is again evident. The slump in volume of business in 1836 stands out clearly. For purposes of comparison, the series for total lockages on the Erie Canal at Lock No. 26 (three miles west of Schenectady) is presented at the top of the Chart. The very much smaller rate of growth, representing probably the more developed stage reached by the Erie forwarding business, is clear, while it may be noted that the slump in volume occurs in 1837, not in the previous year as on the Welland.

TABLE III

Schooners, boats and scows passing the
Welland Canal, 1831–1841

	Schooners	Boats and Scows
1831	—	—
1832	240	175
1833	433	237
1834	570	334
1835	636	660
1836	474	463
1837	718	769
1838	769	518
1839	1,169	736
1840	1,971	762
1841	—	—

Source: *Annual Reports of the Welland Canal Company*, 1831–1841

TABLE IV

Total lockages at Lock No. 26,
Erie Canal, 1831–1841

1831	16,284
1832	18,601
1833	20,649
1834	22,911
1835	25,798
1836	25,516
1837	21,055
1838	25,962
1839	24,234
1840	26,987
1841	30,320

Source: New York State Assembly Document 145, *Annual Report of the Canal Commissioners for 1856*, pp. 260–262.

CHART III

Annual Gross Revenue from Tolls on Erie,
Oswego, and Welland Canals
(*uniform logarithmic vertical scale*)

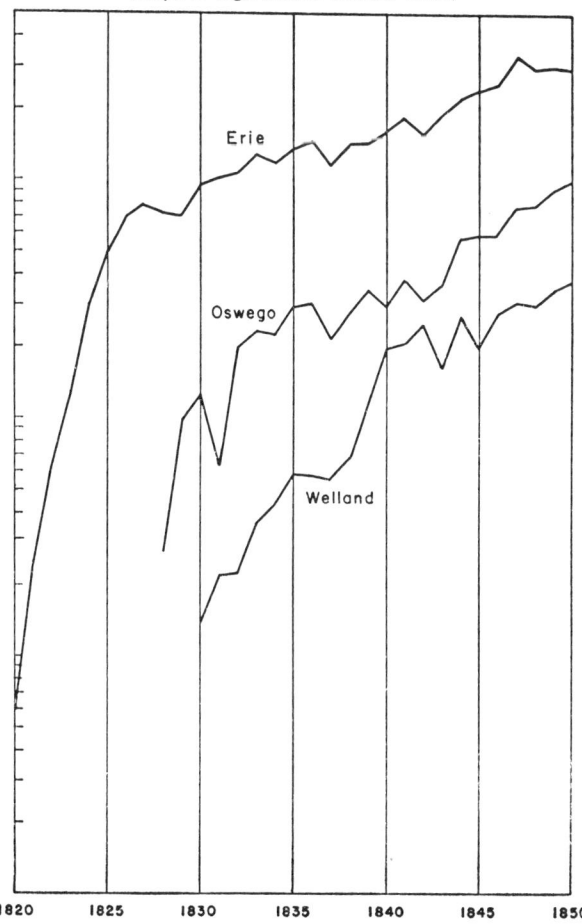

III. GROSS REVENUE

Chart III presents series for gross revenue from tolls on the Erie, Oswego, and Welland canals from their respective dates of completion to 1850. Data for the American canals are taken from the Reports of the New York State Canal Commissioners. Regarding the Welland Canal figures, a few words of caution are necessary. The figures for the earlier years are extremely doubtful, and it is not too much to say that the whole series up to 1840 must be treated with extreme scepticism. The various sources do not agree, and in one case the *Annual Reports* of the Company

TABLE V

Annual Revenue from Tolls on the Welland,
Oswego, and Erie Canals, 1820–1850

(All figures rounded to the nearest pound or dollar)

	Welland	Oswego	Erie
1820	—	—	$ 5,695
1821	—	—	23,002
1822	—	—	60,447
1823	—	—	125,991
1824	—	—	294,547
1825	—	—	492,664
1826	—	—	687,977
1827	—	—	775,919
1828	—	$ 2,758	727,650
1829	—	9,439	707,883
1830	£ 1,349	12,335	943,545
1831	2,171	6,271	1,001,714
1832	2,203	19,768	1,085,612
1833	3,618	22,950	1,290,163
1834	4,300	22,168	1,180,968
1835	5,807	29,203	1,376,673
1836	5,754	30,470	1,440,540
1837	5,516	21,093	1,144,170
1838	6,740	27,372	1,414,174
1839	11,757	34,162	1,427,032
1840	19,175	29,523	1,597,334
1841	20,792	38,244	1,813,651
1842	24,976	31,222	1,568,947
1843	16,159	36,204	1,880,315
1844	26,134	56,165	2,190,147
1845	19,888	58,347	2,361,884
1846	27,410	58,185	2,499,276
1847	30,549	77,933	3,333,347
1848	29,064	79,793	2,947,701
1849	34,741	91,220	2,962,132
1850	37,925	98,528	2,933,126

Sources: *Annual Reports of the Welland Canal Company*, 1830–1841; Reports of the Board of Works, Government of Canada, 1842–1850; New York State Assembly Document 145, *Annual Report of Canal Commissioners for 1856*; Noble E. Whitford, *History of the Canal System of the State of New York* (Albany, 1906) Vol. II, pp. 1064–1065.

for two successive years (1834 and 1835) give conflicting figures. The tolls for 1830 and 1831 are so merged in the Forwarding Account that separate treatment is impossible. Revenue from tolls on the Welland was not distributed; it was plowed back into the canal for repairs and maintenance and probably not even the directors themselves knew what their revenue really was. The situation is complicated by the fact that the financial affairs of the Company were drawn into public controversy. The annual figures given here should be regarded as nothing more than an attempt to follow the preponderance of evidence in each year. For the period after 1840 the figures given by the Board of Works have been used, and these are presumably reliable.

The trend for each series, but most clearly that of the Erie Canal, seems to be adequately represented by a logarithmic parabola, with a relative rate of growth decreasing at a constant rate of retardation. The apparent break in trend in the Welland series around 1840 is probably illusory, and this in spite of the fact that the reconstruction and enlargement of the canal was begun in that year. The trend is best represented by a smooth curve, the rate of growth of which after 1841 is approximately the same as that of the Erie. The trend of the Oswego series appears to be slightly steeper after 1840 than either the Welland or the Erie series. As regards fluctuations about the trend line, the Oswego and Erie series appear to move roughly in step with each other after 1832, while the Welland series fluctuates independently. This suggests that the anticipated link-up between the Welland and Oswego canals, as a through route from Lake Erie to Syracuse, did not take place, or at least that it did not result in a volume of through traffic large enough to leave its mark on the gross revenue series. The effects of the depression of 1837 are marked in the Erie and Oswego series, and can perhaps be discerned in the Welland series also. But the dip in revenues for the years 1836 and 1837 is probably also due to the increase in tolls at the end of 1835 and to the fact that the canal was closed to traffic during a large part of the 1836 season.

IV. COSTS

The Board of Works took over in 1841 a ship canal of 8 feet depth, with 40 wooden locks measuring 22 feet by 100 feet; three harbors, Ports Dalhousie, Maitland, and Colborne; an aqueduct over the River Welland built of wood and measuring 365 feet by 24 feet; a dam across the Grand River; about 13,400 acres of land; and various water power rights, the rents from which amounted to over £1000 per annum. The direct line from Lake Erie to Lake Ontario was 28 miles in length, while the whole canal, including all branches and feeders, had a length of about 88 miles.

What had this property cost, and who had paid for it? Up to the end of 1837 the total expenditure on the canal appears to have been £451,529 6s. 2d. currency. This was obtained from the following sources:

TABLE VI

Total Expenditures on the Welland Canal, 1824-1837

Stock Subscriptions:

Government of Upper Canada	£107,500	0	0
Government of Lower Canada	25,000	0	0
Individuals in Upper Canada	3,712	10	0
Individuals in Lower Canada	13,825	0	0
Individuals in New Brunswick	500	0	0
Individuals in New York	69,625	0	0
Individuals in England	30,137	10	0
Forfeited stock	540	0	0
	£250,840	0	0

Loans:

Government of Upper Canada	£100,000	0	0
Government of Great Britain	55,555	11	2
	£155,555	11	2

Miscellaneous:

Tolls	£22,243	16	4
Land and hydraulic rents	1,110	3	3
Profits on foreign exchange	7,156	15	5
Bank of Upper Canada, loan account	1,370	2	3
Donation from Catholic Bishop of Quebec	25	0	0
Issue of Welland Canal notes	8,115	15	0
Rents from special water privileges	2,157	4	2
Other minor items	2,954	18	7
	£45,133	15	0
	£451,529	6	2

Source: William Hamilton Merritt, *Brief Review of the Origin, Progress, Present State, and Future Prospects of the Welland Canal* (St. Catharines, 1852), p. 21 (slightly abbreviated).

In addition, the Company had paid no interest on loans made by the province since 1828. The amount due the provincial government on this account was estimated at £44,690. No interest was ever paid or demanded on the loan from the British government, the amount payable on this account being some £20,000. Loss of interest to the province and to the imperial government should be included in estimates of total cost, for the Company was under a legal obligation to make these payments. As a tentative estimate of the total amount expended by the Welland Canal Company during the period of private control, a figure of £516,219 currency is suggested.

The total amount expended on the Welland Canal by the provincial government of Upper Canada, by loans and subscriptions, between 1824 and 1837 was £275,644. The following table lists the amount and date of the various grants:

TABLE VII

Grants by Government of Upper Canada to the Welland Canal
Company, 1826–1837

Statute	*Date*	*Amount*	*Form of Grant*
7 Geo. IV, c. 20	1826	£25,000	loan
8 Geo. IV, c. 17	1827	50,000	subscription
11 Geo. IV. c. 11	1830	25,000	loan
1 Wm. IV, c. 18	1831	50,000	loan
3 Wm. IV, c. 54	1833	7,500	subscription
4 Wm. IV, c. 39	1834	50,000	subscription
7 Wm. IV, c. 92	1837	68,144	subscription

The total amount of the outstanding public debt of Upper Canada in 1840 was £1,179,949 11s. 2¼d. Assistance to the Welland Canal Company therefore amounted to approximately 23.3 per cent of the total provincial debt in 1840. In 1843 further debentures to the amount of £117,800 were issued as compensation to the private stockholders. The total net increase in the provincial debt on account of the Welland Canal Company was therefore £393,444.

NOTES

CHAPTER I. UPPER CANADA: THE INLAND PROVINCE

1. A. Shortt and A. G. Doughty, *Documents Relating to the Constitutional History of Canada, 1759–91* (Ottawa, 1918), p. 664.

2. The older estimate of the number of Loyalists who came to the province of Quebec was 10,000, but according to the analysis given by A. L. Burt in his *The Old Province of Quebec* (Toronto, 1933), pp. 262–263, only 6800 Loyalists had arrived by 1785. There are no really reliable figures for the number of Loyalists who reached Canada over land, and there were many later arrivals who called themselves Loyalists but whose claim to the title was of doubtful validity. See M. L. Hansen and J. B. Brebner, *The Mingling of the Canadian and American Peoples* (New Haven, 1940), pp. 64–65.

3. W. S. Wallace, "Overland Loyalists," *Canadian Magazine*, XLIII, no. 6 (October 1914), 577.

4. Burt, pp. 360–361; R. L. Jones, *History of Agriculture in Ontario, 1613–1880* (Toronto, 1946), p. 19.

5. See E. A. Cruikshank (ed.), *The Correspondence of Lieut. Governor John Graves Simcoe* (5 vols., Toronto, 1923; cited hereafter as *Simcoe Papers*); W. R. Riddell, *The Life of John Graves Simcoe* (Toronto, 1926).

6. *Simcoe Papers*, II, 18, Simcoe to Banks, January 18, 1791.

7. La Rochefoucault-Liancourt, *Travels in Canada, 1795* (13th Report of the Bureau of Archives for the Province of Ontario, 1916: Toronto, 1917), p. 60.

8. *Simcoe Papers*, I, 178, Dundas to Simcoe, July 1792.

9. *Ibid.*, II, 109–110, Simcoe to Dorchester, December 2, 1793.

10. Until about 1800, when roads began to be built along the south shore of Lake Erie, the most convenient route from New York and New England to the Ohio territory passed through Upper Canada. This complicates the problem of estimating the number of Americans who entered Upper Canada to settle there. See Hansen and Brebner, p. 82.

11. Michael Smith, *A Geographical View of the Province of Upper Canada* (New York, 1813), p. 83. The proportion is sometimes given as eight out of ten.

12. Hansen and Brebner, p. 90.

13. *Seventh Census of Canada, 1930* (Ottawa, 1936), I, 146–147. The figure given in the text is obtained by intrapolation. Smith (*Geographical View*, pp. 62–63) gives a figure of 136,000 for 1811, not including Indians, but this is certainly too high.

14. Michael Smith remarked that in 1812 two thirds of the members of the elected Legislative Assembly of Upper Canada were natives of the United States; one third of the justices of the peace were Americans, while the sheriffs were either Europeans or Loyalists. See Smith, *Geographical View*, p. 70. See also F. Landon, *Western Ontario and the American Frontier* (New Haven, 1941), pp. 16–22; Hansen and Brebner, chap. IV.

15. *Simcoe Papers*, I, 18, Simcoe to Banks, January 8, 1791.

16. For the text of the act, see Shortt and Doughty, *Documents*, pp. 694–708.

17. See, for example, Grenville to Dorchester, October 20, 1789 (Shortt and Doughty, *Documents*, p. 665).

18. Shortt and Doughty, *Documents*, pp. 646–647.

19. E. A. Cruikshank and A. F. Hunter (eds.), *The Correspondence of the Honourable Peter Russell* (3 vols., Toronto, 1935; cited hereafter as *Russell Papers*), II, 84, John Elmsley to D. W. Smith, February 18, 1798.

20. *Russell Papers*, III, xiv.

21. The most authoritative work on this subject is Gilbert Patterson, *Land Settlement in Upper Canada, 1783–1840* (16th Report of the Department of Archives for the Province of Ontario, 1920; Toronto, 1921); but Cruikshank's introduction to the *Russell Papers* is also useful, together with R. G. Riddell, "A Study in the Land Policy of the Colonial Office, 1763–1855," *Canadian Historical Review*, XVIII, no. 4 (December 1937), 385–405.

22. *Russell Papers*, I, 163–164, Russell to Portland, April 18, 1797.

23. In 1824 the population of Upper Canada was just under 150,000. Yet approximately eleven million acres of land had been granted and appropriated. See R. K. Gordon, *John Galt* (Toronto, 1920), p. 53.

24. W. S. Wallace, *The Family Compact* (Toronto, 1915); W. R. Riddell, "Mr. Justice Thorpe, the Leader of the First Opposition in Upper Canada," *Canada Law Times*, November 1920, pp. 907–924; W. R. Riddell, "Joseph Willcocks, Sheriff, Member of Parliament, and Traitor," Ontario Historical Society, *Papers and Records*, XXIV (1927), 475–499; A. H. U. Colquhoun, "The Career of Joseph Willcocks," *Canadian Historical Review*, VII, no. 4, 287–293; John Mills Jackson, *A View of the Political Situation of the Province of Upper Canada* (London, 1809).

25. E. A. Cruikshank, "The Government of Upper Canada and Robert Gourlay," Ontario Historical Society, *Papers and Records*, vol. XXIII (1926); W. R. Riddell, "Robert (Fleming) Gourlay," Ontario Historical Society, *Papers and Records*, vol. XIV (1916); R. F. Gourlay, *The Banished Briton and Neptunian* (Cleveland [?], 1836).

26. For the membership of the Compact, see A. Ewart and J. Jarvis, "The Personnel of the Family Compact, 1791–1841," *Canadian Historical Review*, vol. VII, no. 3 (September 1926). These writers present a list of individuals who were members of the Legislative Council or the Executive Council or both between 1791 and 1841. This list is then identified with the Family Compact. This procedure seems far too mechanical and results in the inclusion of Robert Baldwin, who was certainly not a member of the Compact.

27. W. S. Wallace, *The Family Compact* (Toronto, 1915). Patterson writes (p. 12): "The original members of the official group were men of good tradition, upright, faithful, and adequately efficient. They owed their position to the fact that they were the original creators of the state. They gave Upper Canada perhaps the cheapest and best public service possible under the existing conditions. But the system was undeniably bad."

28. The Bank of Upper Canada was chartered in 1821 and began operations in 1822. Of the fifteen original directors, nine were either members of the Executive or Legislative councils, or held important government offices, while most of the others occupied such positions within a few years. A large part of the capital was subscribed by the government. See A. Shortt, "The Early History of Banking in Canada," *Journal of the Canadian Bankers' Association, 1896–97*, pt. V, p. 21.

29. Jones, *History of Agriculture*, pp. 17–25.

30. Hansen and Brebner, pp. 75–76.

31. Jones, *History of Agriculture*, pp. 25–27.

32. M. M. Quaife (ed.), *The John Askin Papers* (2 vols.; Detroit, 1928–31), p. 343, Robert Nichol to John Askin, June 15, 1901.

33. C. E. Cartwright (ed.), *Life and Letters of the late Hon. Richard Cartwright* (Toronto, 1876), p. 82.

34. Jones, *History of Agriculture*, p. 27.

35. It should be noted, however, that a very similar type of commercial organization developed around other seaports than Montreal. See F. M. Jones, *Middlemen in the Domestic Trade of the United States, 1800–1860* (Urbana, Ill., 1937); N. S. Buck, *The Development of the Organization of Anglo-American Trade, 1800–1850* (New Haven, 1925); L. E. Atherton, *The Pioneer Merchant in Mid-America* (Columbia, Mo., 1939).

36. Thus Forsyth, Richardson & Co., who had amalgamated with Parker, Gerrard & Ogilvie to form the XY Company in 1800, and who had united with the North West Company in 1804, turned to the importing business in 1821 when the latter company dissolved. See R. H. Fleming, "The Origin of 'Sir Alexander Mackenzie and Company,'" *Canadian Historical Review*, IX, no. 2 (June 1928), 137–155.

37. *Simcoe Papers*, II, 54–55, Simcoe to Dundas, December 23, 1793. See also Simcoe to Dorchester, June 15, 1794 (*ibid.*, p. 265) for the measures taken by Simcoe to offset the influence of Hamilton and Cartwright.

38. *Ibid.*, II, 150–151, McGill to Simcoe, January 8, 1793.

39. See R. F. Gourlay, *Statistical Account of Upper Canada* (London, 1822), I, 226. Gourlay stated that in 1810 there were 132 licensed retailers in Upper Canada, together with 76 licensed peddlers, who carried on the trade of the country by "a species of indirect barter."

40. *Simcoe Papers*, II, 151–152, McGill to Simcoe, February 10, 1794.

41. Robert Hamilton had accumulated 35,625 acres by June 18, 1799 (*Russell Papers*, III, 241–242). As we might expect, this tendency to accumulate land was not entirely a matter for self-congratulation to the merchants.

42. John Howison, *Sketches of Upper Canada* (Edinburgh, 1821), p. 81.

43. E. A. Cruikshank, "A Country Merchant in Upper Canada," Ontario Historical Society, *Papers and Records*, XXV (1929), 145–190.

44. For all practical purposes, £1 currency may be taken as having been equivalent to $4.00 or 18s. sterling.

45. A. Shortt, "Economic Effect of the War of 1812 on Upper Canada," Ontario Historical Society, *Papers and Records*, X (1913), 79–85; Jones, *History of Agriculture*, p. 26.

46. J. W. Pratt, *The Expansionists of 1812* (New York, 1925) and A. L. Burt, *The United States, Great Britain, and British North America from the Revolution to the Establishment of Peace after the War of 1812* (New Haven, 1940). Pratt emphasizes the grievances and ambitions of the American West as contributing to the outbreak of war, while Burt seems to ascribe to them only minor importance. For an irenic interpretation, see J. B. Brebner, *North Atlantic Triangle* (New Haven, 1945), pp. 81–83.

47. Michilimackinac, which the British forces, with the help of the North West Company, took pains to seize in the early stages of the war, played a similar role, though in addition it had a symbolic importance for the Indians. See on this subject C. P. Stacey, "The Myth of the Unguarded Frontier," *American Historical Review*, LVI (October 1950), 1–18; A. T. Mahan, *Sea Power in its Relation to the War of 1812* (London, 1905).

48. *Simcoe Papers*, I, 90, Simcoe to Dundas, December 7, 1791.

49. "Tacitus" (De Witt Clinton), *The Canal Policy of the State of New York* (Albany, 1821), pp. 18–19.

50. *Ibid.*, pp. 19–20.

51. *Ibid.*

52. Charles G. Haines (ed.), *Public Documents Relating to the New York Canals*

(New York, 1821), pp. 77–100, Memorial of the Citizens of New York, March 1816.

53. *Ibid.*, pp. 87–88.

54. Thus James Geddes, surveyor and engineer, argued in 1808 that "it would be bad policy in the United States to open a communication for sloops between Erie and Ontario, as the products of all the upper lakes would, on their passage to the ocean, come into Ontario and when there, the lockage to the tide in the St. Lawrence being only 206 feet, while it is 574 feet to the tide in the Hudson, there would be danger of the whole lakes trade being diverted to a port in the territory of another nation." See Henry W. Hill, "Historical Sketch of Niagara Ship Canal Projects," Buffalo Historical Society, *Publications*, XXII (1918), 201–266. It should also be noted that there were political advantages in a longer route, since more communities could be expected to support the project in the legislature. In the case of the Erie Canal, the longer route had the further advantage that it would tap and stimulate local traffic in northern New York State, thus providing an important source of revenue independent of the Erie's competitive success in the through trade.

55. "Tacitus", *Canal Policy*, speech of De Witt Clinton to New York legislature, 1819.

56. Haines, p. xxxiv.

57. D. G. Creighton, *The Commercial Empire of the St. Lawrence, 1760–1850* (Toronto, 1937) ; "The Commercial Class in Canadian Politics, 1792–1840," Canadian Political Science Association, *Papers*, 1933.

58. The phrase is taken from J. P. Merritt, *Biography of the Hon. William Hamilton Merritt, M.P.* (St. Catharines, 1875), p. 75.

59. H. C. Pentland, "The Role of Capital in Canadian Economic Development before 1875," *Canadian Journal of Economics and Political Science*, XVI, no. 4 (November 1950), 457–474.

60. The number of immigrants arriving at Quebec each year rose from 12,648 in 1827 to 15,945 in 1829, 28,000 in 1830, 50,254 in 1831, and 51,746 in 1832. About two thirds of these immigrants came from Ireland. See A. Shortt and A. G. Doughty (eds.), *Canada and its Provinces* (22 vols., Toronto, 1914–17), IV, 577.

61. Pentland, "Capital in Canadian Development," p. 458.

CHAPTER II. PROMOTION

1. J. J. Talman (ed.), "Memoirs of Thomas Merritt, Esq.," in *Loyalist Narratives from Upper Canada* (Toronto, 1946).

2. Public Archives of Canada, *Merritt Papers*, vol. 17, Merritt's journal for 1823.

3. Catharine Rodman, daughter of Dr. Jedediah Prendergast, of Mayville in New York State, whom he married on March 13, 1815.

4. Can. Arch., *Merritt Papers*, vol. 17, Merritt's journal for 1823; *ibid.*, vol. 1, W. H. Merritt to Catharine Merritt, June 3, 1817, to Mary Hamilton Merritt, September 18, 1817.

5. *Ibid.*, vol. 17, Thomas Adams to W. H. Merritt (bond), March 27, 1816.

6. *Ibid.*, vol. 17, abstract of invoices of merchandise (1815) ; J. P. Merritt, *Biography of the Hon. W. H. Merritt* (St. Catharines, 1875), pp. 38–40.

7. See F. M. Jones, *Middlemen in the Domestic Trade of the United States, 1800–1860* (Urbana, Ill., 1937) ; R. L. Jones, *History of Agriculture in Ontario, 1613–1850* (Toronto, 1946), pp. 29 ff.

8. Cartwright to Davison & Co., November 4, 1797, in C. E. Cartwright (ed.), *Life and Letters of the late Hon. Richard Cartwright* (Toronto, 1876), p. 76.

9. W. A. Langton (ed.), *Early Days in Upper Canada: Letters of John Langton from the Backwoods of Canada and the Audit Office of the Province of Canada* (Toronto, 1926), p. 201.

10. Can. Arch., *Merritt Papers*, vol. 28, field notes of a level taken between Chippawa and Twelve Mile Creek, September 28, 1818.

11. This is not to be taken literally. The Niagara River, in a distance of 32 miles between Lake Erie and Lake Ontario, drops 326 feet; only about half of this drop takes place at Niagara Falls. See L. J. Chapman and D. F. Putnam, *The Physiography of Southern Ontario* (Toronto, 1951), p. 113.

12. See J. F. Caley, *Palaeozoic Geology of the Toronto-Hamilton Area, Ontario* (Geological Survey, Memoir 224, Ottawa, 1940), p. 8.

13. John Clark, who represented Niagara in the Assembly, voted in favor of the first charter for the Welland Canal Company in 1824, and in consequence lost his seat at the next election; but he was returned again in the election after that, as "its effects were so prominent . . . by money being then in the country from the canal." See "Memoirs of Col. John Clark," Ontario Historical Society, *Papers and Records*, VII (1906), 157–192.

14. Upper Canada Assembly *Journals*, November 4, 1818.

15. Perhaps partly because he had at the same time a petition before the Assembly in his own name. This was a prayer for a bounty on the domestic production of salt, or a duty on the importation of American salt. Merritt stated in this petition that he had already bored through 176 feet of solid rock and had gone to considerable expense to erect works and boiling kettles. See Upper Canada Assembly *Journals*, November 4, 1818.

16. Niagara *Gleaner*, October 29, 1818, in E. A. Cruikshank, "The News of Niagara a Century Ago," Ontario Historical Society, *Papers and Records*, XXIII (1926), 54–55.

17. Upper Canada Assembly *Journals*, November 6 and November 17, 1818.

18. H. P. Hill, "The Construction of the Rideau Canal, 1826–1832," Ontario Historical Society, *Papers and Records*, XXII (1925), 117; E. A. Cruikshank, "The Inception of the Welland Canal," *ibid.*, p. 60; C. P. Stacey, "An American Plan for a Canadian Campaign," *American Historical Review*, XLVI (January 1941), 348–358.

19. Cruikshank, "Inception of the Welland Canal."

20. On May 20, 1793, Hamilton had proposed to Simcoe the construction of a "Tract Road for dragging boats from the Welland Creek to Fort Erie," and a canal with a lock at the rapids below Fort Erie. (*Simcoe Papers*, I, 332–333.) Six years later, on June 15, 1799, he petitioned the legislature, in company with Thomas Clark and George Forsyth, for permission to improve the highway between Queenston and Fort Erie and "to construct a canal with locks to facilitate the passage of boats at the rapids of this latter place." (Upper Canada Assembly *Journals*, June 15, 1799.) A bill was introduced to give the necessary authority, but it aroused wide opposition and was therefore dropped. See E. A. Cruikshank, "The Centenary of the Welland Canal," Welland County Historical Society, *Papers and Records*, I (1924), 1–35.

21. Cruikshank, "Inception of the Welland Canal," p. 60.

22. Upper Canada Assembly *Journals*, February 21 and February 24, 1818.

23. *Ibid.*, March 10, 1818.

24. *Ibid.*, October 30, 1818.

25. *Ibid.*, November 19, 1818.

26. *Ibid.*, 1819.

27. Cartwright, *Life and Letters*, p. 66; Shortt, "Economic Effect of the War of 1812," p. 80; Jones, *History of Agriculture*, p. 26.

28. James Stevenson, *The War of 1812 in Connection with the Army Bill Act* (Montreal, 1892).

29. The rapid conversion of Army Bills is demonstrated by the following figures of bills in circulation at various dates during 1815: February 19, £1,300,000; April 24, £1,211,857; May 22, £1,207,192; June 19, £1,193,531; September 11, £504,376 15s. 0d;

October 9, £434,990 15s. 0d.; November 6, £407,151; December 4, £396,778. See Stevenson, *Army Bill Act*, pp. 58, 63, and *passim*.

30. D. G. Barnes, *A History of the English Corn Laws from 1660–1846* (London, 1930), chapters VII and VIII.

31. Jones, *History of Agriculture*, pp. 39–40.

32. John Howison, *Sketches of Upper Canada* (Edinburgh, 1821), p. 81.

33. The problem had been foreseen by Richard Cartwright in 1792, when he wrote: "As long as the British Government shall think it proper to hire people to come over to eat our flour we shall go on very well, and continue to make a figure, but when once we come to export our produce, the disadvantages of our remote inland situation will operate in their full force, and the very large portion of the price of our produce that must be absorbed by the expense of transporting it to the place of export, and the enhanced value which the same cost must add to every article of European manufacture, will give an effective check to the improvement of the country beyond a certain extent." (*Life and Letters*, pp. 49–50, Cartwright to Todd, October 21, 1792.)

34. Upper Canada Assembly *Journals*, March 31, 1821.

35. For a more detailed treatment of this episode in Merritt's career, see the author's "A New Way to Pay Old Debts," in William Miller (ed.), *Men in Business* (Cambridge, Mass., 1952).

36. Upper Canada Assembly *Journals*, March 31, 1821.

37. Report of the Commission on the Improvement of Internal Navigation (1823). See Can. Arch., Series Q, 335–2, pp. 287–309.

38. T. C. Keefer, *The Canals of Canada* (Montreal, 1894), p. 5.

39. C. P. Stacey, "The Myth of the Unguarded Frontier," *American Historical Review*, LVI, no. 1 (October 1950), 1–18.

40. Can. Arch., Series C, 43, p. 35, Sir J. S. Smyth to General Mann, August 17, 1826.

41. I have been unable to secure any information regarding the personal history or technical qualifications of Hiram Tibbet beyond that given in the text; nor does there appear to have been any serious surveying for an American Niagara canal in progress at this time.

42. Can. Arch., Upper Canada Sundries, report of Hiram Tibbet, May 10, 1823.

43. Can. Arch., *Merritt Papers*, vol. 17, Merritt to Mrs. Merritt, March 9, 1823.

44. J. L. McDougall, *The Welland Canal to 1841* (unpublished M.A. thesis, University of Toronto, 1923), chap. II.

45. For the various abortive projects for an American Niagara canal, see Henry W. Hill, "Historical Sketch of Niagara Ship Canal Projects," Buffalo Historical Society, *Publications*, XXII (1918), 201–266. In 1798 the legislature of New York State had incorporated a Niagara Canal Company, but apparently nothing further was done. In 1808 James Geddes surveyed a route for a canal between Lakes Erie and Ontario as a part of the general surveys for the proposed water communication between Lake Erie and the Hudson River, and in 1826 Nathan Roberts carried out a similar survey for a group of private individuals.

46. Can. Arch., Upper Canada Sundries, Merritt to Hillier, June 2, 1823.

47. It is interesting in this connection to recall Lord Elgin's appraisal of Merritt at a rather later stage in his career: "Merritt is I think an honest man, that is to say I do not believe that he is actuated by any mean or personal motive in the course which he takes — nor do I concieve that he attempts to decieve others until he has first succeeded in decieving himself. He is very illogical however, and like most one idead men, utterly unscrupulous in his mode of grouping together facts and figures when he has a case to make." See A. G. Doughty (ed.), *The Elgin-Grey Papers, 1846–*

1852 (4 vols., Ottawa, 1937), II, 762 ff., Elgin to Grey, December 11, 1850. (Spelling as in original.)

48. The dates for the petition and charter given by W. H. Merritt in his *Brief Review of the Origin, Progress, Present State, and Future Prospects of the Welland Canal* (St. Catharines, 1852), p. 3, are not correct.

49. For a more extended discussion of this point, see the article by the author entitled "The Family Compact and the Welland Canal Company," *Canadian Journal of Economics and Political Science*, XVIII, no. 1 (February 1952), 63–76.

50. The scale was as follows: one vote for each share not exceeding four; five shares, four votes; six or seven shares, five votes; eight or nine shares, six votes; ten shares, seven votes; and one vote for every five shares above ten. This provision was amended in 1825.

51. Upper Canada Assembly *Journals*, 1826–27, appendix, report of select committee on Welland Canal, evidence of J. B. Yates.

52. Section 29 provided that the Company should be managed by five directors, who had to be stockholders (though no minimum stockholding was specified) and inhabitants of the province. Two of the directors chosen each year, except the president, were ineligible for reëlection for one year after the expiry of their term of office.

53. Ernest Green, "John De Cou, Pioneer," Ontario Historical Society, *Papers and Records*, XXII (1925), 92–116.

54. Robert Keefer, *Memoirs of the Keefer Family* (Burlington, Ontario, 1935).

55. Niagara *Gleaner*, January 1, 1824, in Cruikshank, "The News of Niagara."

56. Department of Archives for the Province of Ontario, *Merritt Papers*, vol. 12, Merritt to Prendergast, January 11, 1824.

57. Can. Arch., Upper Canada Sundries, Merritt to Maitland, February 21, 1824.

58. *Ibid.*

59. J. P. Merritt, *Biography*, p. 60.

60. Merritt to Mrs. Merritt, March 14, 1824, in J. P. Merritt, *Biography*, pp. 60–61.

61. Can. Arch., Upper Canada Sundries, Merritt to Hillier, March 16, 1824.

62. Their reports are partially summarized in Can. Arch., Pamphlet 1168.

63. J. H. Dunn to president and directors of the Welland Canal Company, May 30, 1824, quoted in Cruikshank, "The News of Niagara," pp. 77–78.

64. The figures which follow are taken from various sources. For shares sold in Upper Canada, see the original subscription list in Can. Arch., *Merritt Papers*, vol. 28; for subscriptions in Lower Canada, see president and directors of Welland Canal Company to Maitland, August 8, 1824, Can. Arch., Series Q, 336–2, pp. 509–510. The board had hoped to have $100,000 taken up in the Canadas, and $50,000 elsewhere, but Merritt had not succeeded in this; see the speech by W. H. Merritt at the commencement of the Welland Canal, November 30, 1824, as given in J. P. Merritt, *Biography*, pp. 63–67. This may be a convenient point at which to warn the reader that I do not consider the formal biography of Merritt written by his son, Jedediah Prendergast Merritt, a reliable source and have therefore used it as evidence only where all other sources have failed me.

65. First stockholder list (1824). In many cases these promised subscriptions were later defaulted, and the stock forfeited for nonpayment of calls.

66. Niagara *Gleaner*, August 14, 1824, in Cruikshank, "The News of Niagara," p. 78.

67. Can. Arch., Series Q, 336–2, pp. 509–510, president and directors of Welland Canal Company to Maitland, August 8, 1824.

68. For an extended discussion of the operations of this firm, see the article by the author entitled "Yates and McIntyre: Lottery Managers," *Journal of Economic History* (Winter 1952–53).

69. See Henrietta M. Larson, "S. & M. Allen — Lottery, Exchange, and Stock Brokerage," *Journal of Economic and Business History*, III (1931), 424–445.

70. Speech by W. H. Merritt, November 30, 1824, in J. P. Merritt, *Biography*, pp. 63–67.

71. Upper Canada Assembly *Journals*, 1836–37, appendix, II, 27, Third Report of the Select Committee appointed to Examine and Enquire into the Management of the Welland Canal. (This source will be referred to hereafter as *Third Report*.)

72. *Third Report*, p. 253, Benjamin Wright to Merritt, October 1, 1824.

73. Ont. Arch., *Merritt Papers*, vol. 12, Merritt to Mrs. Merritt, October 18, 1824.

74. Speech by W. H. Merritt, November 30, 1824, in J. P. Merritt, *Biography*, pp. 63–67.

75. Ont. Arch., *Merritt Papers*, vol. 12, Merritt to Mrs. Merritt, November 24, 1824.

76. *Third Report*, p. 196. Originally it was to be only nine feet wide, but the dimensions were enlarged at the suggestion of the New York stockholders to give the same "clearance" as the Erie Canal; see *Third Report*, pp. 14–15, New York stockholders to Keefer, December 22, 1824, and *Welland Canal Company Directors' Report*, February 1, 1825.

77. *Third Report*, pp. 14–15, New York stockholders to Keefer, December 22, 1824.

78. Can. Arch., Series Q, 336–2, pp. 290–292, Barrie to Maitland, June 15, 1824.

79. *Ibid.*, pp. 506–507, Maitland to Bathurst, November 8, 1824.

80. Can. Arch., Series Q, 371–A, p. 5, Bathurst to Maitland, January 29, 1825.

81. Ont. Arch., *Merritt Papers*, vol. 12, Merritt to Mrs. Merritt, November 24, 1824.

82. *Ibid.*, Merritt to Mrs. Merritt, January 13, 1825.

83. *Ibid.*, Merritt to Prendergast, January 13, 1825.

CHAPTER III. CONSTRUCTION

1. *Welland Canal Company Directors' Report*, February 1, 1825; John H. Thompson (ed.), *Jubilee History of Thorold Township and Town* (Thorold, Ont., 1897–98), pp. 111–112.

2. *Third Report*, p. 242, evidence of W. H. Merritt. In this testimony, taken in 1835, Merritt stated: "My own judgment was at the time against the enlarged dimension, as I did not view the propect of obtaining so large a capital as favorable as those who I admitted to be far more competent judges." This is hardly consistent with his arguments in favor of enlargement quoted above, p. 55.

3. Upper Canada Assembly *Journals*, 1825–26, appendix, report of select committee on petitions of president and directors of the Welland Canal Company.

4. The reasons given for this hostility are not entirely without an element of humor. The "Petition of Sundry Inhabitants of the District of Niagara" (*ibid.*) stated that the proposed change in the route would "overflow some hundreds of acres of the best meadow lands in the Township of Thorold with a mass of stagnated water much to the injury of your petitioners, and His Majesty's subjects in general, both in health and property; throwing back water over roads, and bridges, and on Mr. John Crook's kitchen floor. . ." More seriously, the successful construction of the canal would mean the eclipse of Niagara as a commercial entrepôt.

5. *Papers respecting Claims of Shareholders in the late Welland Canal Company for Arrears of Interest* (Quebec, 1853), statement by W. H. Merritt.

6. Upper Canada Assembly *Journals*, 1833–34, appendix, letter from J. B. Yates to chairman of select committee on Welland Canal petition.

7. *Annual Report for 1825*.

8. Upper Canada Assembly *Journals*, 1825–26, appendix, report of select committee on petitions of president and directors of the Welland Canal Company, evidence of J. H. Dunn.

9. *Ibid.*

10. *Annual Report for 1826.* It should be noted that the dimensions had again been changed, this time to twenty-six feet width on bottom and fifty-six feet on the surface, with a depth of eight feet. The dimensions of the Deep Cut remained unchanged.

11. Can. Arch., Upper Canada Sundries, By to Hillier, March 1, 1827.

12. The substance of his report may be found in John MacTaggart, *Three Years in Canada, an Account of the Actual State of the Country in 1826–28* (London, 1829).

13. Thomas resigned on June 9, 1827, for reasons unknown. For information on Barrett, see Noble E. Whitford, *History of the Canal System of the State of New York* (2 vols., Albany, 1906), p. 1148.

14. *Annual Report for 1827.*

15. *Ibid.,* but see also W. H. Merritt, "Account of the Welland Canal, Upper Canada," *The American Journal of Science and Arts* (Benjamin Silliman, ed., New Haven), XIV (July 1828), 159–168. Phelps' machine was merely a simple pulley, by which the weight of an empty cart descending the bank was used to help raise a loaded cart. This was apparently the first use of machinery of any kind (beyond ox-carts, plows, and shovels) on the Deep Cut.

16. Ont. Arch., *Merritt Papers,* vol. 12, Merritt to Prendergast, April 29, 1827.

17. *Annual Report for 1828.* William Kingsford in his *The Canadian Canals* (Toronto, 1865) takes the Company to task for this decision, arguing that the correct policy would have been to persevere with the Deep Cut. "Any engineer knows, that by the help of good drainage and with banks of sufficient slope protected by sods, any cut may be secured" (p. 76). One wonders how Geddes and Barrett could have failed to think of a remedy so simple and practicable. And some scepticism as to the reliability of Kingsford's views is perhaps pardonable in the light of the fact that as late as 1871 the Canadian Department of Public Works was still wrestling with the same problem. If, in spite of the assistance of steam dredges and the accumulated technical know-how of four decades of intensive canal-building, the government engineers in 1871 still had not succeeded in reducing the Deep Cut to Lake Erie level, it is difficult to be very critical of Geddes and Barrett in 1828. See the statement by Langevin, Minister of Public Works, in *Parliamentary Debates,* Dominion of Canada, 1st Parlt., 4th Session (Ottawa, 1871), p. 239.

18. *Third Report,* p. 382; Whitford, p. 1154.

19. *Third Report,* p. 383, reports of Geddes and Barrett.

20. Water level on Lake Erie was normally 12 feet above water level on the River Welland. The Grand River dam would raise the water level in the reservoir 5 feet above Lake Erie, and therefore 17 feet above the Welland. Allowing 2 feet total fall in the cutting from Grand River to the Deep Cut (Geddes insisted on ¾ inches declivity per mile), the new water level in the Deep Cut would be 15 feet above the old or Welland River level — ample to permit raising the bottom of the canal above the quicksands.

21. Upper Canada Assembly *Journals,* 1830, appendix, report of select committee on Welland and Burlington Bay canals, evidence of W. H. Merritt.

22. In judging the seriousness of Barrie's objections, it is well to remember that the Rush-Bagot agreement between Great Britain and the United States, concluded in 1817 and ratified in April 1818, limited each of the contracting parties to one vessel not over one hundred tons burden and armed with one eighteen-pound cannon on Lake Ontario, and on the upper Lakes to two vessels of like tonnage and armament. Captain Basil Hall, the well-known British traveler, visited this so-called naval base at Grand River in July 1827 and described it as a scene of utter desolation. See his *Travels in North America* (3 vols., Edinburgh, 1829), I, 241.

23. For these incidents, see Can. Arch., Upper Canada Sundries, Barrie to Col-

borne, March 16 and March 30, 1829; *Supplementary Annual Report for 1829*; Can. Arch., Series C, 48, pp. 63–71, 231, and 281–286; and McDougall, chap. II.

24. Barrett's Report, December 10, 1829.

25. Merritt, *Brief Review*, p. 8.

26. Barrett's Report, December 10, 1829.

27. *Supplementary Annual Report for 1829*; see also the Appendix to this volume.

28. *Third Report*, p. 404, prospectus for Erie and Ontario Transportation Company.

29. *Third Report*, p. 442, minutes of board.

30. The board stated that "no rational person can, for a moment, hesitate in declaring that the work cannot, and must not, stop short of the original design" (*Supplementary Annual Report for 1829*). If by "the original design" they meant the plans proposed in 1824 and 1825, they were talking nonsense, for the slides in the Deep Cut had made both these plans impossible, and a direct cut to Lake Erie had been a feature of neither. The proposal for the new cutting was really a recognition of the inadequacy of the "original design."

31. *Annual Report for 1830*.

32. Port Robinson (named after John Beverley Robinson, the attorney general) was the name given to the point at the south end of the Deep Cut where vessels locked down to the Welland River.

33. By the end of 1831 the canal-building program of the state of Ohio, begun in 1825, was almost completed, 343 miles of canal out of the 400 originally planned having been constructed. See Chester E. Finn, "The Ohio Canals: Public Enterprise on the Frontier," *Ohio State Archaeological and Historical Quarterly*, LI, no. 1 (January-March, 1942); C. P. McClelland and C. C. Huntington, *History of the Ohio Canals* (Columbus, 1905).

34. One of the two directors appointed by the legislature.

35. *Annual Report for 1831*.

36. *Ibid.* The rumor was false, but in September the embankment near the aqueduct did give way, causing an interruption of one month at the busiest part of the season.

37. *Ibid.*

38. *Annual Report for 1832*.

39. *Ibid.*

40. John Macaulay, W. B. Robinson, and Absalom Shade.

41. Upper Canada Assembly *Journals*, 1833–34, appendix, report of commissioners of the Welland Canal.

42. *Ibid.*; Wright stated: "Taking the whole work as it now exists, the greatest error I have seen is the plan of constructing the locks: I do not object to wooden locks, in a case like the Welland Canal, but I think the plan of block work for the sides of the locks is very objectionable, and more particularly the plan of securing the ties by dovetails not passing through the front or face timbers; and for this reason, a little bad workmanship, or decay in the timber, makes a weak place in the work; and this with a clay puddle behind it, will certainly cause these ties to loose their hold upon the front timbers, being only let in."

43. *Ibid.*

44. Upper Canada Assembly *Journals*, 1833–34, appendix, letter of J. B. Yates to chairman of select committee on Welland Canal petition, January 9, 1834.

45. *Ibid.*, report of select committee on Welland Canal petition.

46. *Annual Report for 1834*.

47. *Ibid.*; but see footnote 51.

48. *Annual Report for 1835*.

49. This crop failure was not, however, reflected in Erie Canal tolls. Tolls on the

Erie rose from $1,179,744.97 in 1834 to $1,375,821.26 in 1835 (Whitford, p. 1064). The Erie had, of course, the benefit of a considerable volume of local traffic from western New York, while the Welland was almost entirely dependent on the through trade.

50. The notice appeared in the New York press on October 20, just when fall shipments were being arranged. It stated: "The Commissioners of the Welland Canal contemplate closing the Canal on the 1st November, in order to commence the improving of the Canal, and having it in perfect order by the time the Erie Canal opens in the spring. Goods will not be shipped from Oswego, destined for Lake Erie, after the 25th of October."

51. These figures are very unreliable. The *Third Report* gives £4300 for 1834 and £5807 for 1835. The *Annual Report for 1835*, however, gives £3719 for 1834, while Merritt's statement in *Papers Respecting the Claims of Shareholders* . . . gives £3719 for 1834 and only £3807 for 1835. The discrepancies may arise from the inclusion of water power rents, profits from forwarding operations, and so on, in certain of the figures and not in others, but this is nowhere expressly stated.

52. At the end of 1837 these notes were being accepted by the Bank of Upper Canada in settlement of outstanding debts, an indication of their general acceptance at a time of great financial stringency. See Coventry's Memoir in Can. Arch., *Merritt Papers*, vol. 17.

53. *Annual Report for 1836.*

54. *Ibid.*, and Hill, "Niagara Ship Canal Projects." This was the survey carried out by Captain William G. Williams of the U. S. Topographical Engineers for a ship canal between Lakes Erie and Ontario. Williams surveyed four possible routes, the estimated costs of which varied between $2½ and $5 million. There was considerable pressure in certain quarters in New York State at this time for an American Niagara canal, to supplement the strained facilities of the Erie. In 1834 the Utica Convention memorialized the state legislature and Congress to construct a navigable communication between Lake Ontario and the Hudson River and also between Lake Erie and Lake Ontario, but Congress made no response. In 1840 the Assembly and Senate of the state resolved "That the consent of the Legislature is hereby given to the construction, by the Governor of the State, of a ship canal around the Falls of Niagara," and that Congress be requested to pass a bill for the purpose. Again nothing was done. In 1853 a private corporation was formed with a capital stock of $5 million to construct the canal, but did not commence operations. A similar fate befell the Niagara Ship Canal Company, formed in 1866 with a capital of $6 million.

55. Only a fraction of this large subscription was actually raised; see the preamble to the purchase act of 1843 (7 Vic., c. 34).

56. Their report is summarized in Lieutenant Colonel George Phillpotts, *First and Second Reports on the Inland Navigation of the Canadas, 1839–40.*

57. Can. Arch., Series C, 59, pp. 200–211, Cooper to Rowan, with enclosures, October 19, 1839.

58. For the Cornwall Canal, see G. P. de T. Glazebrook, *History of Transportation in Canada* (Toronto, 1938), p. 84; Kingsford, *Canadian Canals*, pp. 52–57.

59. Lt. Col. Phillpotts, *First and Second Reports on the Inland Navigation of the Canadas* (Can. Arch., Series C, 59, and pamphlet 1876).

60. Report of directors to Sir Francis Bond Head, February 12, 1838, in Merritt, *Brief Review*, pp. 43–44.

61. Upper Canada Assembly *Journals*, 1839–40, appendix, pt. II, p. 23, memorial of New York stockholders, March 18, 1839.

CHAPTER IV. FINANCE

1. Upper Canada Assembly *Journals*, 1825.

2. Can. Arch., Upper Canada Sundries, Merritt to Hillier, March 21, 1825; *ibid.*, Burton to Maitland, April 2, 1825.

3. Divided into 16,000 shares of common stock of a par value of £12 10s. 0d. currency ($50.00 or £11 5s. 0d. sterling).

4. J. P. Merritt, *Biography*, p. 74; *Third Report*, p. 211, evidence of W. H. Merritt.

5. Merritt, *Brief Review*, pp. 9–10.

6. See Adam Shortt, "Founders of Canadian Banking," *Journal of the Canadian Bankers' Association*, XXX (January 1923), 154–166.

7. Can. Arch., Series Q, 338, pt. 1, pp. 300–301, Maitland to Bathurst, May 19, 1825.

8. Can. Arch., Series G, 104A, Bathurst to Maitland, August 31, 1825.

9. The Canada Company was formed by John Galt in 1824, and chartered in 1826. It purchased from the British government 1,000,100 acres of land in Upper Canada, known as the Huron Tract, agreeing to pay to the British government the sum of £295,000 sterling in sixteen annual installments in consideration for this grant. Almost the whole of the capital stock of the Company was owned in London. The opening up of the Huron Tract depended very directly upon the improvement of transportation facilities, both to bring out settlers and their effects and to provide a remunerative market for their produce. This may explain the interest of the Canada Company in the Welland Canal. See John Galt, *Autobiography* (London, 1833); R. and K. M. Lizars, *In the Days of the Canada Company* (Toronto, 1896); Shortt and Doughty, *Canada and its Provinces*, III, 333–336 and IV, 514–515. For biographical information on Galt and McGillivray, see W. S. Wallace, *Dictionary of Canadian Biography* (2 vols., Toronto, 1945), I, 224–225 and II, 401.

10. Upper Canada Assembly *Journals*, 1825–26, report of select committee on petition of president and directors of Welland Canal Company, evidence of J. H. Dunn; minutes of board, April 14, 1825; *Third Report*, p. 268, evidence of W. H. Merritt.

11. *Third Report*, evidence of W. H. Merritt, letter from Simon McGillivray to J. H. Dunn and W. Allan (no date).

12. Upper Canada Assembly *Journals*, 1825–26, report of select committee on Welland Canal, evidence of J. H. Dunn; *Journals*, 1826–27, report of select committee on Welland Canal, evidence of J. B. Yates; *Annual Report for 1825*.

13. Upper Canada Assembly *Journals*, 1825–26, report of select committee on Welland Canal, evidence of J. H. Dunn.

14. For biographical data on H. J. Boulton, see Wallace, *Dictionary of Canadian Biography*, I, 65.

15. Minutes of board, November 22, 1825.

16. Can. Arch., *Merritt Papers*, vol. 2, McGillivray to Merritt, September 21, 1825.

17. Ont. Arch., *Merritt Papers*, vol. 12, Boulton to Merritt, September 26, 1825.

18. Upper Canada Assembly *Journals*, 1825–26, report of select committee on Welland Canal, evidence of William Allen.

19. *Third Report*, evidence of W. H. Merritt, letter from Merritt to Dunn, October 31, 1825.

20. Upper Canada Assembly *Journals*, 1825–26, report of select committee on Welland Canal, evidence of William Allan.

21. *Third Report*, evidence of W. H. Merritt, letter from McGillivray to Dunn and Allan (no date).

22. *Ibid.*, Merritt to Dunn, October 31, 1825.

23. *Ibid.*, Allan to Merritt, October 15, 1825.

24. *Ibid.*, Dunn to Merritt, November 7, 1825. As late as June 1827 Dunn was still worrying: "Altho' I cannot assure myself of a knowledge of anything very wrong, yet that transaction of Mr. Boulton's is what I cannot reconcile at all. He makes a charge for going to England on the affairs of the Welland Canal, and leaves the Country without any Documents or instructions, or anything else, and then makes a charge for his expences to England when he knows well that his own Private Business carry'd him there." (Can. Arch., *Merritt Papers*, vol. 2, Dunn to Merritt, June 23, 1827.) Boulton finally refunded the £300.

25. Can. Arch., *Merritt Papers*, vol. 2, Dunn to Merritt, June 23, 1827.

26. This incident is tactfully glossed over in the *Annual Report for 1826*. Mc-Gillivray proved a broken reed; the 122 shares which had been sold to him were forfeited and sold at auction at the end of 1826 (*Third Report*, p. 300).

27. Upper Canada Assembly *Journals*, 1825–26, report of select committee on Welland Canal, evidence of William Allan.

28. Ont. Arch., *Merritt Papers*, vol. 12, Merritt to Prendergast, December 25, 1825.

29. Upper Canada Assembly *Journals*, 1825–26, report of select committee on Welland Canal, evidence of J. H. Dunn.

30. *Ibid.*

31. *Ibid.*, report of committee.

32. Proctor's failure involved the Company in a loss of £3428. See Upper Canada Assembly *Journals*, 1830, appendix, report of select committee on Welland and Burlington canals; *Third Report*, pp. 211 ff.

33. Minutes of board, June 22, 1826.

34. *Annual Report for 1826.*

35. Upper Canada Assembly *Journals*, 1826–27, appendix, report of select committee on Welland Canal, evidence of W. H. Merritt. For information on Prime, Ward & Sands, see Ralph W. Hidy, *The House of Baring in American Trade and Finance* (Cambridge, Mass., 1949), pp. 49, 70. The Barings held the account of this firm from 1810.

36. *Annual Report for 1826.*

37. Minutes of board, September 2, 1826. Bosanquet, Pitt & Co. were appointed the Company's bankers for this transaction.

38. Minutes of board, September 2, 1826.

39. Ont. Arch., *Merritt Papers*, vol. 2, Nehemiah Merritt to W. H. Merritt.

40. Can. Arch., Series Q, 344, pt. 1, pp. 148–153, Dunn to Hillier, March 10, 1827.

41. Upper Canada Assembly *Journals*, 1826–27, appendix, report of select committee on Welland Canal.

42. Can. Arch., Series Q, 371A, pp. 127–129, Bathurst to Maitland, September 30, 1826.

43. Can. Arch., Series C, 43, pp. 33–53.

44. This was an estimate made in 1825 for a canal from the River Welland to Lake Ontario only.

45. Can. Arch., Series Q, 344, pt. 1, pp. 41–42, Dunn to Hillier, December 26, 1826.

46. Upper Canada Assembly *Journals*, 1826–27, appendix, report of select committee on Welland Canal.

47. Can. Arch., Series Q, 179, pt. 1, pp. 383–391, Dalhousie to Bathurst, April 20, 1827.

48. Can. Arch., Series Q, 344, pt. 1, pp. 148–153, Dunn to Hillier, March 10, 1827.

49. Twenty-seven per cent still due on £83,000 of stock was £22,410. The "one-ninth" grant amounted to £16,360 sterling, or £18,177 currency. Adding to this the

£50,000 subscribed by the provincial government, we get a total of £90,587. Dunn's arithmetic erred on the generous side.

50. Can. Arch., Series Q, 344, pt. 1, Maitland to Bathurst, March 12, 1827; 345, pt. 1, pp. 71–72, Hill to Stanley, December 18, 1827; 371A, pp. 273–274, Huskisson to Maitland, December 25, 1827; 344, pt. 2, pp. 573–575, Maitland to Huskisson, December 31, 1827.

51. Can. Arch., *Merritt Papers*, vol. 2, Yates to Merritt, December 12, 1827. According to the *Annual Report for 1827*, the capital stock was at this time distributed as follows:

Private individuals	6893 shares	£86,162	10s.	0d.
Government of Upper Canada	4000 shares	50,000	0s.	0d.
Government of Lower Canada	2000 shares	25,000	0s.	0d.
Unsubscribed	3107 shares	38,837	10s.	0d.

There had actually been paid in and expended on the canal the following amounts:

81 per cent on 8893 shares held by Government of Lower Canada and individuals	£90,041	12s.	6d.
100 per cent on 4000 shares held by Government of Upper Canada	50,000	0s.	0d.
Provincial loan	25,000	0s.	0d.
	£165,041	12s.	0d.

52. *Annual Report for 1827*; *Third Report*, p. 382, evidence of W. H. Merritt.

53. *Third Report*, minutes of board, February 14, 1827.

54. J. P. Merritt, *Biography*, pp. 90–92, extracts from Merritt's journal for 1828.

55. McDougall, chap. III.

56. Ont. Arch., *Merritt Papers*, vol. 12, W. H. Merritt to Thomas Merritt, May 13, 1828.

57. J. P. Merritt, *Biography*, pp. 95–99, extracts from Merritt's journal for 1828.

58. Can. Arch., *Merritt Papers*, vol. 17, prospectus "The Welland Canal" (1828); vol. 27, list of subscribers to Welland Canal (1829); vol. 28, Merritt's memorandum book, 1827–43; vol. 29, Welland Canal Ledger.

59. Upper Canada Assembly *Journals*, 1830, report of select committee on Welland and Burlington canals, evidence of W. H. Merritt.

60. Upper Canada Assembly *Journals*, 1833–34, appendix, report of select committee on Welland Canal, letter of J. B. Yates to chairman.

61. Minutes of board, December 15, 1828, in *Third Report*. As Yates was the only large stockholder in close communication with the board, the opinion quoted may be taken as illustrative of his views.

62. *Annual Report for 1828*; *Third Report*, pp. 382 ff., evidence of W. H. Merritt.

63. *Annual Report for 1828*.

64. *Ibid.*

65. *Ibid.*

66. Minutes of board, November 21, 1828. Dunn drew on the Treasury in favor of Ellice & Co., and then on Ellice in favor of the Bank of Upper Canada, which was the Company's treasurer. There is no indication of the commission charged by Ellice & Co., but the charges made by the Bank of Upper Canada were a subject of complaint on at least one occasion. See, for example, *Third Report*, p. 415: "It appears that on a part of the loan from England the Bank only allowed a premium of 8 per cent, although the rate of exchange was higher at New York at the time the bills were sold, while drafts on that city had a premium here — nor has the Bank allowed the Company any premium on the instalments paid in New York, in current money, by the stockholders."

67. Can. Arch., Series Q, 354, pp. 89–96, Colborne to Murray, March 10, 1830, with enclosures.

68. Bosanquet, Pitt & Co. had been appointed, also on November 21, 1828, bankers to the Company in London, to receive installments on the stock and dividends, should any materialize. They were immediately drawn on for £2500, and there seems to have been no difficulty in this connection. For future negotiations with E. and R. Ellice & Co., see Yates' report to the president and directors in *Third Report*, p. 469. Ellice told Yates that "he considered the delay of the Company in not immediately answering the terms of his former conditional arrangement with Mr. Merritt to have released him from all honorary and legal obligations to comply with them, and the person who was to have united in the engagement had utterly refused when they heard of the accident in the Deep Cut, considering the whole project . . . to have wholly failed; such was still [summer of 1830] the prevailing opinion, and nothing but an actual use of the canal would ensure confidence."

69. On September 21 he wrote to Merritt: "I did all I could to advise the Bank Company to advance the £6000 on the security agreed upon, but I fear circumstances will prevent its being done" (J. P. Merritt, *Biography*, p. 121). The bank finally lent at least £3000 to pay off the laborers. (Minutes of board, October 29, 1829)

70. Minutes of board, October 29, 1829.

71. On September 24, 1829 the board resolved: "That in order to meet the present expenditure . . . it is expedient to obtain the sum of £10,000 which it is understood by the Directors the Lieutenant Governor will sanction provided the Directors guarantee His Excellency from all personal responsibility." (Minutes of board, September 24, 1829) On September 28, Dunn wrote to Merritt: "I did hope no more money would be required until the water was through, but expect when that takes place we shall have no difficulty in obtaining a loan — at least through the medium of Sir John — for £10,000." (Cited, J. P. Merritt, *Biography*, p. 121.) At a later meeting the board resolved: "That the President, Directors, and Agent do hereby agree to save, defend, and bear harmless the Lieutenant Governor of this Province of and from all personal risk and responsibility for making the advance sanctioned at the previous meeting." (*Ibid.*) The Bank of Upper Canada could hardly refuse to discount a note endorsed by the lieutenant governor, and Colborne was freed from liability by the directors' guarantee. The strength of the informal ties between the board and the various lieutenant governors, up to the appointment of Sir Francis Bond Head in 1836, is one of the most remarkable features of the story.

72. *Supplementary Annual Report for 1829*; Can. Arch., Series Q, 354, pp. 89–96, Colborne to Murray, March 10, 1830. In justice to the Company, it should be noted that this sum is considerably smaller than the amount lost by the failure of Ellice & Co. and the Canada Company to honor their pledges.

73. At the end of January 1830 the provincial debt amounted to £131,722 4s. 5½d., on which 6 per cent interest was paid. £75,000 of this sum represented assistance to the Welland Canal. (Upper Canada Assembly *Journals*, 1831, appendix, p. 41.)

74. Upper Canada Assembly *Journals*, 1830, appendix, report of select committee on petition of Welland Canal Company.

75. Can. Arch., Upper Canada Sundries, Colborne to Kempt, March 8, 1830. This loan could be expended only on certain specified pieces of work — widening the cutting and making towpaths on the Niagara, Welland, and Grand rivers. It could not be used to liquidate the Company's debts.

76. As on a previous occasion (see above, p. 87), the increase in capital was Merritt's idea. Yates expressed himself frankly on the subject, in a letter which also illuminates his motives for investing in the canal: "You again speak of an increase of capital stock. My dear Sir, what good will that do when we cannot dispose of what we have? Unless the powers of banking are also given there can certainly be

no use in an increase of capital; but if that can be done, it may be advantageous to increase the capital. If however I was anxious to make a permanent investment I would rather have the canal stock if the company had no banking powers than if it had." (Can. Arch., *Merritt Papers*, vol. 2, Yates to Merritt, January 2, 1830.)

77. *Ibid.* The question of what "undoubted" security Yates was offering is a difficult one. The best he had to offer was a second mortgage.

78. Can. Arch., *Merritt Papers*, vol. 2, Yates to Merritt, January 18, 1830. It should be noted that Yates' lottery business was involved in extensive litigation at this time. Who the "Gentlemen" were against whom he inveighed so bitterly and incoherently is not indicated. But his denunciations should perhaps be taken with a grain of salt, for on February 6 he wrote: ". . . you have perhaps acted wisely in not shewing my letters, you know the people better than I do. I wrote in the expectation that what I said should be named if you thought it prudent, supposing, no doubt erroneously, that it would induce greater efforts on the part of the persons for whom it was meant, and as addressed to their better feelings in favor of the undertaking. I did not mean to convey the idea in my letter that I would not meet my engagements; but perhaps such inferences might be drawn by others . . ." (Can. Arch., *Merritt Papers*, vol. 2, Yates to Merritt, February 6, 1830.)

79. *Third Report*, p. 409, report of J. B. Yates to president and directors.

80. Can. Arch., Series Q, 355, pp. 34–35, J. Stewart to R. W. Hay, July 22, 1830; Can. Arch., *Merritt Papers*, vol. 27, Hay to Yates, July 31, 1830; *ibid.*, Yates to Bosanquet & Co., August 20, 1830.

81. *Third Report*, pp. 409 ff., report of J. B. Yates to president and directors.

82. Upper Canada Assembly *Journals*, 1831, appendix, report of select committee on Welland Canal petition, February 11, 1831.

83. Merritt, *Brief Review*, pp. 10–11.

84. See above, note 73. During 1830 J. H. Dunn, in his capacity as receiver general, wrote to Edward Ellice, Baring Brothers, Overend & Co., and Nathan Rothschild & Co. in an attempt to negotiate an issue of provincial debentures to the amount of £90,000 sterling (£100,000 currency) at par at 4 per cent per annum. He found no one willing to handle the issue.

85. Minutes of board, October 26, 1830.

86. Minutes of board, May 11 and June 2, 1831; Upper Canada State Papers, vol. 96, Dunn to lieutenant governor, July 15, 1834, and minutes of Executive Council thereon. Early in May 1834 Dunn saw Biddle, president of the Bank of the United States, in Philadelphia to arrange for the redemption of these debentures by drafts on London at the current rate of premium in Upper Canada, or by payment in specie at Dunn's office. Biddle refused, on the ground that the premium in Upper Canada was higher than in the United States, while Upper Canada currency was depreciated there. He demanded payment either by drafts on London at the rate of exchange in New York or in American specie. Dunn estimated that compliance with Biddle's demands would mean a loss to the province of about £1000 and refused to meet his wishes. The Executive Council instructed him to seek a delay. What followed is obscure. Apparently Biddle threatened to sell the debentures for what they would bring (in July 1834 Yates estimated they would sell at 90 instead of the 110 he thought they were worth), thus causing something little short of panic in the canal management. The situation was finally cleared up, it seems, through Yates' intervention. Every statute authorizing the issue of Upper Canada debentures included a clause that they were not to be sold at less than par. See Can. Arch., *Merritt Papers*, vol. 3, Yates to Merritt, July 24, 1834 and December 14, 1835.

87. Minutes of board, October 26, 1830.

88. Minutes of board, November 3, 1830.

89. *Third Report*, p. 573, examination of A. Y. Macdonell. The board decided to

make the sale by unanimous vote. See *Annual Report for 1831* for a justification of the transaction.

90. Particularly was this true of the lands which would be taken over by the Canal Company for the direct cutting to Lake Erie. This cutting had not yet been begun, but the lands and water rights involved were included in the sale to the Hydraulic Company. Wherever the new harbor on Lake Erie might be, Yates would own the best parcels of land and the most valuable mill sites.

91. *Third Report*, conclusions of committee on Mackenzie's charge number eighteen.

92. Upper Canada Assembly *Journals*, 1836, appendix, p. 27, Merritt to Rowan, May 9, 1833.

93. Thus Barrett, the engineer, reported to Merritt early in 1830: "Mr. Phelps' work goes slow from the frost. *Money will take out the frost.*" Can. Arch., *Merritt Papers*, vol. 2, Barrett to Merritt, February 7, 1830. (Italics in original.)

94. See, for example, Can. Arch., *Merritt Papers*, vol. 2, Newlove and Porter to Merritt, May 3, 1830: "H. Merritt or Black Esqs. Send by the bearer my son one hundred dollars if [you] can any way or I shall have to quit work on the Deep Cut for I have nothing to feed my Cattel on after this day and they cannot work without feed and I have three men working for me and their land is advertised for sale for the tax and I cannot releve them without your help."

95. Can. Arch., *Merritt Papers*, vol. 2, T. G. Ridout to Merritt, October 6, 1831.

96. *Ibid.*, Allan to Merritt, April 29, 1830.

97. Can. Arch., Series Q, 374, pt. 2, pp. 304–307, Colborne to Goderich, February 22, 1832.

98. Can. Arch., Series Q, 376A, pp. 75–76, Goderich to Colborne, May 30, 1932.

99. Upper Canada Assembly *Journals*, 1832–33, appendix, Welland Canal Company's balance sheet, November 1832.

100. Minutes of board, February 19, 1833. It may be noted that the bond had already been assigned to Dunn as collateral for a loan of £3000 for which he had become liable to the Bank of Upper Canada. (Minutes of board, November 19, 1832.) Apparently by February 1833 this loan had been paid off.

101. Upper Canada Assembly *Journals*, 1836, appendix, Merritt to Rowan, February 16, 1833.

102. *Ibid.*, p. 27, Boulton to Rowan, March 28, 1833.

103. *Ibid.*, Macdonell to Rowan, March 23, 1833.

104. *Ibid.*, p. 27, Merritt to Rowan, May 9, 1833.

105. *Ibid.*, Merritt to Dunn, May 9, 1833.

106. J. P. Merritt, *Biography*, p. 142.

107. See the correspondence quoted in J. P. Merritt, *Biography*, pp. 140–141.

108. Upper Canada Assembly *Journals*, 1833–34, appendix, report of commissioners of the Welland Canal.

109. *Ibid.*

110. *Ibid.*, report of committee on Welland Canal petition, letter of J. B. Yates.

111. *Ibid.*, report of commissioners.

112. *Ibid.*, p. 116, Baring Brothers & Co. to the receiver general, June 21, 1833.

113. There had previously been no statutory provision for the appointment of government directors, although, with the consent of the Company, two had been appointed each year since 1827.

114. Can. Arch., Series Q, 381, pt. 2, pp. 487–490, address from the Assembly to the King, April 1, 1834.

115. Can. Arch., Series Q, 384A, pp. 95–96, Spring Rice to Colborne, July 30, 1834.

116. Can. Arch., *Merritt Papers*, vol. 3, Yates to Merritt, April 16, 1834. In this and all other quotations the spelling of the original has been retained.

117. These were town lots and therefore valuable, selling at this time for about £25 per acre.

118. For this reason among others, the two "purchases" completely mystified the committee of investigation in 1835, who stated: "This transaction to your committee is inexplicable, no statement that they have heard has satisfied them of the justice or even expediency of an arrangement which, if applied to the ordinary transaction of life, would not only be deemed ruinous but the result of insanity. The value of the property sold, or the amount of profits received by the Hydraulic Company, is quite uncertain." (*Third Report*, conclusions of committee.)

119. Can. Arch., *Merritt Papers*, vol. 3, Yates to Merritt, November 3, 1834.

120. *Ibid.*, Yates to Merritt, January 7, 1835.

121. *Ibid.*, Yates to Merritt, April 26 and September 22, 1835.

122. *Ibid.*, Yates to Merritt, November 10, 1835.

123. Can. Arch., Upper Canada Sundries, Creighton to Rowan, December 28, 1835.

124. Can. Arch., *Merritt Papers*, vol. 3, Creighton to Merritt, January 21, 1836.

125. *Ibid.*, Yates to Ridout, transcribed in Creighton to Merritt, February 4, 1836. Yates' offer at this time was as follows: "I propose that the whole [amount] due by us to the Province be consolidated; that the Stock of the Province be [purchased]; that we give the Bond of the Company with a pledge of the Canal and Tolls for the annual interest, at such rates as shall be deemed reasonable, and the payment of the principal in 25 or twenty years — this will be fair, giving the Stockholders an opportunity untrammelled by the fear of offence to attend to their property as they should."

126. *Ibid.*, Yates to Merritt, February 27, 1836.

127. *Annual Report for 1836.*

128. On May 12, 1836 the editor of the St. Catharines *Journal* remarked that "there is not one bank in the country that will discount a note for the most paltry sum." The experiment of issuing "Welland Canal Money" was surprisingly successful, a total of $33,463 in denominations of one, five, and ten dollars being issued during 1836. It may be noted that on August 4, 1836 a meeting of the "Merchants, Farmers, Mechanicks, and other men of business in St. Catharines and vicinity" pledged themselves to accept the Company's notes at par in their business transactions. (St. Catharines *Journal*, August 4, 1836.) At the same time, the editor commented: "We feel only surprise, that the Directors did not carry their plan earlier into effect . . . we have scarcely a Bank note in circulation, except a few from Ohio." This newspaper is not, however, the most reliable of sources, as Merritt appears to have had a substantial financial interest in it.

129. Can. Arch., Upper Canada Sundries, Clark to Joseph, November 14, 1836.

130. Can. Arch., *Merritt Papers*, vol. 3, Macaulay to Merritt, August 15, 1836.

131. Can. Arch., pamphlet 2412, *Papers Respecting Claims of Shareholders in the late Welland Canal Company for Arrears of Interest* (Quebec, 1853), memorial of shareholders.

132. Can. Arch., *Merritt Papers*, vol. 4, Peter McGill to Merritt, May 20, 1837.

133. Merritt, *Brief Review*, pp. 43–44, report of directors to Sir Francis Bond Head, February 12, 1836. They gave the following figures:

Average annual cost of administration		£ 3,085	12s.	0d.
Average annual cost of repairs and improvements		13,985	3s.	6d.
Annual interest on £66,144 8s. 10d.		3,968	13s.	3d.
		£21,039	8s.	9d.
Average amount of tolls	£4,999 6s. 6d.			
Average amount of rents	2,000 0s. 0d.			
		£ 6,999	6s.	6d.
Average annual loss		£14,040	2s.	3d.

This crude average of tolls over the previous five years to provide an estimate of future earnings ignored, of course, all possibility of future increases in traffic, while the figure given for average maintenance costs included much that was not maintenance but construction.

134. Upper Canada Assembly *Journals*, 1839–40, appendix, pt. 2, p. 23.

135. Can. Arch., Series Q, 417, pt. 1, pp. 82–84, Sir George Arthur to the Marquis of Normanby, June 8, 1839.

136. Upper Canada Assembly *Journals*, 1839–40, appendix, pt. 2, report of select committee on petition of shareholders in the Welland Canal.

CHAPTER V. ENTREPRENEURSHIP

1. *Third Report*, p. 268.

2. Can. Arch., *Merritt Papers*, vol. 17, Merritt's memorandum book for 1827.

3. *Hamilton Free Press*, quoted in *British American Journal*, September 30, 1834: ". . . Hamilton Merritt, with a red Yankee pocket-book chock full of plans and estimates for a canal to connect Athabasca and the Columbia River."

4. Merritt was of course frequently a member of the board and occasionally president, as well as being agent. It is hard for us, as it undoubtedly would have been for Merritt, to say precisely in what capacity he was acting at any given time. But the point is not of much importance, for his behavior had but little connection with his particular official position.

5. Can. Arch., *Merritt Papers*, vol. 2, Dunn to Merritt, June 23, 1827.

6. Ont. Arch., *Merritt Papers*, vol. 12, Mrs. Merritt to Mrs. Prendergast, March 11, 1828.

7. Compare above, p. 111.

8. Upper Canada Assembly *Journals*, 1836–37, appendix 3, report of committee on Welland Canal.

9. Can. Arch., *Merritt Papers*, vol. 5, J. B. Robinson to Merritt, June 6, 1850.

10. J. B. Robinson to Merritt, December 13, 1833, quoted in St. Catharines *Journal*, February 25, 1836.

11. *British American Journal*, February 11, 1834.

12. *British Colonial Argus*, August 20, 1833.

13. Many must have thought their worst suspicious confirmed when there appeared a notice in the Upper Canada *Gazette* of July 19, 1834, announcing that a bill would be introduced in the next session of the legislature to tax all cultivated lands in the Niagara, London, and Western districts 3*d.* per acre to pay for the Welland Canal. The notice was unsigned and caused the Company considerable embarrassment. Its author was one Thomas Clark of Niagara, a legislative councillor and a land speculator, then engaged in promoting the Erie and Ontario Railroad, a potentially dangerous source of competition for the Welland.

14. *British American Journal*, February 18, 1834, report of debate on Welland Canal loan bill.

15. *Ibid.*

16. *Ibid.*

17. In this connection Francis Hincks gave an early demonstration of the ability to straddle a difficult issue which was to serve him in good stead in his later political career. Called in by the select committee investigating the Company's affairs in 1835–36, Hincks, then cashier of the Bank of the People, stated that the Company's books were "full of false and fictitious entries, so much so that if I was on oath I could hardly say whether I believe there are more true or false ones." See Charles Lindsey, *The Life and Times of William Lyon Mackenzie* (2 vols., Toronto, 1862), I, 347, footnote. Yet in his testimony before the committee he stated: "I really do

not think that any fraudulent intent can attach itself to any individual connected with the Books of the Company." (*Third Report*, p. 210)

18. *Third Report*, W. H. Merritt to board of directors, March 10, 1831.

19. *Ibid.*, p. 192, testimony of W. H. Merritt.

20. *Ibid.*, p. 160, testimony of David Thorburn.

21. St. Catharines *Journal*, February 25, 1836, report of Merritt's speech in the Assembly.

22. Can. Arch., *Merritt Papers*, vol. 3, J. B. Robinson to W. H. Merritt, December 4, 1835.

23. *Third Report*, p. 14, testimony of Love Newlove.

24. Can. Arch., *Merritt Papers*, vol. 2, Dunn to Merritt, June 23, 1827.

25. Upper Canada Assembly *Journals*, 1830, appendix, report of select committee on Welland and Burlington canals.

26. *Third Report*, p. 102, testimony of W. L. Mackenzie.

27. *Ibid.* The author was a certain "Mr. Bennett of New York."

28. Confidence in the superiority of the accounting methods used by these companies is by no means encouraged by such statements as the following, contained in a letter from J. H. A. Cameron (accountant to the Canada Company) and C. S. Murray (bookkeeper to the Bank of Upper Canada) to the Welland Canal Company directors, dated June 8, 1835: ". . . we have to remark upon the whole investigation, that in consideration of the expenditure of so large a sum of money, throughout a period of twelve years, in payment of accounts kept with upwards of two thousand individuals, that it is very surprising how few errors have occurred; and we believe that there are few undertakings of similar magnitude, the accounts of which have been so correctly kept . . ." (St. Catharines *Journal*, July 14, 1836, "Refutation of Slanders against Welland Canal Managers.") The reliability of this statement must be assessed in the light of the political affiliations of both institutions.

29. Can. Arch., Upper Canada State Papers, vol. 94, memorial of president and directors of Welland Canal Company, referred for consideration of Executive Council, October 23, 1829.

30. Kingsford, *Canadian Canals*, pp. 76–77.

31. St. Catharines *Journal*, February 25, 1836, reporting Mackenzie's testimony before the select committee of the Lower Canada Assembly on the Welland Canal petition.

32. Louis Hartz, *Economic Policy and Democratic Thought: Pennsylvania, 1776–1860* (Cambridge, Mass., 1948), p. 89. It may be observed that discussions of the proper spheres of activity of the state and private enterprise in Upper Canada are conspicuous by their absence in this period, at least so far as canals are concerned. Only a few stray comments in legislative debate show any disposition to treat this as a policy issue.

INDEX

Aberdeenshire, 10
Account books, of Welland Canal Company, 104, 114, 126, 127
Accountancy, *see* Bookkeeping methods
Act of incorporation, *see* Charter
Adams, George, named provisional director, 42–44
Adams, Thomas, 43
Address to the King, 102
Address to the Queen, 108
Agent, of Welland Canal Company, 45, 111, 112, 135, 163n
Albany, N.Y., 19, 21, 26, 49, 50, 54, 91, 115, 119, 130, 135
Allan, William, 78, 80, 90, 96, 131
Allanburgh, Upper Canada, 30, 103
American contractors, 50, 51, 52, 61
American immigration, 7, 8, 12, 149n
American invasion, fear of, *see* Defence
American Revolution, 2–5, 25, 43
Amherstburg, 40
Appalachians, 13, 17
Aqueduct, over Welland River, 63, 64, 147, 158n
Aristocracy, 5, 7, 8
Armour & Davies, 27, 37
Army Bills, in War of 1812, 35, 36, 159n
Arthur, Sir George, 108
Ashes, toll charge on, 65, 139, 140
Assembly, of Lower Canada, 21, 34, 84, 85, 91
Assembly, of New York State, 159n
Assembly, of Upper Canada, 7, 11, 34, 36, 37, 58, 69, 71, 77, 78, 81, 84, 91, 92, 94, 97–102, 108, 112, 115, 117, 123, 132, 133, 149n, 153n
Astor, John Jacob, 87
Athabasca, 167n
Atlantic Ocean, 1, 18, 73
Auldjo, Maitland & Company, 16

Bacon, toll charge on, 140
Baggage, toll charge on, 140
Baird, N. H., 72, 73
Baldwin, Robert, 10, 150n
Baltic, 13
Baltimore, 26
Bank of Montreal, 45
Bank of the People, 167n
Bank of the United States, 95, 164n
Bank of Upper Canada, 11, 22, 71, 78, 90, 96, 98, 99, 101, 118, 130, 134, 148, 150n, 159n, 162n, 163nn, 165n, 168n

Banks, Sir Joseph, 7
Banks, in New York State, 91; in Upper Canada, 22
Baring, Alexander, 88
Baring Brothers, 82, 101, 161n, 164n
Barley, toll charge on, 140
Barrels, toll charge on, 140
Barrett, engineer to Welland Canal Company, 61–63, 89, 114, 157nn, 165n
Barrie, Commodore, 63, 64, 90, 134, 157n
Bateaux, 14
Bathurst, Henry, third Earl, 53, 78, 83, 88
Beach, General, 51, 61
Beaton, bookkeeper to Welland Canal Company, 126
Beef, passing Welland Canal, 141, 142, 144
Beer, toll charge on, 140
Beeswax, toll charge on, 140
Biddle, Nicholas, 164n
Bidwell, Marshall Spring, 10, 11
Bishop of Quebec, donation by, 148
Black, secretary to Welland Canal Company, 125, 126, 165n
Blacow, Reverend Richard, 88
Board of Trade (Quebec), 45, 46
Board of Works, 74, 132, 147
Boards, toll charge on, 140
Boats, passing Welland Canal, 65, 70, 143, 144; toll charge on, 140
Bookkeeper, 113, 114, 126
Bookkeeping, in country store, 27; in Welland Canal Company, 126–130, 168n
Bosanquet, Charles, 82
Bosanquet, Pitt & Company, 161n, 163n
Boston, Mass., 26, 95
Boulton, D'Arcy, 78
Boulton, Henry John, 60, 78, 80–82, 94, 98, 99, 130, 131, 161n
Bran, toll charge on, 140
Bricks, toll charge on, 140
Bridgewater, N.Y., 51
British Colonial Argus, 121
British constitution, 5
British Empire, 2
British government, 12, 20, 21, 32, 38, 46, 56, 61, 69, 83, 85–89, 91–95, 97, 102, 104, 108, 114, 134, 135, 148, 154n, 160n
British North America, 25, 72, 144
Buchanan, J. C., 78
Buffalo, N.Y., 20–22, 40, 49, 52, 60, 64, 66, 67